The Folklore of Hereford & Worcester

The Folklore of Hereford & Worcester

by

Roy Palmer

Logaston Press 1992

LOGASTON PRESS
Little Logaston Woonton Almeley
Herefordshire HR3 6QH

First published by Logaston Press 1992
Copyright © Roy Palmer 1992

ISBN 1 873827 02 4

Photoset in Times 11/13 point by Logaston Press
and printed in Great Britain by Ebenezer Baylis & Son, Worcester

Dedicated to the memory of Dave Jones (1940-91)
singer, musician, dancer, impresario—'one of the doers'

CONTENTS

.

INTRODUCTION AND ACKNOWLEDGEMENTS

For a thousand years Herefordshire and Worcestershire were separate counties. In 1974, to the chagrin of many, they were joined in unholy wedlock. Fortunately, there now seems to be a prospect that they might regain their autonomy, but although the two counties have a marked difference they have much in common, too, in history, geography, agriculture—and folklore.

Neither county can boast a recent monograph of substance on its folklore. A magnificent book, *The Folk-lore of Herefordshire*, by Mrs. E.M. Leather (1876-1928), was published in 1912, and re-issued in 1991. In the eighty years which have passed since it was written many traditions have declined or disappeared, while others have enjoyed a new lease of life or even emerged for the first time. Another major work, *On the Ancient British, Roman, and Saxon Antiquities and Folk-lore of Worcestershire*, by Jabez Allies (1787-1856), appeared as long ago as 1852, and incorporated material from an earlier book, *On the Ignis Fatuus, or Will-o'-the-Wisp, and the Fairies* (1846). It is true that *Customs and Folklore of Worcestershire*, by Lavender Jones (born 1900), came out in 1970, but although this was a very welcome piece of work it runs to only thirty-two pages.

The present book, the first to deal with the folklore of the two counties together, attempts to give fair coverage to both. It is a wide and far-reaching survey, though full of detail rather than generalisation. It leans towards living folklore—that which is current or was so within recent memory—rather than dead traditions, but reference is nevertheless made to earlier records for the sake of providing perspective.

An invaluable source has been printed materials of all kinds: books, pamphlets, articles, newspaper reports. Some items here are culled from very obscure works, or printed for the first time from manuscripts. Letters and verbal accounts from living people have also been extremely useful, though one wonders for how long oral tradition—already severely depleted—will be able to survive.

The study of folklore if it is a science at all is an imprecise one, concerned with what people perceive. This book is therefore full of words like said, suspected, reported, suggested. Nevertheless it is a contribution to social and cultural history which in a time of alienation should appeal to those seeking their heritage, their roots.

Just as no man is an island, neither is any county. Folklore is a national—and indeed international—phenomenon. Nevertheless it is interesting to see variations on a theme in a particular part of England, and to observe how motifs are given a local habitation and a name.

To have printed over and over again Herefordshire or Worcestershire after the huge number of towns and villages mentioned in the text would have been tedious. There are two Kingtons and two Orletons, differentiated by context.

I have spent a good deal of time and covered many miles in checking on the ground—such things as the site of a holy well, the existence of an epitaph, the whereabouts of a haunted house or standing stone—but inevitably some things have been taken on trust. Any further correction or enlightenment is welcome from readers, as are stories or songs—or variants on those given here.

I am indebted to Lavender Jones, who generously passed on to me her collection of notes and cuttings; Heather Hurley, who discovered the story of *Tom Reece's Ghost* and other Hoarwithy material; K. Stanley Yapp, who provided a wealth of information and anecdote; and my wife, Pat, who did musical transcriptions and accompanied me on numerous fact-finding missions to public houses.

In addition, I should like to thank these institutions and individuals: Bodleian Library, Folklore Society Library, Hereford and Worcester Record Offices, Hereford and Worcester Libraries, Royal College of Music Library, Trinity College Library (Cambridge), Vaughan Williams Memorial Library; H. Baber, Joyce Banbury, Rose-Marie Bradly, Alan Buckwell, Richard Churchley, Mrs. F.V.V. Coe, Peter Garnett, Rev. John Henscher, Bob Jenkins, Annie Jones, Peter C. Jones, Betty and Robin King, Stuart Knight, Maureen Martin, Douglas Miller, Rev. J.R. Parkinson, Jack Perry, Roger Pye, Rev. A.F. Ricketts, S. Rickhuss, Miss S.F.G. Robinson, Doreen Ruck, Paul Ryder, Mrs. Sue Spackman, Susie Stockton-Link, Mrs. Jacqueline Taverner, E.P. Thompson and Katherine Thomson.

For permission to reproduce material I should like to thank Daphne Davies (song, *Have you not heard*), Annie Jones (Cradley Play and song, *I Loves My Sarah*) and Ursula Vaughan Williams (songs collected by Ralph Vaughan Williams); and for illustrations: author's collection, 19b (photo: Pat Palmer), 43, 81 (photo: Valerie Grosvenor Myer), 117, 157 (photo: Juergen Koenigsbeck), 167, 181, 261 (photos: Bob Etheridge), 128, 153, 189, 234 (photo: John Howes), 252 (photo: Catherine Side); Cheltenham Newspaper Co., v; Reed Midland Newspapers 85, 258; Brassington *Historic Worcestershire*, 53; Bentley *History of Bewdley*, 61;

Anderson, *Witch on the Wall*, 73; Lawson, *Nation in the Parish*, 137; Bodleian Library, 187; W. Sykes, *British Goblins* (1880), 251; Dudley Library, 163; Leominster Priory Church, 97; Much Marcle Church, 102; Hereford Cider Museum, 169; Hereford Library, 103, 172, 255 (and Ken Hoverd for the reproduction of the two Watkins' photographs); Hereford Museum, 155; publisher's collection, 96 (re-drawn by Eric Bottomley), 15, 19a, 23, 41, 42, 47, 66, 77, 129, 131, 147, 229 (photos: Ben Corbett); Worcester Library, 29, 110 (from Jordan's *Bewdley*), 83; setting of music samples by Robert Kay.

Cover illustration from *Prospect of Worcester from the East* c.1750, attributed to John Harris reproduced by permission of the City Museum and Art Gallery, Worcester.

Roy Palmer
August 1992

I
PLACES

Hills and caves, wells, springs and streams, rocks and stones, fields and farms, even single trees: all these have been or are the subject of beliefs, traditions and stories. Towns and villages have popular etymologies and long-standing reputations, not always of the best. But one of the functions of folklore seems to be to provide possible explanations—unscientific but not unsatisfying—of how people's everyday surroundings came about.

Pride and prejudice
Sayings like 'All about Malvern Hill a man may live as long as he will' and 'Blest is the eye between Severn and Wye' certainly express local pride. So does the claim that something 'shines like Worcester agen Gloster'. Yet the ladies of Worcester were proverbially held to be 'poor, proud and petty.' Herefordshire boasted its six W's—wool, water, wood, wheat, wine (cider) and women—but shared with several other counties the disparaging rhyme:

> Herefordshire born, Herefordshire bred,
> Strong in the arm, weak in the head.

Even so, its inhabitants boast the sobriquet of 'white-faced uns', after the county's famous breed of cattle.

The mention of several places—including Letton, Orcop, Pencombe and Pershore—once elicited the invariable comment of 'God help us', a reference to the fabled poverty of their inhabitants. People of Orcop had alternative responses such as 'Lord be praised' (in summer), 'where the sun never sets' or 'where the treacle mines are'. Pencombe was also said to be where they:

> Put the pig on the wall to watch the band go by,
> And thatched the river to keep the ducks dry.

Luston had the label of being 'the dirtiest place you ever did see', and was known as:

> Luston short and Luston long,
> At every house a tump of dung.

13

Weobley was the place 'where they sweep the tide away with a broom', the reference being to a stream liable to cause sudden floods. Other expressions are more mysterious. Why were people advised to 'go to Ross and be sharpened'? Why was Ballingham Hill a spot 'where the sun never shines'? Tibberton, near Oddingley, had:

> A stone church, a wooden steeple,
> A drunken parson, a wicked people.

Complaints of this kind were not uncommon, and the language was direct:

> Acton Beauchamp, the poorest place in all the nation,
> A lousy parson, a nitty clerk and a shabby congregation.

One rhyme makes no comment; perhaps none is needed:

> Naunton Beauchamp,
> Peopleton and Crowle,
> North Piddle, Wyre Piddle,
> Piddle in the Hole.

There was once bitter hostility between many neighbouring settlements. For example Kidderminster and Bewdley where perhaps the latter town blew its own trumpet too loudly:

> For ringers, singers and a crier,
> Bewdley excelled all Worcestershire.

On occasions, both praise and disparagement were offered, as in:

> Lusty Tarrington, lively Stoke {Edith},
> Beggars at Weston {Beggard}, thieves at Woolhope.

Even this, though, was altered so that the first line ran 'Dirty Tarrington, lousy Stoke'. Woolhope does seem to have had an unsavoury reputation. Even today some Ledbury people pass on the axiom that when God had rubbish left over after making the world he dumped it at Woolhope.

Some villages liked to emphasise their superiority over neighbouring towns. The little settlement of Dodderhill looks down on Droitwich both literally and figuratively:

The tower of Evesham Abbey

Who'er has been to Dodderhill
And down on Droitwich gazed
Will not, if he has been to hell,
Be very much amazed.

Church Honeybourne made the claim that:

> There was a church at Honeybourne
> When Evesham was but bush and thorn.

This leads us on from derogatory and congratulatory remarks to the derivation of place names. A thirteenth century seal of Evesham Abbey shows a swineherd looking up at a vision of the Virgin Mary. The inscription beneath (translated into modern English) reads:

> Eoves dwelt here and his swine,
> Therefore call ths Evesham.

The story is that a swineherd, Eoves or Eof, was tending his pigs by the River Avon where he heard celestial harmonies and saw a vision of the Virgin. He reported the experience to his master, Egwin, Bishop of Worcester (later canonised; for more information see chapter 2), who hurried to the spot and saw the same vision. The Virgin told him to build an abbey there in what was the wilderness of Blackenhurst. The new church was dedicated in 714, and the place came to be called Eovesholm—later Evesham.

Such attempts at etymology are often disputed by scholars. Kidderminster comes from Cydda's minster but that does not prevent a different—and no doubt tongue-in-cheek—explanation:

> King Cador saw a pretty maid,
> King Cador would have kissed her.
> The damsel slipped aside and said:
> 'King Cador, you have missed her'.

Equally fanciful is the suggestion that Vowchurch (meaning multi-coloured church) and Turnastone (probably signifying thorn thicket) came about because of a do-gooding but quarrelsome woman who said to her sister: 'I vow I will build my church before you turn a stone of yours.'

The pedigree of Oddingley is also far-fetched. Two Saxon giants, Odd and Dingley, fought on a common until the former was obliged to give best, with the words:

> O Dingley, O Dingley, spare my breath.
> This shall be called Oddingley Heath.

There may not have been a Dingley, but there was an historical Oddo or Odda, a Mercian nobleman who is buried in Pershore Abbey. Dudley and Doddingtree are both named after him, and so is Oddingley, which means 'clearing of the people of Odda'.

The name of Bromsgrove is supposed to stem from Boar's Grove, after the place where a legendary wild boar was slain. The man responsible, Sir Humphrey Stafford, was himself killed in 1450 during the rebellion of Jack Cade, and buried in Bromsgrove Church. Another version of the story—and there usually is another version—claims the victor to be Sir Ryalas Bolton, who was the subject of a ballad entitled *The Jovial Hunter*.

Until 1806 two stones weighing several tons stood in front of Bromsgrove Town Hall. When the road was paved they were too big to move, so great pits were dug and they were buried on the spot. Originally they were put in place by the Jovial Hunter, who shook them out of his shoe because they were hurting his feet. Another explanation is that there was a disagreement between the Hunter and his rival, who lived at Malvern. They launched huge stones at each other—the Hunter from Lickey and the other from the Malvern Hills—and these collided in flight, to fall to the earth in Bromsgrove.

Stones
The durability of stones made them useful as boundary markers. The Four Shire Stone near Moreton-in-the-Marsh shows where four counties—Worcestershire, Gloucestershire, Warwickshire and Oxfordshire—meet, or rather used to meet. It so happens that a battle was fought thereabouts in 1016 between the English under Edmund Ironside and the Danes under Canute. The English won after 'great slaughter'.

A boundary dispute accounts for the existence of the stone at Colwall near the Crown Inn. Two giants were at odds over territories but finally agreed that one of them should hurl the stone from the Malvern Hills and both would accept the place where it fell as their boundary. Alfred Watkins heard another explanation: a giant living in a cave on the Malverns 'saw his wife with another fellow down at Colwall, and chucked a big stone at her, which killed her'. (Some say the reference is to Clutter's Cave; if so, it was a very small giant). However, a roadman whom Watkins met in the Yew Tree at Colwall Green told him that 'the devil was carrying it (the stone) in his apron, the string broke, and there it fell'. Yet another suggestion is that the stone turns round nine times when it hears midnight strike. The operative word here is 'when'. In fact the stone has been in its present position only since the late eighteenth century when it was dragged there from a quarry at the foot of the Wyche by a team of oxen. Why anyone went to this trouble remains unclear.

At roughly the same time four standing stones were being set up on one of the Clent Hills on the orders of Lord Lyttleton of Hagley, who wanted a picturesque vista from his house. Various beliefs about the stones quickly emerged: they were of druidical origin; they stood in memory of the Scots bard, Ossian; they marked the meeting of four counties—Staffordshire, Worcestershire, Shropshire and Warwickshire. Even today some people claim that the stones go down to the brook to drink when they hear the chimes of midnight.

Similarly, the Whetstone on Hergest Ridge above Kington goes down to the Buck Brook to drink when it hears the morning cock crow. The stone may be a waymark, its name deriving from the wheat which together with other produce was sold there when disease raged in the town of Kington in the tme of Edward III.

By the roadside three miles out of Hereford on the way to Sutton St. Nicholas stands the Wergin or Wergins Stone. It has a cup-like recess probably once used for the deposit of an annual ceremonial payment. Daniel Defoe heard this story about the stone when he visited Herefordshire in the 1720's:

Between Sutton and Hereford, is a common meadow called the Wergins, where were placed two large stones for a water-mark; one erected upright, and the other laid a-thwart. In the late Civil Wars, about the year 1652, they were removed to about twelve score paces distant, and no body knew how; which gave occasion to a common opinion, that they were carried thither by the Devil. When they were set in their places again, one of them required nine yoke of oxen to draw it.

Arthur's Stone, in reality a group of stones from an uncovered chambered tomb, is the most famous stone in Herefordshire. It stands on Merebach Hill between Bredwardine and Dorstone. Parson Kilvert, who spent the last years of his life at Bredwardine, knew it well. Joseph Gwynne told him in 1878 that one of the stones had imprinted 'the marks of a man's knees and fingers ... made by King Arthur when he heaved this stone up on his back and set it upon the pillars.' Some who still feel that the site has mystical powers gather there to paint pentangles and signs of the zodiac on the grass.

In a hollow below the crown of Bredon Hill is a group of rocks twenty yards round called the Bambury or Banbury Stones. This was a single enormous stone until a movement of the ground caused it to split apart in

Arthur's Stone, above Dorstone

The Bambury, or Banbury Stones, Bredon Hill

the nineteenth century. Despite such bulk it, too, was said to go down to the Avon to drink when it heard a church clock strike midnight, or alternatively when it heard the bells of Pershore Abbey. The stone may have been used in prehistoric times as a sacrificial altar. More recently, it was customary for people to climb the hill on Good Friday and kiss the stone.

On another part of Bredon Hill, above Westmancote, are the King and Queen Stones. Until the end of the eighteenth century the sessions of the manorial court were proclaimed here—the stones having been ceremonially whitewashed beforehand—and then adjourned to the Royal Oak in Bredon's Norton below. Until the late nineteenth century people were passed between the two stones in the belief that the ritual would charm away aches and pains and restore the weakly to good health. There is a suggestion that a baptismal rite for witches was carried out at the same spot.

In his classic book, *The Old Straight Track*, Alfred Watkins has a chapter on the stones which marked tracks and ley lines.

Hills

As well as having a secure place in folklore, Bredon Hill also appears in fiction, from Henry Fielding—in whose *Tom Jones* it is disguised as Mazard Hill—to John Moore and Fred Archer. The Malvern Hills, too, have many literary connections, starting as early as the fourteenth century with the Colwall-born,—some say Ledbury-born, at Langlands Farm— William Langland and his vision in the poem *Piers Plowman*, of a 'fair feeld ful of folk' seen 'on a May morwenynge on Malverne hilles'. A much lesser figure was Charles F. Grindrod, who published in 1888 a novel entitled *The Shadow of the Raggedstone*. In it he tells the story of how a monk from Little Malvern Priory defies a vow of chastity and falls in love wth a local woman. As a penance he is made to crawl up Raggedstone Hill on his hands and knees each day. In his torment, just before dying, he utters a curse 'May all upon whom the shadow of this stone falls untimely die'. The story stuck, and has confidently been repeated ever since. During the First World War it inspired a poem by Wilfrid Gibson about a soldier and his sweetheart:

> As I was walking with my dear, my dear come back at last,
> The shadow of the Ragged Stone fell on us as we passed;
> And if the tale be true they tell about the Ragged Stone,
> I'll not be walking with my dear next year, nor yet alone.

However, much of Grindrod's story seems to have been his own invention. A version claimed to be authentic concerns a dispute over land between the monks of Little Malvern and Sir John Nanfan of Birtsmorton. Nanfan enclosed land, some of which the monks claimed as theirs. One day Sir John found a monk on Raggedstone Hill, part of the area in contention, and ordered him off. The monk retorted that this was the monastery's land, and if Nanfan failed to restore it God's judgement would be called down on him. 'Do your worst', replied Sir John. The monk pronounced the formula of excommunication, and when Nanfan remained defiant, prophesied that whenever the shadow of the hill fell on Birtsmorton Court the oldest son of the house would die within twelve months. As he spoke, the shadow fell on the house. Nanfan's oldest son died within the year.

The respective positions of the house and the hill mean that the shadow can only fall on a particular day in November, providing, of course, that the sun is shining, which is not necessarily the case every year. Nevertheless over the centuries unexpected deaths among Nanfan heirs—a fall from a horse, a casualty during the Civil War (the only royalist to die in a skirmish in the Leadon Valley), a duelling victim after the Restoration—were attributed to the curse. In 1704 the elder branch of the Nanfan family was extinguished, and the malediction transferred to a junior branch which itself died in poverty at Worcester in the nineteenth century.

On parts of the Malvern ridge, including the Raggedstone Hill, a trench known as the Red Earl's Dyke is still visible. It was cut in 1287, sometimes from solid rock, by Gilbert de Clare, Earl of Gloucester, after a series of boundary disputes with Bishop Cantilupe of Hereford (for whom, see chapter 2). It was so designed that deer could easily leap into the earl's land, but not out.

The Gloucestershire Beacon (or Chase End) lies at the southern end of the eleven-mile range. On the Worcestershire Beacon towards the northern end Macaulay tells us that a fire was lit in 1588 to warn of the Spanish Armada, and 'twelve counties saw the blaze from Malvern's lonely height'.

In between the two rises the Herefordshire Beacon, otherwise known as the British Camp, which is reputed to have been the place in 50 A.D. of the last stand of Caractacus (or Caratacus), prince of the Atrebates, against the Romans. Some disagree. Fosbroke, the historian of Ariconium, says that Caractacus was indeed at the British Camp, but retreated across Herefordshire to a cluster of strong positions—the *montes ardui* (steep hills) of Tacitus—near the confluence of the Rivers Clun and Teme: Borough Hill, Tongley Hill, the Whettleton Hills and Coxall Knoll. He argues Caractacus was defeated at Coxall by Ostorius Scapula—whose name is said to provide the derivation for Capler Camp, near Fownhope—but escaped, only to be betrayed and handed over to the Romans by Cartimandua, Queen of the Brigantes.

Henry Card, an early nineteenth century vicar of Great Malvern, nevertheless stuck in his writings to the British Camp as the site of Caractacus' last stand. A plaque at the foot of the hill by the A4104 mentions the Red Earl but not Caractacus. Close to this point, which used to be called Burstners Cross, a gold coronet encrusted with precious stones was unearthed in 1650. Oddly enough it had probably belonged to a British prince who lived at the time of Caractacus.

The Clent Hills, which are within sight of the Malverns, have a furrow thought to run from Clent village to St. Kenelm's Church. The groove was made, so it was said, by an old woman's plough when her oxen ran away in protest at being made to work on St. Kenelm's Day (28 July; for Kenelm himself see chapter 3). A variant is that when the woman attempted to start ploughing on a Sunday she became blind and her oxen escaped. Her piece of land, somewhere in a hollow of hills, has grown unnaturally greener grass since as a warning to others.

Wormelow Tump is shown on maps a few miles south of Hereford on the Monmouth road. It is now merely the name of a hamlet, the mound having been removed for road widening in the nineteenth century. A thousand years earlier the Welsh antiquary, Nennius, claimed that Anir, the son of King Arthur, was buried in the tump, which 'sometimes measures in length seven feet, sometimes fifteen feet, and sometimes nine feet'. Local people held a similar belief, namely that no one could step over or round the tump with the same number of paces. Further south on the same road, the A466, lies the village of St. Weonards which still has its tump, close to the church—the only one in England dedicated to the obscure Welsh saint who settled hereabouts as a woodcutting hermit. People believed that Weonard was buried beneath the mound in a golden coffin on top of a golden chest inscribed:

> Where this stood
> Is another twice as good,
> But where that is, no man knows.

Inspired, perhaps, by the story, archaeologists excavated the tump in 1855 and found two cremation burials, but no gold. Folk memory nevertheless proved to have at least some basis, as is often the case. Feasts and morris dancing were regularly held on the tump. A ghostly pig can sometimes be seen at midnight at the nearby crossroads. Just south of the village a standing stone shares a story with many other places in England. A sheepstealer was carrying home his prize, its body over his back and its legs tied together in front of him. He stopped to rest by the stone and leaned against it, but the sheep slipped down behind it and the rope pulled his neck against the stone and strangled him. Next morning the man was found dead, a convenient warning to others.

Even quite small hills, especially when they rose inexplicably from level ground, presented a challenge to people's imagination. The devil often features in the aetiological stories which resulted. For example, he is vexed at the piety of Bewdley, so determines to dam the Severn and drown the town. He takes up a spittleful (spadeful) of earth and sets off towards Bewdley from Kidderminster. On the way he meets a cobbler carrying a bundle of worn-out shoes for repair, and asks him how far it is to Bewdley. The quick-witted cobbler, realising that his interlocuter means no good, replies: 'Well, I've worn out all these shoes coming from there'. The devil drops his spittleful in disgust—it is reassuring that he can be so easily deceived—and stamps off. The evidence can still be seen. The hill is marked on the OS map close to the railway line at Blackstone Farm, about half way between Kidderminster and Bewdley.

A similar story is told of the Cobbler's Mound at the eastern end of Shobdon village, near Leominster, where the devil was diverted from his

Pyon Hill and Butthouse Knapp, near Canon Pyon

project of obliterating what claimed to be the finest church then known. The cobbler in this case claimed to be ignorant of the whereabouts of Shobdon. When the villagers heard the story, though, they were so afraid that the devil would try again that they dismantled the church. (The old church was indeed dismantled in 1752 on the orders of the lord of the manor, and parts of it were removed to Shobdon Park).

A few miles away, close to Kings and Canon Pyon, the same theme crops up again. Two conical hills marked on the map as Pyon Hill and Butthouse Knapp (near the A4110) are locally called Robin Hood's Butts. One tradition is that the devil abandoned two sacks full of earth after being dissuaded from overwhelming Hereford with them. Either he swallowed the suggestion that Hereford was so wicked as to be on his side already, or he accepted a trusty cobbler's familiar tale of wearing out so many shoes on his way from that city.

Another story claims that two men attempted for a wager to jump over Wormsley Hill to Canon Pyon. Each clipped the top, knocking out enough earth to form one of the smaller hills. In a further tale the devil is replaced by Robin Hood and Little John, each carrying a spadeful of earth to bury the monks at Wormsley but abandoning it to form one of the hills. As a boy in Ledbury in the 1880's John Masefield was told yet a different story:

Robin Hood used to stand on one (hill), to shoot at the other; then crossed over ...., picked up the arrows and shot them back. ...Another man ... said that they were Robin Hood's treasure rooms, and that there was an underground passage between them.

Below Ground
Real finds such as the one at Burstners Cross must have stimulated the many traditions of buried treasure. Bronsil Castle—now a ruin, near Eastnor—still keeps the secret of the whereabouts of a hoard of gold and silver concealed by Lord Beauchamp before going on crusade. Beauchamp told his wife that if he died the treasure would be easily found, provided his body was brought home for Christian burial. He was indeed killed, outside Jerusalem, but although his remains were brought back to Bronsil the treasure could not be recovered. In those days the practice was for the flesh to be boiled off, and the bones only to be returned. If some of these were lost the condition laid down by Beauchamp might have been thwarted. There is another clue—the croak of a raven, perhaps a descendant of the tame raven Beauchamp set to watch over his hoard, can apparently be heard at midnight close to the place where the treasure still lies.

Another bird—this time a jackdaw—stood guardian over the treasure hidden at Penyard Castle, near Ross-on-Wye. There, two hogsheads full of money were in a vault protected by iron doors. A farmer dragged the doors open with a team of twenty steers, revealing the jackdaw perched on one of the casks. He was so delighted at the prospect of reaching the treasure that he called out: 'I believe I shall have it'. Immediately the doors clanged shut and a sepulchral voice intoned:

Had it not been for your quicken-tree goad and your yew-tree pin,
You and your cattle had all been drawn in.

According to Alfred Watkins, a 'crock of French gold' was unearthed at Castle Farm, Madley, early in the nineteenth century; he obtained the information from the granddaughter of a servantmaid present when the find was made in the cellar. The same farm also has a ghost and a reputed passage leading to the church a mile away. Kinnersley Castle, a mansion of the late Elizabethan and early seventeenth century periods, is said to have a similar tunnel running to the nearby church. The Manor House at Ashton-under-Hill claims to have passages leading both to the church and to the monastery at Beckford, two miles away. White Ladies, a house in the Tything at Worcester, incorporates fragments of the nunnery founded in about 1250 by Bishop Cantilupe. (The nuns also owned land at the village which came to be called White Ladies Aston). Tradition held that the Worcester house had passages leading to the cathedral and also to Hindlip House. The likelihood seems remote, but there certainly was a passage of some kind for it was explored by the historian, Nash, who penetrated a hundred yards before foul air put out his lantern and forced him to retreat. Worcester Cathedral was also supposed to be connected by a secret passage to Malvern Abbey, and the priory of St. Guthlac at Hereford was similarly linked to its vineyard on the banks of the Wye. This passage was investigated by Watkins, who found it to be 'some kind of natural "fault" or long crevice, not man made'.

Stories of such passages could be capped with accounts of whole settlements swallowed beneath the ground. A field by Arthur's Stone is said to have deep below it a village engulfed by an earthquake. People claimed to be able to see the top of the old church steeple at the bottom of a pond in the field.

Old Pembridge was lost in Shobdon Marshes. A fiddler who had played for a dance at Pembridge arrived home at Eardisland, then remembered a fine pair of white gloves tied with red ribbons which he had left behind. He retraced his steps, but the village had disappeared into a swamp. Until the twentieth century people believed that a stone dropped down a well on the site could be heard striking the top of the church spire far below.

Wells and Waters

Early peoples valued water for practical reasons but also felt it had a sacred dimension. Springs and wells connected the world of every-day life with a mysterious realm below the ground.

Great Malvern may owe its origin to the spring known as St. Ann's Well, which was perhaps in the first place dedicated to Anu, a Celtic water Goddess. A Christian missionary, possibly in Saxon times, may have noticed the veneration in which Malvern water was held, and resolved to harness this to his own purposes by using the spring for baptism. Eventually, Anu became Anne (mother of the Virgin).

St. Anne's Well was famous in mediaeval times. Its water healed skin and eye diseases, the spiritual element having acquired a literal dimension. The same power came from the water of the Holy Well and Eye Well (at present Malvern Wells), of which a homespun poet wrote in 1622:

> A little more I'll on their curing tell,
> How they help sore eyes with a new found well.
> Great speech of Malvern-hills has late reported
> Unto which spring people in troops resorted.

Later in the same century John Evelyn recorded in his diary:

We set out towards Worcester, by the way (thick planted with Cider-fruit) we deviate to the holy Wells trickling out of a vally, thro a steepe declivity toward the foote of great-Maubern hills: They are said to heale many Infirmities, As Kings-evill, Leaprosie, etc: sore Eyes ...

In the eighteenth and nineteenth centuries the springs led to Malvern's prosperity as a spa town. They are still sought out by those who are dissatisfied with the quality of local tap water.

Many wells have now disappeared or fallen into disuse. The Holy Well at Worcester enjoyed the reputation of curing eye troubles. In the eighteenth century its water was used to brew beer, and during the nineteenth was sold at a halfpenny a can as the purest in the town. In the 1870's, though, it was bricked up.

On Bredon Hill some 300 yards east of the Banbury Stones is a spring traditionally associated with St. Catherine of Alexandria. Close by stood a chapel where a yearly fair celebrated St. Catherine's Day (25 November).

After the Reformation the chapel was allowed to fall into ruin, and in 1871 the last stones were levelled. The holy well is still shown on today's maps but demand for its healing water has long ceased.

Herefordshire was particularly famed for its large number of healing wells. There were three at Peterchurch alone, two for eyes and one for rheumatism. The stories of others—at Dorstone, Hereford, Marden and Stoke Edith—are told in chapter 3. Job's Well at Bosbury, once renowned for curing eye troubles and boils, now seems to be unknown to villagers. Bromyard's Eye Well is now in a private garden in Highwell Lane. The water of St. Waum's Well on the Malvern Hills, just below Waum's (or Clutter's) Cave, was often drunk by John Masefield who knew of its power 'to cure broken hearts, weary eyes and rheumatism'. By the 1950's, though, he found the spring dry.

Until within living memory another St. Anne's Well, this time at Aconbury, was prized for its healing powers. Speaking in 1990 a local forester, Arthur Crum, recalled seeing as many as twenty or thirty people at times washing their hands and swilling their faces at the well. They were 'mostly city folk from Hereford', he said, somewhat wryly. A blue mist was reputed to rise from the well at midnight on Twelfth Night. Water drawn then—known as 'the cream of the well'—was carefully bottled and saved to be used when its curative powers were needed. The well is still there (on private land), cut into solid rock at the back of a thirty-yard recess, but tangled undergrowth points to its present neglect.

Rivers and streams have their own traditions. The Wye was considered a greedy river, needing an annual victim. After a child had been drowned near Bredwardine a woman is said to have reassured mothers about the safety of their children with these words 'You needn't worry about them, m'dears. The river has took his toll and they'm safe for the rest of the year'. Bodies of the drowned were thought to rise on the ninth day. The number may not have scientific backing, but it is certainly of mystical significance.

The River Lugg had a water nymph, at Marden. When a bell was allowed to fall into the water she ensured that it stayed firmly at the bottom. A wise man said the bell might be recovered if a team of white freemartins (heifers) were to pull it with yokes of yew tied with bands of wittern (rowan), provided the whole operation were carried out in complete silence. As the bell broke surface the nymph was seen in it, asleep. As it started to come up the bank one of the drivers, unable to contain his excitement, said:

> In spite of all the devils in hell,
> Now we'll land Marden's great bell.

The mermaid awoke, and plunged back into the river with the bell, breaking the yokes and screaming:

> If it had not been for your wittern bands and your yew tree pin
> I'd have had the twelve freemartins in.

The story is very similar to that of the buried treasure at Penyard Castle. At Marden a bronze bell which can now be seen in Hereford Museum was found eighteen feet below ground level in a pond a few yards from the church in a field belonging to the vicar. The question arises as to whether the find inspired the story or confirmed it.

On his way to victory at the battle of Bosworth Henry Tudor crossed the River Arrow between Pembridge and Eardisland. He took the opportunity to remind his followers of the ancient saying that 'he who would win a national strife must shoot the arrow first'.

Downstream from Bewdley the Severn is overlooked by a beetling crag called Blackstone Rock. High on its sandstone cliff is the entrance to some caves where hermits once lived. There is a tradition that the holy men regularly rescued from the river unwanted babies who had been set adrift at Bewdley. They brought up and educated the children, all of whom were given the surname of Severn.

In the same hermitage Sir Harry Wade once lived while waiting to take his revenge. He was bethrothed to Alice Clopton of Stratford-on-Avon. The Clopton family was notoriously unlucky, and Alice seems to have been no exception. She was seized by a rival suitor, blindfolded, and carried away on horseback. Wade gave chase, and was about to catch up when the fugitive threw Alice into the River Rea at Deritend, in Birmingham. Wade naturally stopped to help her, but she drowned. He then tracked the murderer through Edgbaston, Hagley Wood, Blakedown and Kidderminster, but lost him when he took sanctuary in Bewdley. Wade, his patience matched only by his hatred, lived for ten years as a hermit at Blackstone Rock until the murderer at last ventured there for confession, only to be summarily thrown to his death in the river below.

Less sensationally, the Sapey Brook near Clifton-on-Teme was renowned for a series of circular marks on its sandstone bed. Two—at Jumper's Hole (for which, see also chapter 7)—were particularly clear, with other good specimens between Clifton and Stanford Bishop. Some of these were removed from the bed of the stream by Jabez Allies, and taken to Worcester Museum. Most scholars agreed that the marks were caused simply by the action of the water, though one argued that prehistoric beasts had left them. Tradition says that St. Catherine of Ledbury (see also

Blackstone Rock, 1788

chapter 3) and her servant, Mabel, had a mare and colt stolen one night as they were travelling this way. The thief led the animals along the brook to avoid leaving tracks, but Catherine prayed that their tread and that of the thief (who turned out to be a girl wearing pattens) should remain visible. Her request was granted. The animals were traced to Ledbury, and recovered. The marks remained. There were similar markings in the bed of the Dick Brook at Rock. In this case the explanation offered is that a church was being built on one side of the brook, but each night the stones were carried across to the other by a mare and foal which permanently imprinted the bed with their hooves.

Between Chaddesley Corbett and Bromsgrove runs a brook which can be seen from the M5 motorway. As a boy Edward Corbett was told that its water ran red with blood on the day of a battle, thus giving it the name of Battlefield Brook. The battle in question, Corbett claims, involved the defeat of a Roman force on Walton Hill during the first century A.D. If so, the power of oral tradition has been strong enough to carry the story for some 1,800 years.

What's in a name?

As well as of brooks, the names of fields and farms often convey glimpses of long-past events. Scotland Bank near Dorstone is so called because the last few Highlanders left alive after the battle of Worcester fled there, only to be cut down by Welshmen who loosed powerful dogs on them.

Hangman's Cross is the name of a field off Lincomb Lane, Hartlebury. It commemorates a gibbet which stood nearby. Gibbet lane and Gibbet Wood at Stourton recall a highway robber and murderer of 1812. He was hanged at Stafford, but his body was brought back to be exhibited at the scene of the crime. This is said to have been the last instance of gibbeting in the Midlands.

Chase Well at Chase End was formerly called Deadwoman's Well because a woman was murdered there while fetching water. Alternatively she was torn to pieces by hounds.

The Devil's Bib is a field at Heightington in north-west Worcestershire. In the same parish is a Devil's Spadeful, which must have the same kind of pedigree as the hill mentioned earlier. Foxhall's Field at Tenbury bears the name of a farmer from Queen Anne's time. The man owed money to a neighbour, and to avoid repaying laid a charge that the neighbour had robbed him. The creditor in turn accused him of perjury. To avoid arrest Foxhall jumped into the River Teme and was drowned. At Ewyas Harold a field is called Queen Anne's Bounty. The name goes back to 1704, when an act of parliament apportioned the rent of certain fields for the support of poor clergy.

Next to the old pound in the village of Wolverley is Knight's Meadow. A whole saga explains its name. One day a milkmaid, accompanied by an old dog, was crossing the field on her way to milking when she saw a man asleep on the grass. He was thin, ill-kempt, and in fetters. She was alarmed, but the dog seemed to recognize the man, who woke up and claimed to be Sir John Attwood. He was taken to Lady Attwood, who had despaired of her husband's return from crusading—this was in the fourteenth century—and was on the point of re-marrying. She could not recognize the man as her husband after so many years of separation but he produced the broken half of a ring which perfectly matched the half kept by his wife when they parted. The fetters were struck off, the new marriage was cancelled, and Sir John came home.

He explained that he had been miraculously transported from imprisonment abroad after praying and seeing a vision of an angel or the Virgin Mary. He travelled on the back of a swan, and as they were coming in to land his foot touched the top of the church steeple. In gratitude for his deliverance and in fulfilment of a vow he gave land at Wolverley to Worcester Cathedral. His funeral monument in Wolverley Church showed him with a swan as his crest and a dog (or possibly a lion) at his feet. When the old building was demolished in 1772 the effigy was removed to Wolverley Court. The fetters were also preserved; one account says at least until 1988.

The story is full of well-known motifs. The faithful dog and impending re-marriage recall Ulysses' return to Ithaca. The obliging swan comes from northern mythology, the foot touching a pinnacle from oriental romance. The broken ring or token was a favourite theme in British traditional song until this century.

There was no English crusade during the fourteenth century but Sir John Attwood could have joined a group of knights on one of Bertrand du Guesclin's expeditions against Pedro the Cruel, King of Castile. He could have been taken prisoner, exhausted his fortune in paying a ransom, and then made his way home penniless and weary in 1368 or '69. One sceptic has suggested that the whole thing was made up by monks to explain how they had come into possession of certain lands. Another has pointed out that it might be a fantasy based on the swan and the dog of the effigy. Nevertheless for many years there was a rent charge on the Knight's Meadow which went to pay someone 'who should keep the irons polished and show them to all who would like to see them'.

Apostles Farm at Kingswood traces its pedigree even further back. St. John is supposed to have preached there. The nearby Apostles Lane and Apostles Stone reinforce the message, though a gibbet once incongruously stood where the lane crosses the Kington to Hereford road.

At Bretforton are to be found fields called Porridge Yats, Bull Butts and Pumbleditch. Kilpeck has a Starveacre and Ledbury a Baregains, both pointing to a struggle for survival. Blackhole always points to a burial place. The mysterious Moneyfarthing Hill at Clodock is a corruption of the Welsh, Mynydd Ferddynn: Ferddyn's Hill. Killdane Meadow, Field and Orchard near Bromsash are as sinister as they sound: they commemorate the killing of Danes on the periphery of his kingdom carried out on St. Brice's Day (13 November) 1002 on the orders of King Ethelred.

It is a great pity that many field names are disappearing. Sometimes they are simply lost as old people die and newcomers replace them. Sometimes the removal of hedgerows deprives fields of their names along with their identity.

The Tuppeny Cake is a small, triangular green at Bournheath, three miles from Bromsgrove. Until the 1930's tenants of the adjoining cottages had to pay an annual fee of twopence to its owner, the squire of Fockbury. Friday Street at Pebworth is said to be so called because Shakespeare liked to go and drink there on Fridays, and so many people came to join in the conversation that the street was very busy on that day of the week. In the rhyme which Shakespeare is supposed to have made about various villages in the locality, Pebworth came out as 'piping'—a reference to the pipe and tabor players who accompanied the morris dancers.

Even trees and woods had their stories. The famous Whitty Pear of the Wyre Forest is described in chapter 5. Until 1974 at Kempsey there was a Revolution Elm, the last of three planted in 1688 to mark the Glorious Revolution. On Rushock Hill, close to Offa's Dyke and near to Kington, there are three yew trees which were planted in the eighteenth century. The Three Sisters, as they are called, may salute the memory of three human sisters at Knill Court, or represent three local shepherds lost in a bitter snowstorm as they were tending their flocks.

There are many Gospel Oaks (see chapter 3) and Holy Thorns (chapter 12). A famous oak tree is supposed to mark the place where St. Augustine met a synod of British bishops in 603, during the time of King Ethelbert. Five places in Worcestershire claim the honour of St. Augustine's Oak: Alfrick, Martin Hussingtree, Stanford Bishop, Rock and Hartlebury. The name itself of Rock means 'at the oak'. A tradition at least two centuries old when it was written down in 1670 claimed that a particular tree there was Augustine's. It stood till 1775, about a mile from the Hundred House on the road to Abberley. However, the Mitre Oak at Hartlebury, mentioned by Camden, claims to come from an acorn from Augustine's original tree. It stands beside the main Worcester road. Queen Elizabeth I was met there on one of her progresses by the Bishop of Worcester and local gentry. It is possible that the tree was merely used as a landmark. Again, a mitre could have been hung in the branches as an inn sign or the name could have arisen because of the tree's proximity to the Bishop's Palace.

II
PEOPLE

The two counties have many saintly connections, of which two, Egwin and Cantilupe, are covered here. (Others appear in chapter 3). Sinners are represented by Jack of Kent and Oliver Cromwell, both of whom were alleged to have made pacts with the devil. Richard Foley succeeded by his own efforts, though these included industrial espionage. Two further celebrities were Hannah Snell, a woman soldier of the eighteenth century, and Tom Spring, a prizefighter of the nineteenth. All these were historical figures, covering a span of a thousand years, but the facts of their lives mingled with story, song or speculation have persisted to our own time.

Egwin and Cantilupe
Egwin (or Ecgwine) was bishop of Worcester from 693 until 711. At one stage enemies accused him of unspecified crimes, so he decided to go to Rome to appeal to the pope. Before setting out he had his legs chained and padlocked, then threw the key into the Avon close to where Evesham Abbey would later be built. He also proclaimed that only divine intervention would release him from the chains.

When Egwin arrived in Rome all the bells rang in welcome of their own accord, an auspicious start for him. He told his followers to wait by the Tiber while he went into St. Peter's to pray. To while away the time they went fishing in the river and caught a salmon. As the fish was being prepared for the bishop's evening meal a key was found inside, which proved to be the one thrown into the Avon. Egwin was released from his chains, and the pope must have been suitably impressed for he acquitted him of the accusations which had been levelled.

Back in England, Egwin was given land by Ethelred, king of Mercia (to whom he may have been related) for the purpose of building an abbey at what came to be called Evesham. The miraculous choice of site is related in chapter 1. In 709 Egwin was again travelling to Rome, this time with Offa, who had succeeded Ethelred. In the Alps the party—perhaps surprisingly—was in danger of perishing from thirst. Egwin saved the situation by causing a spring to issue from the ground. At other times he made a dumb man speak, saved a friend from imminent shipwreck, and foretold the end of smithing in Alcester (some say caused it, so as to punish smiths for working on Sundays).

Egwin resigned his see in 711, and became the first abbot of Evesham. Long after his death in 717 monks from Evesham took his relics on a fund-raising trip, and claimed miracles at Dover, Oxford and Winchester. Until the Reformation Evesham Abbey's coat of arms included a lock and chain.

Some 50 years after the time of Egwin, Thomas Cantilupe (or Cantelupe) was elected bishop of Hereford by the canons of the cathedral. He was red-haired, short tempered, learned, austere, and no doubt charismatic. One day he was returning to Hereford from his palace at Stretton Sugwas when the bells of the cathedral rang to welcome him without human agency, just at the bells of Rome had rung for Egwin. The White Cross was erected at the spot to commemorate the event, and its successor still stands there.

After becoming embroiled in a dispute with Archbishop Peckham, Thomas was excommunicated. Like Egwin, he decided to appeal to the pope. He travelled to Italy but died (in 1282) before matters could be resolved. Part of his body was buried at Orvieto but his heart and bones were brought back by his secretary, Richard Swinfield, who succeeded him as bishop of Hereford.

During the journey miracles occurred. At Hereford the bones began to bleed in the presence of the Red Earl who had quarrelled with Thomas over boundaries between their land. The tomb attracted so many visitors that in 1287 a decision was made to move it from the Lady Chapel to a more prominent place. The occasion was important enough for King Edward I to attend. Masons were nonplussed as to how to move the heavy slab. Two young pages found they could shift it without effort, but after that no one could move it from its new position. A cripple who touched it was restored to health.

By 1307 221 miracles (by some accounts 400) were credited to Thomas, and the pope sent a commission to Hereford to investigate. The cases included not only those already mentioned but people cured of paralysis and brought back to life after hanging or drowning. Some claims were found to be fraudulent; others stretched credulity to breaking point. In four weeks the commission investigated seventeen cases and on the strength of these recommended that Thomas be canonised. In 1320 he officially became St. Thomas of Hereford.

Through his cult the cathedral became the most important centre for pilgrimage in western England, and the gifts of the faithful helped to build the great west tower. As late as 1610 some of St. Thomas' relics were secretly carried through the city by night in time of plague, 'giving total succour to the same'. By some thirty years later, early in the Civil War, the bones were all dispersed.

Jack of Kent

Herefordshire mothers once frightened their children into good behaviour and due obedience by saying 'Jackie Kent'll 'ave you'. A common comparison in Kentchurch was 'As great as the devil and Jack o'Kent'. The identity of this awesome personage is a mystery.

Some have suggested Sir John Oldcastle, a Herefordshire man, one-time MP and subsequently a member of the House of Lords, who also served as part-model for Shakespeare's Falstaff. Oldcastle, a Lollard, rebelled against the catholic religion of his day, and was hanged for his trouble in 1417. Owain Glyndwr was fighting the English at roughly the same time, and he also has been put forward as a candidate. He owned the castle at Huntington, close to the Welsh border. If things became too difficult he could take refuge at Kentchurch Court or Monnington Court, the homes of his daughters, both of whom had married Englishmen. Although Glyndwr was defeated he was never captured. One tradition says that he lies buried in Monnington churchyard beneath a flat broken stone by the porch.

At Kentchurch Court there is a painting of a man in a white habit which could be a portrait of Jack of Kent. Equally, it might be a Lollard priest or the John Kent who was vicar of Kentchurch at the time of Oldcastle and Glyndwr. Another John Kent who has been equated with Jack was a fifteenth century astrologer and writer on witchcraft. Yet another possibility is Dr. John Gwent, a Welsh Franciscan friar who died in 1348.

Whoever Jack was, and whether he existed or not, stories of his deeds were told for many centuries not only in Herefordshire but in Gloucestershire and Monmouthshire. He is supposed to have made a pact with the devil which allowed him to perform such deeds as building a bridge over the River Monnow near Kentchurch (some say at Monmouth) in a single night. As usual, a condition reserved for the devil the first being to cross, so Jack threw a bone and a dog ran across after it. The dog was of no use to the devil because he had no soul.

Once Jack went from Kentchurch to London with a mincepie for the king. He set off at daybreak and the pie was still hot when he arrived in time for breakfast. On the way he lost a garter which became caught in the weathercock on a church spire as he flew past. Back at home, a farmer wanting to go to Hereford Fair told Jack to keep the crows out of the corn while he was away. Later in the day he came across Jack at the fair and furiously asked him what the game was. Jack assured him that the crows were not in the corn, and when the farmer returned he found it was true. The crows were sitting in an old barn with no roof; a big bird which the farmer took to be the devil was keeping order, perched on an old beam.

One Christmas as Jack was preparing to drag a Yule log into the house some bystanders remarked that it was too heavy to be moved inside. In response he fetched four goslings and harnessed them to the log, whereupon they drew it to the hearth with the greatest of ease.

Despite his alliance with the devil Jack seems to have spent a great deal of time in outwitting or holding trials of strength with him. One day the devil challenged him to thresh a whole bay of corn in a single day. Jack took off his boot and put it on the stack, where it kicked down the sheaves one by one. He set a flail on the floor and it threshed corn by itself as he sat playing the fiddle and murmuring from time to time:

> Nobble, stick, nobble.
> Play, fiddle, play.

The task was finished well within the allotted time.

On another occasion, Jack offered the devil his choice of the pigs in a consignment. When the devil opted for those with straight tails Jack fed them beans so that their tails curled. Next time the devil chose curly tails so Jack drove the animals through water to make their tails go limp.

In a field where the wheat was just springing up Jack asked the devil whether he preferred tops or butts. He chose butts, and when the harvest came he had the straw, and Jack the ears. The following year the devil changed to tops but since the field had been sown with turnip seed Jack had the better bargain once more. In a grass-mowing contest Jack won again by sticking harrow tines into the devil's ground so that his scythe constantly lost its edge. At threshing the devil was induced to take up his stance on a hurdle, so that all the corn fell through for Jack to collect underneath. (Similar contests from Worcestershire between the devil and a farmer are recorded in chapter 10).

Some of these trials of wit or strength left marks on the landscape, or so we are led to believe. One of the explanations of Robin Hood's Butts (see also chapter 1) is that they were produced by spadefuls of earth thrown from Burton Hill by Jack and the devil. Tumbled outcropping rocks on Garway Hill are suposed to have been spilled from the devil's apron when he was trying to help Jack build a fishpond at Orcop. The devil could not pick up the stones because he had to return home at cock crow.

Jack and the devil had a stone-throwing contest on a stretch of heath called Poors' Allotment, part of Tidenham Chase in the Forest of Dean. The devil managed a mile and a half. His missile, Broad Stone, still stands by the railway line near the village of Stroat. Jack's stone has not survived but he threw it over the River Severn and won by a good three miles.

More of Jack's feats were remembered in Monmouthshire, where an old countryman commented:

Why, one day he jumped off the Sugar Loaf mountain right on to the Skirrid, and there's his heel mark to this day, and when he got there he began playing quoits, he pecked {threw} three stones as far as Trelleck, great big ones, as tall as three men (and there they still stand in a field), and he threw another that did not go quite far enough, and it lay on the Trelleck road, just behind the five trees, till a little while ago, when it was moved so as the field might be ploughed, and this stone, in memory of Jack, was always called the Pecked Stone.

The time came when Jack's death approached, and his score with the devil would have to be settled. Their agreement stipulated that whether his body was buried inside a church or outside Jack's soul must go to the devil. Jack chose to have himself interred within the thickness of the church wall at Kentchurch (or Grosmont, or Skenfrith, say other versions), thus being neither in nor out. In addition Jack wished to arrange a public sign that he had cheated the devil, so he gave deathbed instructions that his 'liver and lights' were to be exposed on spikes projecting from the church tower. He predicted that a dove and a raven would come to fight over the remains, with a victory by the former showing that Jack's soul was saved. There seems to be doubt as to the outcome.

Foley the Fiddler

The Foley Arms is not uncommon as an inn sign. The family, which still has members living in Herefordshire, owes its original propserity to the iron trade, and nailmaking in particular. The chief founder of the fortune was Richard Foley (1580-1657), who was born at Dudley and later moved to Stourbridge. In 1627 he set up a mill at Kinver which mechanically slit the thin sheets of iron needed for nail-making, so replacing the laborious cutting by hand. Despite infringing the patent of a slitting-mill established in Kent twenty-eight years earlier Foley was able to establish himself in a dominant position in the Midland nail trade.

A much more romantic account attributes the source of the Foley fortune to an instance of industrial espionage. Its earliest source seems to be a passage written in 1812 by the poet S.T. Coleridge, and repeated approvingly by Samuel Smiles in his book *Self Help* (1859), with the added information that the place in Sweden twice visited by Foley was Dannemora near Uppsala. This is Coleridge's version:

The most extraordinary and the best attested instance of enthusiasm, existing in conjunction with perseverance is related of the founder of the Foley family. This man, who was a fiddler living near Stourbridge, was often witness of the immense labour and loss of time, caused by dividing the rods of iron, necessary in the process of making nails. The discovery of the process called splitting, in works called splitting mills, was first made in Sweden, and the consequences of this advance in art were disastrous to the manufacturers of iron about Stourbridge. Foley the fiddler was shortly missed from his accustomed rounds, and was not seen again for many years. He had mentally resolved to ascertain by what means the process of splitting bars of iron was accomplished; and, without communicating his intention to a single human being, he proceeded to Hull, and thence, without funds, worked his passage to the Swedish iron port. Arrived in Sweden, he begged and fiddled his way to the iron foundries, where, after a time, he became a universal favourite with the workmen; and, from the apparent entire absence of intelligence or anything like ultimate object, he was received into the works, to every part of which he had access. He took the advantage thus offered, and having stored his memory with observations and all the combinations, he disappeared from amongst his kind friends as he had appeared, no one knew whence or whither.

On his return to England he communicated his voyage and its results to Mr. Knight and another person in the neighbourhood, with whom he was associated, and by whom the necessary buildings were erected and the machinery provided. When at length everything was prepared, it was found that the machinery would not act, at all events it did not answer the sole end of its erection—it would not split the bar of iron.

Foley disappeared again, and it was concluded that shame had driven him away for ever. Not so: again, though somewhat more speedily, he found his way to the Swedish iron works, where he was received most joyfully, and to make sure of their fiddler, he was lodged in the splitting mill itself. Here was the very aim and end of his life attained beyond his utmost hope. He examined the works and very soon discovered the cause of his failure. He now made drawings or rude tracings, and, having abided an ample time to verify his observations and to impress them clearly and vividly on his mind, he made his way to the port, and once more returned to England. This time he was completely successful, and by the results of his experience enriched himself and greatly benefited his countrymen. This I hold to be the most extraordinary instance of credible devotion in modern times.

Another version of the story relates that Foley was drinking one day in an alehouse when his wife came to tell him that the cow had been seized for rent. Richard went off in shame and returned three years later from Holland with the technique of the slitting mill. There he had played not the fiddle but the flute, and had disarmed any suspicions on the part of his hosts by pretending to be a fool.

By whatever means—and there is written evidence in the Foley archives that he did travel to Uppsala—Richard undoubtedly made a fortune and established a dynasty whose wealth was displayed in imposing mansions at Great Witley and Stoke Edith (though, ironically, both were subsequently destroyed by fire). He lies buried in front of the chancel steps at Oldswinford Church, having left a will which shows him to have been a deeply religious man. Perhaps he repented his wild years as Foley the fiddler.

Cromwell and Charles
Well over thirty places in Hereford and Worcester have connections with the Civil War. In 1642 the first serious fighting of the war took place at Powick where after 'a confused and bloody mêlée' a parliamentary force fled, leaving Prince Rupert master of the field. A tree known as Rupert's Thorn survived until 1860, when it was removed to make way for a house. The recollection of Mrs. Martha Sherwood, the novelist, who lived at Wick in the early nineteenth century, was that the tree was a yew.

Cromwell's decisive victory in the last important battle of the Civil War was partly achieved also at Powick, though mainly in Worcester. The city supported the king but surrendered to Parliament in 1646 after a siege. The governor during the siege was Colonel Henry Washington, an ancestor of George, the first president of the United States. The family arms—three stars and five horizontal stripes—can be seen at Wickhamford Church on the grave of Penelope, the colonel's daughter. The design formed the basis for the flag of America, the Stars and Stripes.

In August 1651 the small parliamentary garrison at Worcester retired on the approach of a large royalist army, mainly composed of Scotsmen. Prince Charles—or King Charles II, for he had been so proclaimed a few weeks earlier at Carlisle, having spent the previous night at the Swan Inn, Tenbury, entered Worcester unopposed. He set up his headquarters in Sir Rowland Berkeley's house, a Tudor building on the corner of New Street and the Cornmarket which has been known ever since as King Charles' House.

Cromwell arrived outside Worcester in late August. He is known to have stayed at Evesham on 27 August (and again on 5-7 September). There are traditions that during the campaign he lodged at the Lygon Arms, Broadway; in the home of Mr. Justice Berkeley at Spetchley; at

Moor, between Fladbury and Throckmorton, on 28 August; and at White Ladies Aston, where he had a friend called George Symonds, on 29 August. He visited Upton-on-Severn during the day on 29 August, and is said to have had a conversation with an old woman in Church Street, an incident which led to the attachment of his name to some buildings there which persists to this day. On unspecified dates Cromwell is supposed to have rested his horse at Hampton Lovett, and to have planted poplar trees at Shrawley.

Outside Worcester Cromwell's main force was drawn up on Red Hill, which is now a suburb off London Road to the south-west of the city. On 31 August 1,500 men sallied out from Worcester with the intention of making a surprise night attack on the camp and killing Cromwell. They wore white shirts over their tunics for mutual recognition in the darkness, but these made them conspicuous to the parliamentary troops. The royalists suffered disastrous casualties because Cromwell had been forewarned of their plan by a Worcester tailor or cloth-worker, William Guise, who had climbed down the city walls by means of a knotted rope. News of his own expedition must have leaked out, for on his return he was arrested and summarily hanged from the Golden Cross in Broad Street. Six days after the battle of Worcester parliament voted his widow £200 a year for life.

Cromwell's secondary force assembled at Powick, and threw pontoon bridges over the Severn and Teme close to their confluence. On 3 September—Cromwell is said to have delayed until the anniversary of his victory at Dunbar the previous year—the first assault was made at Powick. The royalists withdrew, and parliamentary troops were quickly transferred to Red Hill to support the main attack. Worcester fell. Some 3,000 royalist troops were killed, and 10,000 held prisoner, many in the cathedral.

Charles fled, pausing briefly at Rowland Berkeley's house where as parliamentary soldiers were smashing down the front door he slipped out of the back to a waiting horse. His long and difficult road to exile led initially to Ombersley, where he paused at the inn now called the King's Arms. At one stage he passed through Bromsgrove and in the guise of Jane Lane's serving man was having a horse shod when a search-party of soldiers came by. He was speaking to the smith in derogatory terms about the fugitive king so the soldiers congratulated him on being 'an honest man' and went their way. The same story is placed at Erdington in Warwickshire.

Sir Rowland Berkeley, having either fought or assiduously avoided fighting—depending on which account one follows—at Powick, fled on

Statues of Charles I and II by the entrance to Worcester's Guildhall

his rather conspicuous horse to the farm of one of his tenants at Wick, closely pursued by Cromwell's troopers. The farmer, on the hasty promise that he would never be turned out if he helped, hid the incriminating horse and put in its place another mount of similar appearance. The troopers who arrived soon afterwards accepted that no one could have ridden from the field on so fresh a horse, so Sir Rowland was saved from arrest or perhaps worse. He kept his promise, and the farmer's descendants were still in possession 300 years later.

Cromwell was so delighted by the victory at Worcester that, according to a story current locally until at least the 1920's, he called his soldiers together and ordered them to fill their hats with soil. They then marched several miles to the east and emptied the soil to form Whittington Tump close by the present junction 7 on the M5 motorway.

Royalists claimed that Cromwell won thanks only to the help of the devil. On the morning of 3 September, they asserted, he had met the devil in Perry (or Pirie) Wood near Red Hill and offered his soul in exchange for victory. Cromwell asked for a further twenty-one years of life, then tried for fourteen, and finally had to settle for seven. He remarked to Colonel Lindsay, who witnessed the pact: 'Now, Lindsay, the battle is won and I long to be engaged'. In fact the meeting between Cromwell and William Guise took place in Perry Wood, and for royalist propaganda the move from Guise to the devil was not difficult.

Even so, seven years to the day after the battle, Cromwell died. The violent storms which swept the country were seen as proof by some that the devil was taking his soul. The tempest was particularly awesome at the castle of Brampton Bryan where Brilliana, Lady Harley, had held out so tenaciously in 1643-4 against besieging royalists. A similar storm is said to return to Brampton Bryan every year on 3 September to rampage with Cromwell's soul through the grounds of the long-ruined castle.

Cromwell's head above the Guildhall entrance at Worcester

At Worcester Oliver's Knoll, part of what remains of Perry Wood, is now encircled by two roads, Cromwell Crescent and Cannon Street. The Guildhall has fine statues of Charles I and II but Cromwell's carved head is nailed by the ears over the doorway. The Sidbury bridge bears a plaque with Cromwell's summing up of the battle 'It is for aught I know a crowning mercy'. At Bredon rectory twin stone figures some distance apart on the roof are supposed to represent Charles II and Cromwell. Local people say that if they ever come together the end of the world will be nigh.

The Female Soldier

Hannah Snell, the daughter of a hosier and dyer, was born at Friar Street, Worcester, in April 1723. Although she was one of six sisters she enjoyed playing at soldiers, inspired perhaps by stories of her grandfather and brother, both of whom had been killed in war. This account comes from her *Life and Adventures*:

When she was scarce ten years of age, {she} had had the seeds of heroism ... implanted in her nature, and she used often to declare to her companions that she would be a soldier if she lived; ... she formed a company of young soldiers among her playfellows, of which she was chief commander, at the head of whom she often appeared, and was used to parade the whole town of Worcester. The body of young volunteers were admired all over the town, and they were styled 'Young Amazon Snell's Company'.

After the deaths of her parents, Hannah went at the age of seventeen to live with her married sister at Wapping in London. In 1743 she herself married James Summs, a Dutch sailor who disappeared when she was seven months pregnant. Her child lived for only a few months. In 1745 Hannah dressed in a suit of clothes belonging to her sister's husband, assumed his name (which was James Gray), and set off in search of Summs.

First she travelled to Coventry and enlisted in a regiment which soon moved to Carlisle by means of a 22-day march. A Worcester carpenter called George Beck joined there but did not recognize Hannah who soon

Hannah Snell, by Richard Phelps, 1760

after this deserted over some grievance and spent a month in walking to Portsmouth. There she enlisted as a marine, in which capacity she made several voyages and also fought in India. During her travels she met a man who was able to tell her that James Summs was dead, having been executed aboard a Dutch ship for murder.

Only on being discharged after almost five years' service did Hannah Snell reveal that she was a woman. For a time she went on the London stage, dressed as a soldier and singing 'humorous and entertaining songs':

> All ye noble British spirits
> That midst dangers glory sought,
> Let it lessen not your merit,
> That a woman bravely fought.
> Cupid slily first enroll'd me,
> Pallas next her force did bring,
> Pressed my heart to venture boldly
> For my love and for my King.

Later she was married twice more, kept a public house, and received a government pension of a shilling a day. Eventually she became a pensioner at Chelsea Hospital. She died there, insane, at the age of 69 in 1792.

In 1750 a remarkable book was published under the title of *The Female Soldier or The Surprising Life and Adventures of Hannah Snell*. It is full of equivocation. As James Gray, Hannah Snell has an 'intimate acquaintance' with at least three women, one of whom wishes to marry him/her. On the other hand, fellow servicemen find James effeminate; on one ship he mends linen and is called 'Miss Molly Gray' by sailors 'for want of having such a rough beard as they'. Perhaps to compensate James joins in drinking sessions, displays 'as much skill and dexterity as any sergeant or corporal ... in the military exercise', and with 'wonted intrepidity' faces 'numerous hardships, fatigues and dangers'. He also frequently shares a bed with other men, normal practice for the time, without being unmasked. Even a spell in hospital after wounds in the legs and groin received during the siege of Pondicherry fails to reveal his true identity. What is more, so do two floggings, stripped to the waist.

The first of these is at Carlisle:

At that time her breasts were but very small, and her arms being extended and fixed to the city gates, her breasts were towards the wall, so that then there was little or no danger of her comrades finding out the important secret which she took uncommon pains to conceal. At her second whipping on board the ship, when her hands were lashed to the gangway, she was in much greater danger of being discovered; but she stood as upright as possible, and tied a large silk handkerchief round her neck, the ends wherof entirely covered her breasts, insomuch that she went through the martial discipline with great resolution, without being in the least suspected. ... At this time, it is true, the boatswain of the ship, taking notice of her breasts, seemed surprised, and said they were more like a woman's he ever saw; and as no person on board ever had the least suspicion of her sex, the whole dropped without any further notice being taken.

Hannah Snell's story was part of a great vogue for tales of female soldiers, sailors and highwaymen. Some may find it far-fetched—and perhaps it was embellished, but it contains many details which could have been checked. Hannah was billeted at Coventry in November 1745 with a family called Lucas, in Little Park Street. She served on several ships of which she gives the names and captains, and she also refers to various crew members. Finally, she must have been able to make a convincing case to gain the government pension which she enjoyed for many years, and to become at the end of her life a Chelsea Hospital inmate.

Winter-Spring
Between Woolhope and Fownhope, just off the road, stands a monument erected in 1954 to Tom Spring who was prize-fighting champion of England in 1823 and '24. He was born at Rudge End, Fownhope, in 1795, the son of a butcher. His name was Winter but he later changed it to Spring, which he felt had a more cheerful sound.

Young Thomas intended to be a butcher like his father, but chance determined otherwise. He was dancing at a village wake when, according to Spring's obituary in the *Hereford Times*, his partner was insulted by 'the bully and terror of the neighbourhood, a big and mature miller (Hollands, we think, by name)'. Tom immediately lashed out at the man, and proved the victor in the fight which inevitably ensued.

He then began a spectacularly successful career as a prize fighter which he combined with innkeeping. At one stage he was landlord of the Green Man at Fownhope. Another of his inns was the Boothall at Hereford, which he left in January 1827.

Some years earlier, after Spring's second victory over the Irish champion, Jack Langan, six Irishmen turned up at the Boothall one day with the intention of giving him a good thrashing. Spring coolly went upstairs and changed into fighting rig, then took on all six and threw them out after administering a severe beating.

His feats in the ring as well as outside it made him the object of adulation. 40,000 spectators turned up when he met Langan on the Pitchcroft at Worcester on 7 January 1824. The contest went, by some accounts, to 84 rounds (a round ended only when one of the fighters was knocked down), and lasted two and a half hours. In the end Langan, unwilling to concede defeat, was carried away struggling by his seconds.

Printers all over the country relayed the news in ballad form to countless thousands more. *Spring and Langan. A New Song* was printed in Gateshead:

> Ye champions all both far and near,
> I pray now give attention,
> For Spring he is the finest man,
> Of any we can mention;
> A champion came from Ireland,
> And Langan was his name, sir,
> Who thought to beat our champion Spring,
> And bear away the fame, sir.
>
> But oh let's hope that ne'er a one,
> From any other nation,
> Will e'er be fit to take the belt,
> From the English nation.
> January was the appointed time,
> And the 7th was the day, sir,
> That these two champions did meet,
> For to decide the fray, sir.
>
> A stage was then erected for
> Those champions so bold, sir,
> It's for to fight with all their might,
> For the belt which Spring now holds, sir;
> But all the cry it was that Spring
> Was sure to win the day, sir,
> For Langan he will ne'er be fit
> To take the belt away, sir.

Tom Spring's memorial at Rudge End, Fownhope

At twelve o'clock or something more,
They mounted on the stage, sir,
They both were stripp'd, each fac'd his man,
And eager to engage, sir.
The Irish champion said to Spring,
I've come to let you know, sir,
The belt I'll strip from your shoulders.
Whether you will or no, sir.

You'll find your mistake, then says bold Spring,
And that I'll let you know sir,
I'll send you back to Ireland,
Full of grief and woe, sir;
Hats off, they cried around the stage,
When they begun the fight, sir,
And Langan swore that he would kill
Our champion Spring outright, sir.

The first 9 rounds that they did fight,
Langan was sorely beat, sir,
Then the friends of Spring did loudly sing,
20 to 1 we'll bet, sir;
That Spring the champion of our land
Their favourite will defeat, sir,
And send him back to Ireland
His sorrow to relate, sir.

Then Spring with cunning begun the fight
For to get on more bets, sir,
But for 20 rounds or more
He appeared to be quite weak, sir;
The friends of Spring were up to that,
The odds they still kept betting,
And Langan's friends took up the same,
Till they found that Spring was skeeming.

For they began to smell a rat,
And found out Spring's intention
To lead them all into a stake,
And leave their pockets empty;
But as for Langan we must say,
He is just as good game, sir,
As ever came from Ireland,
Or any other place, sir.

2 hours and more it's they did fight,
There stood unto their station,
With courage both these heroes fought,
For the honour of each nation.
Now Langan says I'll fight no more

With your champion Spring, sir,
For the beating I have got from him
I'll remember while I live, sir.

45 rounds these heroes fought,
With courage on the stage, sir,
A better fight has not been seen,
Not for this many an age, sir;
Hard blows on both sides were received,
No bribery was taken.
Langan said to Spring, I'll give in,
For you've thrash'd well my bacon.

So we'll drink and sing in praise of Spring,
In all his undertakings,
And that he ne'er the belt may lose,
But always thrash their bacon;
Says Spring to Langan you are bet,
After your great boasting,
You know you swore that you would be
The champion of this nation.

I say neither Irish, Scotch, nor French,
Nor any other nation
Shall e'er be champion of this land,
While Englishmen are reigning;
So boast no more o'er Englishmen,
Spring unto Langan said, sir,
For Englishmen before they're bet
Will die upon the stage, sir.

You boxers all now drink a health
To Spring upon the stage, sir,
And if any other man comes forth
He soon will be engaged, sir;
To lose the fame of England
We then should think it hard, sir,
But while we have such men as Spring
We defy the world at large, sir.

Chorus
For Englishmen will not be bet
By any other nation,
For is they will fight man to man
They're sure of a good thrashing.

On retiring from the ring Tom Spring kept the Castle Tavern in London's Holborn, where he died in 1851. He was buried in West Norwood Cemetery. The ballad writers who had celebrated his fights also commemorated his death.

III
CHURCHES

Sited in 'God's Acre', the church was once spiritually as well as physically the focal point of most villages and towns. Its central place in the climactic moments of birth, marriage and death is examined in the next chapter. Here are accounts of builders and bells; epitaphs and inscriptions; stories in wood, stone and stained glass. The first memorial inscriptions in this country were in the time of the Romans. The earliest tombs in parish churches date from the twelfth century but tombstones in churchyards came into common use only from the seventeenth century onwards. Even then, the poor seldom enjoyed the luxury of epitaphs. Inscriptions are now carefully controlled but in earlier times a wide range of styles from pious to punning was tolerated. As one might expect, saints bulk large, but there are also a few sinners—and scandals. Finally, the churches have their own traditions, some decayed but others still vigorous.

Builders
Church sites were often chosen—or so persistent reports would have us believe—by supernatural means. At Leominster a holy man of the seventh century dreamed that a lion fed from his hand. The same night Merewald, King of Mercia (who happened to be nicknamed 'the lion'), dreamed that a hermit had news for him. Next day the two chanced to meet and when the hermit related his dream the king gave orders that a church should be built at the spot. The figure of a lion is still to be seen on the great west door. Despite this belief the name of the town is thought to derive from Leofric's Minster. Leofric, Earl of Mercia, who died in 1057, is best known as the husband of Lady Godiva.

The original intention at Kidderminster was to build St. Mary's Church opposite its present position, on the other bank of the River Stour. When the first attempts at construction were made the stones erected were removed every night by an unseen agency to the present site, and the builders eventually followed suit. A carving on the tower showing an angel holding a piece of arch reminds us of the story. The rejected site is called Cussfield: cursed field.

At Inkberrow—model for the fictional Ambridge of the Archers—spirits called Arkbus took exception to the position first chosen for the church, and carried stones nearer the village every night until the masons took the point. Even so the Arkbus were unhappy at the disturbance which the church bells caused them, and made this lament:

> Neither sleep, neither lie,
> For Inkbro's ting-tangs hang so high.

An intervention of a different kind was made when the old church of St. Mary was being built at Worcester soon after 960, where the present cathedral now stands. A huge square block of stone was noticed. Workmen were told to make use of it but were unable to move it. St. Oswald prayed that the hindrance should become clear, and saw a little black devil sitting on the stone. He made the sign of the cross, which made the devil flee and the masons then easily lifted the block. Again in Worcester, when the church of St. Clement was about to be rebuilt on the eastern side of the Severn an angel came at night and moved the foundation stone to the other bank where some land was unclaimed by St. John's. The new church was built there, and the parish extended accordingly.

The original church at Clodock in the far south-west of Herefordshire was built in the sixth century. An account written some 600 years later tells how the site was chosen. A young noblewoman fell in love with Clodock (or Clydawg), King of Ewyas (and grandson of Brychan, the saint-king of Brecknock), and swore to marry no one else. Another man who had designs on the lady took advantage of a hunting trip with Clodock to murder him. When the body was found it was loaded on a cart to be taken to Ewyas Harold but the oxen stopped on the bank of the River Monnow and refused to go any further. There Clodock was buried and a column of fire played over the grave and a spring burst from the ground. A decision was taken to erect a church at the place, but builders preferred another site at Llanwonog, over a mile away. A start was made there but masonry laid each day collapsed at night until the builders returned to the bank of the Monnow. Nothing now remains of their work—the earliest parts of the present church of St. Clodock date from the twelfth century—but the story is not forgotten. St. Clodock's Well is on the river bank not far from the church.

Two other saints—one each in Worcestershire and Herefordshire—met violent deaths, marked by miraculous springs. On the death of his father in the early part of the ninth century Kenelm became King of Mercia. As an infant of only seven he was placed under the tutelage of his older sister, Kendrida. Wishing to take the crown for herself, Kendrida persuaded her lover, Askobert, to kill the child. Kenelm was taken from the royal palace at Winchcombe in Gloucestershire on a hunting expedition which led many miles to the Clent Hills. Knowing that he was about to die Kenelm planted his staff in the ground where it rooted and became a thorn tree. As he knelt to say the *Te Deum* his head was struck off by Askobert with a long-bladed knife. A white dove flew out of the head and made its way to Rome where it dropped a scroll on the high altar at St. Peter's. The document bore a message which in modern English reads:

> In Clent cow-pasture under a thorn
> Of head bereft lies Kenelm, king born.

The Pope ordered enquiries to be made in England. A procession of clergymen headed by the bishop of Mercia was led to Kenelm's grave by a ray of light or—in another version—by a cow which stood there without eating but still growing fat. As the body was disinterred church bells pealed of their own accord and a spring of water gushed forth from the ground. A dispute arose as to whether the churchmen of Worcestershire or those of Gloucestershire should have the body. The two parties agreed to lie down to sleep at Pyriford (possibly Pershore), the first to wake having priority. The Abbot of Winchcombe and his men woke first, and had secured a lead of several miles with the precious body before the Worcestershire men went in pursuit. The Abbot of Winchcombe prayed, and as he put his crozier to the ground a spring came forth. Refreshed by its water the Gloucestershire men were able to outdistance their pursuers and carry their burden safely to Winchcombe.

The rest of Kenelm's story belongs to Gloucestershire,

Figure supposed to represent St. Kenelm, exterior of south wall of St. Kenelm's Chuch, Clent

but at Clent the spring became a place of pilgrimage. A chapel was built and then in the eleventh century a small church with the spring inside. Another spring about half a mile from the church in a field called Cowbatch (the cow-pasture of the rhyme) also claimed to be St. Kenelm's Well; its waters cured diseases of the eye. The one beneath the chancel, prized by lepers, was partly destroyed at the Reformation. Hugh Latimer, Bishop of Worcester from 1535 until 1539, campaigned against what he regarded as superstition. He resided occasionally at Alvechurch and discouraged pilgrims from visiting and bathing in the well at Clent. Nevertheless, visitors continued, albeit in smaller numbers. In the mid-nineteenth century the spring was diverted from the church into the brook but later re-opened a few yards from the east end, where it can still be seen.

The village of Kenelmstowe grew up near the church, with some thirty houses and an inn called the Red Cow after the beast which had stood by the thorn tree. The place was important enough for Henry III to grant a charter for an annual four-day fair starting on the eve of St. Kenelm's Day (17 July, changed to 28 July after the revision of the calendar in 1752. However, the place—by then called Clent—went into a decline after the Reformation, and now only St. Kenelm's Church and a single house remain some distance from the modern village.

At the risk of spoiling a good story one should point out that the historical Kenelm died before his father, possibly in battle with the Welsh, and was buried at Winchcombe Abbey. His sister, Kendrida, was the abbess of Minster in Kent. The first account of the legendary Kenelm was written by William of Malmesbury in the eleventh century.

By the River Lugg at Marden the church of St. Mary stands close to the spot where St. Ethelbert was buried in 794. Ethelbert, King of East Anglia, set off to meet Offa, King of Mercia, with a view to marrying his daughter, Alfrida. The omens were not good. The earth shook as Ethelbert mounted his horse, and the sun seemed to darken. The king and his companions prayed, and the day grew bright again. One night during the journey Ethelbert dreamed that the roof of his palace had fallen, the corners of his bridal bed were torn, and his mother wept tears of blood. Men cut at the roots of a magnificent tree growing in the palace, causing them to run with blood which flowed towards the east. Transformed into a bird with golden wings Ethelbert flew to the top of a column of light brighter than the sun and heard angel voices singing. When he woke he consulted his advisers who interpreted the dream to signify that he would attain greater power.

Ethelbert travelled on to King Offa's palace at Sutton Walls—or, some say, at Marden on the site of the present vicarage. There he was killed.

Different explanations are offered as to the reason. One suggestion is that he aroused Offa's implacable resentment by attempting to seduce his queen, Kenfrith. Alternatively, Kenfrith tried to seduce Ethelbert and when he rejected her advances told her husband that Ethelbert had approached her. A further story is that Kenfrith, jealous of her daughter's love for Ethelbert, went to Offa and claimed that the match would make Ethelbert too powerful, so he should be killed.

Whatever the reason, the decision was made. Offa proposed a large sum of money to whichever of his men would do the murder. The task was accepted by Winebert who had been brought up in the household of Ethelbert's father. Winebert went to Ethelbert and persuaded him to lay aside his sword and dismiss his retinue. As soon as Ethelbert complied the doors were closed behind him and he realised in a flash that the dream had foretold his death. He stood commending his soul to God when Winebert struck off his head.

Another account suggests that the queen drugged Ethelbert's wine before he was murdered; another that she draped over a pit a cloth on which Ethelbert sat and fell to his death. Old maps designated part of Sutton Walls as the King's Cellar which was traditionally taken to be the pit in question.

Scandalised by the murder, Alfrida took a vow of chastity and went to live as a hermit in the marshes of Crowland in Lincolnshire at a place which later became St. Guthlac's Abbey. Offa ordered Ethelbert's body to be buried on the bank of the Lugg where, in a macabre game, the head was rolled along the ground. The night after the burial a light shone over the grave so brightly that it lit up the sky. Offa became fearful of retribution, and arranged to give a tenth of his goods to the church. He also went on a pilgrimage to Rome where Pope Adrian directed him to build a church of wattle at the site of the grave and a church of stone (later to be the cathedral) at Hereford.

Meanwhile, three nights after the burial Ethelbert appeared in the midst of a great light by the bedside of a peasant and ordered him to re-bury his body by the River Wye. The man got up and with a companion lifted the body, washed it, wrapped it in clean linen and placed it in a cart ready for the journey. A blind man who stumbled into the cart obtained his sight. A spring gushed forth from the Lugg-side grave whose waters kept their clarity even when murky floods from the river covered the area. Where the cart stopped to rest the oxen on the journey another spring emerged whose waters were found to be good for ulcers and sores.

In reality it was Eadwulf, Bishop of Lichfield, who ordered the translation of the body to Hereford. It is possible that the move was made by water since St. Ethelbert's Well at the bottom of Quay Street in Hereford is just where a coffin might have been rested after being landed before being carried up the slope towards the cathedral. This well is now dry; so is the one at the west end of Marden Church, near the font. The tomb of St. Ethelbert in Hereford Cathedral where the sick were healed and the feeble-minded restored to reason was destroyed in 1050 by marauding Danes.

One saint's well still runs with limpid water at Stoke Edith, just off the A438 some ten miles east of Hereford. The builders of the first church there were helped by St. Edith in person, who carried water for the mortar until she sank exhausted to the ground and prayed. In response water flowed out at her feet, thus creating the well. The village may take its name from Queen Edith, widow of Edward the Confessor, rather than St. Edith. Nevertheless, St. Edith's Well was for centuries patronised by people suffering from skin diseases. Some even bathed in its water, to the intense irritation of Lady Foley, the landowner, who in the nineteenth century had a large grille fitted. The well, complete with (open) grille, is on private property beside the entrance to Stoke Edith House. This was formerly the vicarage but was taken over by the Foleys in 1927 when their own house was destroyed by fire.

Another saint has no well but she has left a considerable impression on Ledbury, only a few miles from Stoke Edith. St. Catherine—a local or unofficial saint—is said to be represented in the form of a late fourteenth century effigy in the church's clergy vestry, though scholars attribute it to the Pauncefoot or Carew families.

Catherine certainly existed; her signature has even survived on a document dated from Ledbury in 1313. She was born in 1272, the daughter of Sir John Giffard of Brimpsfield, Gloucestershire. She was married at the age of fifteen—not unusual for the time—to Sir Nicholas Audley of Audley, Staffordshire. In 1299 both husband and father died, leaving her between them the castle and town of Llandovery together with estates in Cheshire, Shropshire and Staffordshire. In 1308 she made over all these lands to her son, Nicholas, in exchange for an annuity of £100. At the same time she may have gone with her other son, Thomas, to live at Hellens in Much Marcle with her cousin by marriage, Yseult Audley.

There, or possibly at Audley Cottage in the same village—to which one story says that she had been ejected from Hellens—Catherine had the revelation that she must seek a town where the bells rang of their own accord, and found a hermitage there. She and her faithful servant, Mabel, duly set off on the quest. Their wanderings included the Sapey Brook, where their horses were stolen, and also Pembridge, Bosbury and finally

Ledbury, where the detached towers of the churches are supposed to mark her visit. (Six others in this category in Herefordshire, some of them later joined to their towers—Garway, Holmer, Kington, Richard's Castle, Weobley and Yarpole—do not claim such a connection).

Having arrived close to Ledbury one evening, perhaps after being led there by the trail of the stolen horses, Catherine heard the church bells ringing and sat down on a stone while Mabel went to investigate. Until late in the nineteenth century Cattern's Stone in Cattern's Acre was pointed out to the curious. Catherine's Acre still exists as the name of a house adjacent to the street called Mabel's Furlong. Neither occur in ancient records, so the names are either modern coinages or persisted in oral tradition for many centuries before being written down.

Mabel heard the bells but could see no ringers, perhaps because they were in the detached tower. Even today visitors sometimes look round in puzzlement and ask where the bellringers are. Mabel returned with her good news to Catherine, who set up a hermitage close to the church by one account, perhaps in Audley Cottage which still stands; at Hazle Farm by another—the name was certainly recorded as early as 1086, and the farm supplied Catherine with the 'herbs' (vegetables) and milk on which she lived. A grant registered in 1323 and arranged, we are told, by Yseult Audley, provided the sum of £30 a year on the orders of Edward II towards the expenses of 'the recluse of Ledbury'.

Catherine is often credited with the foundation of St. Catherine's Hospital in Ledbury, but this dates from forty years before she was born, and the dedication was to St. Catherine of Alexandria. Before her death the Ledbury St. Catherine prophesied that should the outer door of her chapel in the church remain closed until it opened of itself the town would become one of the richest in England. However, if human hands intervened it would remain poor. The chapel in question was probably the Chapter House, which may originally have been intended for a shrine to St. Catherine; in the church's own records at one stage it was indeed called St. Catherine's Chapel. The townspeople were careful to keep the door closed till one night some drunken and impious revellers threw it open, thus depriving Ledbury of its potential prosperity. A final remembrance of the local saint is in the form of a tune by John Jenkins, first published in 1662, with the title of *Lady Katharine Audley's Bells*.

Bells

As well as summoning the faithful to prayer or worship, church bells had secular uses. They pealed for victory in war and stood ready in peace to signal invasion or disaster. Bells once announced seedtime, harvest,

57

gleaning; there was even an Oven Bell to proclaim that the lord of the manor's oven was ready to cook his tenants' dough—at a price.

Leominster—and no doubt many other places—had a Pancake Bell; at St. Martin's, Worcester, a Plum Pudding Bell rang nightly for a few days several weeks before Christmas. At Bewdley an early morning bell woke apprentices for their labour, schoolboys for study and people in general for work. The Day Bell as it was called at St. Helen's, Worcester—a church which closed in 1950 to become a record office—rang for fifteen minutes every morning at 4, until about 1750. Kington in Herefordshire had a 5 a.m. bell until 1830. At Pershore the same bell was discontinued after a sexton called Blake on one occasion rang it five hours too early: he woke when midnight was striking but heard only the last five strokes, so dressed and rang what he thought was the five o'clock bell; some market gardeners, trusting him implicitly, loaded their carts and drove off to Worcester or Birmingham.

Pershore's curfew bell rung between Bonfire Night and Candlemas Day (2 February) survived rather longer. Goldsmith's well known line, 'The curfew tolls the knell of parting day', was once literally true. Even though the legal requirement for a curfew bell ended as long ago as 1100 the practice continued with many local variations until recent times—indeed it continues at Presteigne, just over the Welsh border from Herefordshire.

St. Helen's, Worcester, until 1939 had its own bell at 8 p.m. followed by as many strokes as days had elapsed in the month. The young Edward Elgar in the early 1870's sometimes deputised for the ringer when his rheumatism was too painful, and 'took a delight in adding occasionally an extra number or two to the actual date'. Other places with a curfew bell included Bewdley, Evesham, Bromyard, Hereford All Saints', Kington, Leominster, Ross and Weobley. John Masefield recalled that many parishes still rang the curfew when he was a child.

St. Martin's, Worcester, had a special bell on December evenings to guide people through the darkness. At Aymestrey a man claimed to have been led astray by a will o' the wisp in Poke-house (or Puck-house) Wood, across the River Lugg from the village, so he set aside a piece of land, the rental from which provided for a bell to be rung to guide any benighted traveller. Eventually the sum raised was too small so the custom lapsed, but the hole is (or at least was) pointed out in the ringing chamber floor through which a rope passed to the porch for ease of ringing. The rent of a small field at Leysters called Bell Acre was used to provide new bell ropes. Both Bockleton and Tenbury devoted similar rents to providing light in the churches, and at Rochford the income enabled lights to be placed along the river bank road in the winter to stop people falling into the Teme.

The passing bell—where it is still rung—gives news that a death has occurred. Formerly it warned that death was imminent, to enable people to pray for the soul of the departing man or woman. The experience of hearing it must have been awesome for the person concerned. Until the 1920's St. Mary's, Tenbury, had different numbers of rings for a man, a woman and a child. At Kingsland until the Second World War the pattern was four rings for a man and five for a woman, followed by as many more strokes as the years of his or her age.

An inscription on the tenor bell at St. James', Hartlebury, reads:

> For the living I do call,
> To the grave I summon all.

This or a closely similar message is shared with thirteen more churches in Worcestershire and at least fifteen in Herefordshire. No fewer than 66 churches in the two counties have a bell inscribed 'Peace and Good Neighbourhood'. At Bretforton a bell proclaims:

> As Music Hath a Secret Charm
> We May the Atheist Soul Alarm.

While at Himbleton, Grafton Flyford and Severn Stoke the message is:

> All men that heare my rorin sound
> Repent before ye ly in ground.

An Evesham Abbey bell puts this in more measured language:

> I sound the sound that doleful is,
> To them that live amiss;
> But sweet my sound is unto such
> As live in joy and bliss.
> I sweetly tolling, men do call
> To taste on food that feeds the soul.

The number and pitch of bells varied to produce different patterns of sound which in turn were adapted into jingles, often irreverent. 'Roast beef and old perry say the bells of Bosbury' or 'Stick a goose and dress un say the bells of Wesson' (Weston-under-Penyard). Welsh Newton with its two bells just repeated 'Erfen, cawl Erfen'—turnip, turnip soup—an allusion to the poor crops produced by the local soil.

The ringers themselves could be irreverent in their behaviour, and several bell chambers—at Cradley, Kingsland, Mathon, Leominster and Weobley, for example—have or had (some have been removed or whitewashed over) inscribed tablets or painted boards with rules and penalties cast into rhyme. This set, from Cradley, dates from the eighteenth century:

> Ye Gentlemen Ringers both far and near,
> That are disposed for to Ring here;
> Observe this law, and mark it well,
> The Man that Overthrows his Bell;
> Sixpence he to the Clark must pay
> Before that he go hence away,
> If he ring with Glove, Spur, or Hat,
> Sixpence he must pay for that:
> If he either Curse, or Swear,
> Six-pence must pay while you are here,
> This is not a place to Quarrel in.
> To Curse and Swear it is a Sin.

(Overthrowing a bell, caused by too strong a pull, puts it out of action after breaking a restraining stave). Change ringing is a favourite pastime for many. One special set of changes is known as the Hinton Surprise Major, after the village of Hinton-on-the-Green. Another spectacular effort was commemorated in a printed ballad entitled *A Song on the Famous Peal of 7308 Grandsire Cators Rung by the Society of All Saints Ringers, in Worcester, On the 28th of November, 1774*. The names of the ringers were carefully worked into the song, which ends:

> Four Hours and a Half and Six Minutes they were,
> The people with watches in hand did declare;
> And said the performers were worthy of praise,
> For they ne'er heard a peal better rung in their days.
> So here's a good health to those that wish us well,
> And those that do envy us they cannot excell;
> Those that wish us well, boys, we wish them the same,
> And the Youths of All-Saints they shall still bear the name.

There is an interesting footnote:

Thomas Hill dreamed three times, in one night, that he was ringing at All-Saints and each time awakened with the thought of the Tenor's

Clapper falling out at the end of the peal; which was verified this day, for as soon as George Wainwright gave the finishing stroke, the clapper broke through the middle.

Once the bell ringers had called parishoners to church another team of musicians took over: a band provided accompaniment for the choir and congregation before the days when organs became universal. Thomas Hardy in *Under the Greenwood Tree* has left an affectionate portrait of a 'quire' of village musicians just before they were displaced by an organ. J.A. La Trobe, curate of St. Peter's, Hereford, criticised even organists for

Bosbury Tower from a drawing of the nineteenth century

61

their 'frivolous taste' and lamented that 'much impropriety' was caused by admitting women to church choirs. Writing in 1831 he objected to singers' 'want of reverence in the House of God', 'fondness for display', 'obstinate rejection of advice' and 'bad taste'.

Many churches banished musicians from the chancel to a gallery, usually positioned at the west end. Clodock still has one; as does Kilpeck. At St. Margaret's Church in the village of the same name in the Golden Valley the richly-carved rood loft—still in existence, and described by Pevsner as 'one of the wonders of Herefordshire'—was used by singers and musicians alike. At Eckington a gallery was built at the west end of the nave in 1774, then enlarged in 1841 to accommodate both singers and a band of two violins, two cellos, one bass viol, flutes, 'clarionets', trumpet, trombone and bassoon. Items such as these appear in the church register:

> 1783 Paid for a Reed for the Music 6s 6d
> 1825 Paid for Strings for the Church Music £1
> 1826 Bass Viol £5. 19. 0

All of the Eckington musicians were supplanted in 1863 by a harmonium (which had to be repaired three years later at a cost of five shillings), and in 1887 the gallery itself was removed. In 1907 came the organ.

Bromsgrove had a string and reed band, the latter instruments being used not only in church but outside by the waits (see chapter 9) at Advent and Christmas. Church Honeybourne was reduced to one violin and the ''oss's leg' (a bassoon) when the players were replaced in the 1860's by a £5 Alexandre harmonium. Even the Methodist Mill Street Chapel at Kidderminster had fiddles, brass instruments and a serpent during the 1850's. (A serpent is an ancient bass instrument with three U-turns, made of wood covered in leather).

Dorstone once had a cornettist and fiddlers; Longdon (until 1868) a string quartet. A musician called William Smith played at Saintbury near Broadway from 1834 until 1901, first woodwind instruments, then after the loss of his teeth the bass viol. He was succeeded by a Mrs. Mason who played the harmonium for a mere 22 years, and then by Harold Andrews who was still using the same instrument in 1973 after half a century's service.

There was even a vogue for barrel organs programmed to play hymn tunes, and sometimes a man who had previously played an instrument was given the ignominious task of cranking one of the new devices. At Bosbury a barrel has been preserved which played eleven hymn tunes including *Rockingham, Melcombe* and *Stuttgart*. At Bayton a barrel organ was used both for services and dances. One Sunday morning the parish clerk forgot to change the barrel, and instead of a hymn the congregation heard *The Keel Row*.

Samuel George, parish clerk and bellringer at St. John's, Hadzor, died in 1774. His gravestone bears these words:

> I have oft tolled the passing bell,
> And dug the silent grave,
> For many a neighbour dear.
> Have oftimes sat beneath the yew tree shade,
> As up the road was borne with solemn pace
> The poor remains of some dear one deceased.
> My mouldering body now in dust doth lie
> Like theirs, awaiting for immortal day.

Another ringer, this time at Kempsey, has a much more laconic verse on a tablet fixed to the belfry wall:

> Time and Steven are now both even:
> Steven beat time, and Time beat Steven.

At Bromsgrove, rather more sedate lines were composed by a local poet, Waterson, in memory of Charles Ravenscroft who died in 1812:

> Ay, Charles! thy ringing now is o'er,
> Thou'lt call the merry peal no more,
> To Single not to Bob direct,
> To give each change its due effect,
> Nor teach the inexperienced youth
> The course to range with ease and truth.
> Of this no more! give up thou must,
> And mingle with the parent dust!
> Into its place thy Bell is come,
> And ruthless Death has brought thee home.

Epitaphs

Members of other trades and professions also had fitting memorials. A verse traditional for blacksmiths is to be found with variations at Richard's Castle, Claines, Norton and Shrawley. The last example reads:

My sledge and hammer lie reclined
My bellows, too have lost their wind;
My fire is spent, my forge decayed
And in the dust my vice is laid:
My coal is spent, my iron is gone,
My nails are drove, my work is done.
My fire dried corpse here lies at rest,
My soul, smoke-like, soars to be blest.

Again at St. Mary's, Shrawley, a gamekeeper is shown on a tombstone; he shoots partridges and his dog retrieves. The verse says:

He sleeps! no more at early morn
To wake the woods with yellow horn:
No more with willing dog and gun
To rise before the sluggard sun;
No more beside the social can
To-morrow's sport with joy to plan;
Death took his aim, discharged his piece,
And bade his sporting season cease.

Another sportsman—a cockfighter called John Andrews, who died in 1799—is remembered at Peterchurch:

Also, poor Captain, winged by cruel death,
He pecked in vain, o'ermatched, resigned his breath,
Lov'd social mirth, none dare his word distrust,
Sincere in friendship, and was truly just.

John Oakes, a Severn boatman who drowned in 1821 at the age of 27, is commemorated at Ribbesford with suitably nautical metaphors:

Boreas' blast and Neptune's waves
Have tossed me to and fro;
I strove all I could my life to save
At last obliged to go.
Now at anchor here I lay,
Where's many of the fleet;
But now once more I must set sail
My Saviour Christ to meet.

Another boatman has a more laconic, stoic epitaph:

> My anchor's cast—
> My rope's on shore—
> And here I lie
> Till time's no more.

A spectacular headstone—black, with white lettering, and headed by the representation of an early locomotive—stands in Bromsgrove church-yard. The memorial to Thomas Scaife, an engine driver killed at the age of 28 in 1840 on the Birmingham and Gloucester Railway by a boiler explosion was 'erected at the joint expense of his fellow workmen'. The 'lines (were) composed by an unknown Friend as a Memento of the worthiness of the Deceased':

> My *engine* now is cold and still
> No *water* does my boiler fill:
> My *coke* affords its flame no more,
> My days of usefulness are o'er.
> My *wheels* deny their noted speed,
> No more my guiding hands they heed;
> My *whistle* too, has lost its tone
> Its shrill and thrilling sounds are gone;
> My *valves* are now thrown open wide
> My *flanges* all refuse to guide,
> My *clacks* also, though once so strong,
> Refuse to aid the busy throng
> No more I feel each urging breath
> My *steam* is now condens'd in death.
> Life's *railway's* o'er, each *station's* past,
> In death I'm stopp'd and rest at last.
> Farewell dear friends and cease to weep,
> In Christ I'm SAFE, In Him I sleep.

John Abel died in 1674 at the age of 97 and was buried at Sarnesfield. He built handsome black and white market houses at Brecon, Kington, Ledbury and Leominster (of which only the last two survive), and during the siege of Hereford by parliamentary forces in 1645 constructed a powder mill for which he was given the title of King's Carpenter. Abel's tomb shows the tools of his trade—rule, compasses and square—and bears these lines:

John Abel's tomb outside Sarnesfield Church

This craggy stone a covering is for an architector's bed;
That lofty building raised high, yet now lies low his head;
His line and rule, so death concludes, are locked up in store;
Build then who list,
Or they who wist,
For he can build no more.
His house of clay could hold no longer,
May Heaven's joy build him a stronger.

At Holy Trinity Church, Belbroughton, a headstone recalls Richard Phillpotts of the Bell Inn, who died in 1766 at the age of 69:

To tell a memory or a wond'rous tale
Over a chearful glass of nappy ale
In harmless mirth was his supreme delight,

To please his guests or friends by day or night.
But no fine tale, how well so ever told
Could make the tyrant Death, his stroke withhold;
That fatal stroke has laid him here in dust
To rise again once more with joy we trust.

Another publican receives more jocular treatment:

Beneath this stone in hopes of Zion
Doth lie the landlord of the Lion.
His son keeps on the business still
Resigned upon the heavenly will.

The establishment mentioned is the White Lion at Upton-on-Severn, where a series of episodes in Fielding's *Tom Jones* is set. The epitaph, too, may be fictional; an Upton writer of 1869 says it 'has been stated in Sunday magazines and newspapers to have existence in our churchyard (but) we can get no clear memory of its being here'. On the other hand, this was copied from a stone at Upton's old church:

Here lies the body of Mary Ford
Whose soul we hope is with the Lord
But if for hell she has changed this life
It's better far than John Ford's wife.

The state of relationships between married couples often spills over into epitaphs, as in the peremptory farewell by Thomas Weston to his first wife at Bredwardine:

Here lies my wife, here let her lie;
Now she's at rest, and so am I.

By contrast, William Grove says at Hanbury of his wife, Frances who died in 1829 at the age of 50:

She was—but words are wanting to say what;
Think what a mother should be—she was that.

At Eaton Bishop Richard and Margaret Snead, who died in 1678, have a joint epitaph:

One bed we shared; one tomb now holds us,
And our bones, mingled with dust now lie together.
One death was ours; one year took us away.
One day saved us and gave us back to God.

A vicar and his two (successive) wives are commemorated on an eight-eenth century tablet in the chancel at Kempsey: 'Underneath the corrupt-ible parts of a vicar, one husband, two helpmeets, both wives and both Anna, a triplicity of persons in two twains but one flesh, are interred'.

The writers of epitaphs were not above making puns when the opportu-nity arose. At Bromsgrove the name of Knott was too good to miss:

Here lies a man that was Knott born,
His father was Knott before him.
He lived Knott, and did Knott die,
Yet underneath this stone doth lie;
Knott christened,
Knott begot,
And here he lies,
And yet was Knott.

Even eminent people were not exempt. Theophilus Field was succes-sively bishop of Llandaff, St. David's and Hereford. When he died in 1636 this epitaph was deemed appropriate:

The Sun that light unto three Churches gave
Is set; this Field is buried in a grave,
This Sun shall rise, this Field renew his flowers,
The sweetness breathe for age, not for hours.

When Bishop Hurd of Worcester was visited by George III at Hartlebury the king's contingent had to pass through a tollgate at Worcester. (This was a roundhouse called the Barban gate—now a sweet-shop—at the junction of the Ombersley and Droitwich roads). The toll keeper, Robert Sleath, allowed the party through on promise of payment by an equerry. When the money was not forthcoming he refused to allow the king's party to pass on the return journey until both tolls, amounting to 27 shillings, were paid. When Sleath died in Birmingham in 1805 the inci-dent was remembered:

On Wednesday last old Robert Sleath
Passed through the Turnpike Gate of death;
To him would Death no toll abate,
Who stopped the King at Wor'ster Gate.

At times the dead set out by means of their epitaphs to address the living from beyond the grave. Not surprisingly, the mood is inclined to be grim. 'Remember' cries Thomas Barrett (who died in 1747 at the age of 23) from a tablet fixed outside the south wall of the nave at Bosbury:

Remember, all you who pass this way,
As you are now so once was I,
And as I am so will you be,
Therefore prepare to follow me.

Almost the same words occur at St. Mary's, Kington, St. Stephen's Redditch, and no doubt elsewhere too. Similar sentiments are conveyed in another traditional verse which crops up at Mathon (for John Barrett, to the left of the porch) and at Belbroughton (for Joseph Bird who died in 1804):

All you that come my grave to see
As I am now so must you be;
Repent in time, make no delay,
I in my prime was snatched away.
In love I liv'd, in peace I died,
My life was ask'd—but God denied.

Margaret Jones who died in 1805 has sombre words on a tablet in the chancel of Clodock Church:

Oft by the silent grave I once did tread,
Mused on the short memorials of the dead,
Thou too, that readest this must lie supine
Whilst others read some epitaph of time.

A tombstone in the churchyard of St. Mary's, Ripple, marks what is locally known as the Giant's Grave. Here lies Robert Reeve, who died in 1626 at the age of 56. He was a powerful man, 7 feet 4 inches in height, who died of over-exertion—possibly what we should now call a heart attack—while engaged in a mowing contest for a wager in Uckinghall meadow. His epitaph is very simple:

As you passe be, behold my length,
But never glory in your strength.

There is a similar inscription in Welland churchyard. Equally terse and resigned is the following from Evesham:

Here doth ly
All that can dy
Of Ann Haines who ended this life ... May 1717

Other epitaphs struggle to come to terms with grief, especially when they concern children. Daniel Ward died at Eckington in 1706, aged three years and six months:

Sweet Pretty Babe
Soon snacht away
We trust to live
With Christ in iay {joy}.

This was for a baby who died at Kingsland in 1683:

So young and so soon dead, conclude we may
She was too good longer on earth to stay.

The same kind of hope is expressed at Upton Bishop on the north wall of the nave for a woman who died in 1698, aged 29:

Here lies interr'd from Nature's Flesh and Blood,
Being taken in her prime, Susannah Underwood,
Death sunk her Body from on Earth to Rest
Her soule, I hope, sings Hallelujahs with the Blest.

Churchyards

Despite their many gloomy associations churchyards were often used for recreation. At Craswall a levelled area by the north wall of the church was used for playing fives, and a hollow beyond as a pit for cockfighting. A stone bench along the outside of the chancel accommodated spectators. At St. Margaret's, where fives was played against the north wall of the nave, the hinges of shutters which protected the east window can still be seen. At St. Mary's, Kington, the wake held on the Sunday on or following 15 August was ousted by the vicar from the churchyard only in

1795. Pershore Fair managed to survive in the abbey churchyard until 1838.

Various oddities are also found in churchyards. A two-ton mass of rock at Bosbury, thought to have been 'held in veneration in heathen times', said a nineteenth century clergyman, was buried beneath a cross, presumably to nullify its malevolent influence. Then for some reason it was dug up in 1796 and moved to its present position on the south side of the tower. At Ashperton an old font now in the churchyard perhaps served for the christening of Katharine Grandison whose name has been linked with the origin of the Order of the Garter. It was she who dropped her garter at a court ball and had it retrieved by Edward III. His famous comment— *Honi soit qui mal y pense*, (shame to him who thinks ill of it)—has been attributed to a desire not to spare Katharine's blushes but to shield her from a possible accusation of sorcery. The suggestion, based on the notion that the garter was somehow a witch's badge at the time, seems rather fanciful. Daniel Defoe in his *Tour through the Whole Island of Great Britain* mentions the monument in Worcester Cathedral to the Countess of Salisbury (Katherine's married name) 'who dancing before, or with King Edward III in his great hall at Windsor, dropped her garter, which the king taking up, honoured it so much as to make it the denominating ensign for his new order of knighthood'. The *Dictionary of National Biography* calls the story 'palpably fictitious', and points out that its first source, Polydore Vergil, visited England 150 years after the Order of the Garter was set up.

In what was once the northern boundary wall of Bromsgrove churchyard people used to point out Tom Thumb's Monument, probably the lid of an old stone coffin. The unfortunate Tom had made a pact with the devil (like that of Jack of Kent related in chapter 2), to be repaid by the surrender of his soul after death, whether he were buried outside or inside consecrated ground. Tom cheated the devil by having himself placed beneath the wall, and therefore neither in nor out. In 1824, though, the churchyard was enlarged, so what had been the boundary wall fell inside. What happened to Tom's soul at that stage is not known.

The devil's head is seen by some in the small finely worked bronze doorknocker at Dormington Church. The large ring hanging from the grimacing mouth may have secured sanctuary for any outlaw who could manage to grasp it. The original which dates from the twelfth century was stolen in 1980 and recovered only by a fortunate chance. Since then it has been kept in a museum, with only a copy remaining in its place.

Until 1811 a large green dragon could be seen painted on the west wall of Mordiford Church. Although the beast shown was in fact probably a wyvern from the arms of the priory of St. Guthlac (which held the living of Mordiford) it gave rise to a clutch of dragon stories. A girl called Maud found a dragon 'no bigger than a cucumber' wandering in the woods. Ignoring warnings she insisted on treating it as a pet. It soon moved from milk to meat, and started hunting first poultry, then sheep, then cattle. Finally it became a man-eater, living in Haugh Wood and following a path still known as Serpent Lane down to the confluence of the Lugg and the Wye.

The dragon's end came in one of several ways. A condemned criminal after being offered his life as a reward hacked it to pieces while it slept; or hid in a cider barrel by the river and killed it by firing a gun through the bunghole. Alternatively the dragon impaled itself on a knife-studded barrel from which the man emerged to administer the coup de grâce. The three stories unite in saying that the criminal failed to enjoy his triumph because he died from the after-effects of the dragon's noxious breath. A further twist is provided by the notion that the unfortunate hero was no outlaw, but a member of the respected Garston family. Yet another suggestion is that the villagers of Mordiford combined to hack the dragon to death as it slept off the effects of gorging itself on a drowned ox washed down the river. As late as 1875 the rector found two old women trying to drown a couple of newts in the font lest they grow up to renew the scourge. In 1973 to celebrate the centenary of their school local children staged a pageant showing a battle between green and red dragons which ended when the red dragon went to the west to become the symbol of Wales while the green dragon became the picture on the church.

Carved dragons feature in churches at Kilpeck, Shobdon, Chaddesley Corbett (on the font), Clent (St. Kenelm's), Pedmore and Netherton. At Brinsop a dragon writhes in its death throes at the feet of St. George on a twelfth century tympanum in the church dedicated to him. The encounter was believed to have taken place locally, in a field to the north of the church called Lower Stanks; and to the south in Duck's Pool Meadow is the Dragon's Well. However, scholars tell us that although it was executed by Herefordshire craftsmen the sculpture's theme derives from a carving at Parthenay-le-Vieux in western France.

More tractable game in the shape of deer and salmon is shown together with an archer in the Norman tympanum admired by John Ruskin at Ribbesford Church. The local explanation is that John Horshill, Lord of the Manor in the twelfth century, saw a hind coming down to drink on the opposite bank of the Severn. He shot an arrow and killed not only the hind but a salmon which happened to leap at the critical moment. Sceptics say the carving simply showed the characteristic game of the area. Another—

The sheila-na-gig at Kilpeck Church

perhaps fanciful—theory is that it portrays Sigurd the Volsung, a hero of Teutonic mythology and Wagner's *Ring*.

The tiny church at Kilpeck has a wealth of carvings, many of them Norman, both inside and out. Some eighty figures on corbels include real and imaginery birds and beasts, a strange creature playing an unrecognisable instrument, a kilted dancer, and two lovers embracing. Some are missing; they probably showed naked men in a state of arousal. Asked in the 1920's about damage to one figure an old man replied: 'Ah, that wur Miss - - -. A never could suffer that un, so a get her a pole and a pothered un off.' One wonders what the lady thought of the female figure on the south side of the apse, which represents a woman holding open her genitals.

This is a sheila-na-gig, a figure which inspires extensive speculation. A Celtic earth mother who gives life and death; a Norman joke carried out by masons in a period of artistic licence when the decorative features of churches covered a wide range of subject matter; 'the witch on the wall', as some once believed; an illustration of how to give birth unaided (with parallels in the pre-Columbian sculpture of South America); merely 'a quaint representation of the human figure': these are some of the theories. Only eighteen examples of such figures are known in Britain, scattered all over the country. Many clergymen would prefer them not to be there but accept them as part of the fabric of their churches. Some people feel differently, and there was a tradition that a young man would take his bride-to-be and introduce her to the sheila so that their marriage would be blessed with plenty of children.

Object lessons
Within churches, too, are many items which express popular beliefs or have given rise to them. A favourite motif is the foliate head or green man, which some say symbolises sadness and sacrifice, death and ruin; others life and renewal, a potent force erupting from the collective subconscious. (The Green Man of inn signs is probably the Jack-in-the-Green of a spring ritual which dates back only to the eighteenth century). There are examples of foliate heads carved in stone in the churches at Rowlstone, Much Marcle (christianised by the addition of a cross on a chain round the neck) and Bosbury (on the Harford tomb, dating from 1579). A particularly good specimen is in the form of a roof boss in Worcester Cathedral, just opposite the Chapter House door.

The green man is sometimes found in wood on misericords, of which Worcester cathedral has a set of 37, dating from 1379. These were wooden brackets fixed to the underside of choirstall seats so as to give support to singers standing through the long services. Carvings in such a lowly position seem to have been left to the fantasy of craftsmen, so we find not only Biblical scenes but fabulous beasts, traditional sports, rough humour and vignettes from everyday life.

At Worcester the misericords show an old man stirring a pot, a flute player, an angel with a viol, a knight holding a dagger, a butcher slaughtering an ox, the circumcision, the presentation of Samuel, a woman writing, a sower, knights tilting, an angel playing a lute, a huntsman blowing a horn, a knight fighting two griffins, three reapers, three ploughmen, three mowers, Abraham and Isaac, the temptation of Eve, the expulsion from Paradise, Moses bringing the commandments, the judgement of Solomon, Samson and the lion, a man knocking down acorns, a lion and a dragon fighting, a knight hawking, a monster, a sphinx, a cockatrice, a naked woman riding on a goat, Adam delving and Eve spinning, a stag under a tree, and a dragon.

A broadly similar collection of some 60 misericords is to be found in Hereford Cathedral. It includes a naked man seated on horseback facing the tail. Among other offences forgery was punished in this way, and one instance is to be found in the Hereford records for 1535. Misericords found elsewhere include subjects as diverse as pig-killing (Ripple), a monk driving away the devil by inserting a bellows in his backside (Malvern Priory), two mermaids (All Saints', Hereford), a fox running away with a goose (Canon Pyon) and a pair of contending wrestlers (Leintwardine).

Some other items in churches are more orthodox. In St. Peter's Church at Peterchurch on the inside wall over the south door is a carp with a golden chain round its neck. An old man told Parson Kilvert in 1876:

They do say the fish was first seen at Dorstone and speared there, but he got away and they hunted him down to Peterchurch and killed him close by the church. He was as big as a salmon and had a gold chain round his neck. They do say you can see the blood now upon the stones at Dorstone where the fish was speared first.

The Golden Well at Dorstone where the fish was first seen is the source of the River Dore, which then flows down to Peterchurch and beyond. Peterchurch had its own well, consecrated supposedly by St. Peter himself, who dropped in the fish with the golden chain which was to live there for ever.

Another edifying legend is illustrated on a capital at St. Leonard's Church, Bretforton. Maid Margaret, a nun, was tempted by the devil but resisted his advances, whereupon he swallowed her. Only her feet and the bottom of her skirt were left sticking out of his mouth. However, a holy sister or God smote the devil with a cross, causing him to burst open and allow Margaret to emerge unscathed.

Funerary monuments have given rise to unofficial commentaries of various kinds. At Edvin Ralph a tablet to Maud de Edefen dating from about 1325 bears an inscription promising 60 days' pardon from the bishop of Hereford to those saying a *paternoster* and an *ave* for her. A local tradition already in existence in 1656 holds that Maud was loved by the lords of both Edvin Ralph and nearby Edvin Loach. As they fought over her she rushed between their swords and was mortally wounded. The two fenced on until they both fell dead.

A plaque at St. John's Church, Hagley, records the death in 1779 of Thomas, the second Lord Lyttleton, at the age of 35. The wicked Lord Lyttleton, as he was called, dreamed that a bird flew into his room, then changed into a white-robed woman and said: 'Prepare to die'. 'Not soon, I hope', he replied. 'Yes, in three days'. On the third day Lyttleton felt very well and promised that he would 'bilk the ghost' but as he was going to bed he 'put his hand to his side, sank back, and expired without a groan'. A friend, Miles Peter Andrews, said that Lyttleton appeared to him and said 'All is over' at what he later found to be the precise time of his death.

Ornate tombs, often adorned with life-like effigies of the dead, attracted a great deal of attention and exercised the popular imagination. The little crusader at St. Mary's, Tenbury Wells, is a miniature cross-legged knight of the late thirteenth century. The figure holds a heart. 'No doubt the memorial of a heart burial', comments an expert, reflecting the view that this was a crusader killed in the Holy Land whose heart was returned for interment at home. The small size of the effigy caused people to speculate that this was a child who had taken part in the children's crusade (of 1212) or gone with his father on a different expedition.

King John's tomb in Worcester Cathedral—he died in 1216 of a famous surfeit of lampreys—was originally placed between those of St. Oswald and St. Wulstan, no doubt in the hope that some of their sanctity would rub off. (Until the eighteenth century there was a procession to the two tombs every year on January 19, the anniversary of St. Wulstan's death). John made a further attempt to avoid recognition on the Day of Judgement and subsequent punishment for his crimes by having his body covered with the cowl and habit of a monk. This story ran for 700 years until the tomb was opened in 1797 and demonstrated it to be true.

At Much Cowarne the mutilated effigy of a knight dating from the thirteenth century is considered to be that of Grimbald de Pauncefoot. A second figure, now lost, represented Grimbald's wife, Constantia. During the seventeenth century this was described as having 'the left arm couped above the wrist in memory and confirmation of her heroic conduct.' Whether the missing hand preceded the story or followed it will never be clarified but it is said that when Grimbald was captured while crusading, Saladin demanded as ransom 'a joint of his wyffe'. Constantia, living up

The Little Crusader, St. Mary's, Tenbury Wells

to her name, summoned a surgeon from Gloucester Priory, had her hand removed and sent it to Saladin to secure her husband's release.

The church of St. Kenelm at Clifton-on-Teme has the effigy of a cross-legged knight of the fourteenth century, supposedly Sir Ralph Wysham. The conventional dog gave rise to the tale that as Sir Ralph was walking from Woodmanton to Clifton he fell dead under a yew tree where he was found lying with his legs crossed and the faithful animal at his feet.

Finally in this connection, the church at Tardebigge contains a monument showing Lady Mary Cookes, who died in 1693, embracing her husband, Sir Thomas. She is shown with one breast bare, and this gave rise to the tradition that Sir Thomas was kept from starving in prison by his wife's milk. The red dagger shown in the family crest is explained as a symbol that he once killed his butler in a drunken rage. However, the stories seem to be entirely fanciful.

On the whole, pictures in stained glass are more edifying, as they were intended to be. At St. Weonard's Church the east window of the north aisle shows an old man with a book in one hand and an axe in the other. It dates only from 1875 but is based on an earlier original. The saint was a hermit and woodcutter, though the axe has been taken to show that he was decapitated by the Anglo-Saxons.

Another modern window shows St. Dubricius (otherwise, Dyfrig or Devereux) in the tiny church dedicated to him at Hentland. King Pebiau of Archenfield, who was afflicted with incessant dribbling from the mouth, had a daughter called Eurdil. He returned to his palace at Madley from a hunting expedition and told her to groom his hair. As she did so he noticed that she was pregnant, and in a violent rage ordered that she should be thrown into the Wye. She was put into a sack and thrown in the river three times but each time she floated gently back to the bank. Pebiau then decreed that she be burnt alive, and she was cast into a blazing pyre. Next morning messengers sent to recover the bones found Eurdil safe and well, with the newly-born Dyfrig—the name means water baby—at her breast. When they were taken to the king he had a change of heart and welcomed them. The baby touched the king's face and his affliction was immediately cured.

Dyfrig went on to become scholar, bishop and saint. According to Geoffrey of Monmouth he crowned King Arthur at Cirencester. He also founded a college of 1,000 students known as the House of the Brethren, of which traces have been found near Hoarwithy at the farm still called Llanfrother.

On the Skyrrid or Holy Mountain east of Abergavenny an enclosure surrounds the remains of the chapel of St. Michael which was built above rocks said to have been rent at the moment of the crucifixion. The archangel is thought to have appeared to St. Dubricius there. Another angel told him in a vision to search for a white sow with a litter of pigs and to found a monastery on the site. He discovered the place and called it Mochros—pig's moor—now known as Moccas.

Dubricius retired to Bardsey Island and died there in about 550. When his remains were taken to Llandaff in 1120 a seven-week drought came to an end. His birthplace at Madley was marked by a stone which is gone, but may have been replaced by the cross now at the centre of the village.

Malvern Priory Church has a series of pictures in glass showing episodes in the life of St. Werstan who founded an oratory in the third century. The saint arrives at Malvern and angels show him where to site the oratory. The chapel is consecrated and Edward the Confessor bestows a charter. Finally, Werstan is murdered, possibly by Welsh raiders, and his followers are dispersed. All this may be seen (with difficulty) in a celestory window on the north side of the choir.

Scandals

Saintly stories abound in churches but there are also a few scandals. At Broughton Hackett to the east of Worcester a priest at St. Leonard's in the time of Queen Anne is said to have been tried, convicted and executed for baking his shepherd's boy in an oven. His motive has not been recorded.

Registers from the same church have some pages missing; they are alleged to have been destroyed in an attempt to cover up a scandal. Apparently the cleric was having an affair with a farmer's wife. Together they murdered the man and buried his body beneath the parsonage stairs. Now the farmer had a brother who closely resembled him but had not been seen for many years. Having at last decided on a visit the brother arrived during a service and walked into the church. The parson, thinking the dead man had returned to haunt him, fell down in a faint. The story emerged and a savage punishment was inflicted. The parson was shut in a cage and suspended from a big oak tree near Churchill Mill, with food and water in sight but out of reach and was left to starve to death.

At Oddingley near Droitwich the parson himself was the victim of a murder planned at the Speed the Plough public house in neighbouring Tibberton. The Rev. George Parker, a native of Cumberland, was presented to the living in 1793. His predecessors had agreed to accept £135 a year from each farmer in lieu of tithes; Parker wished to raise the sum to £150. Captain Samuel Evans of Church Farm, which adjoins the churchyard on the south side, refused to pay, and persuaded other farmers to follow suit. Parker then reverted to taking tithes in kind, and after a few years the farmers, finding themselves worse off under this arrangement, agreed to accept the earlier proposal. However, Parker then asked for a collective payment of a further £150 to defray the expense he had incurred in erecting a tithe barn. The farmers declined. Collections in kind continued, accompanied by ill-feeling and punctuated by litigation.

On Midsummer Day in 1806 Parker was shot, then bludgeoned to death with the butt of a gun. Immediately afterwards a Droitwich carpenter called Richard Heming disappeared. The rumour circulated that he had committed the murder, then escaped to America.

Not until 1830 was there any more news on the affair. In that year a barn at Netherwood Farm by the road to Crowle was being demolished when the remains of a body were found buried inside, together with a carpenter's rule and other objects. Heming's wife identified the remains as those of her husband. The inquest elicited a dramatic story from Thomas Clewes. Despite being a magistrate Captain Evans together with three other farmers—Clewes himself, George Banks and John Barnett—had instigated the murder of Parker by Heming. Evans had then arranged for a Droitwich farrier called Joseph Taylor to beat Heming to death in Clewes' barn and to bury his body there.

Taylor had died a few years after the murder, and Evans in 1829 (his family vault is at St. Peter's, Droitwich). The inquest jury brought in a verdict of wilful murder in both cases against Clewes and Banks, and found Barnett an accessory before the fact. The three men were tried at Worcester but acquitted. The case was thrown out because the law at the time did not allow accomplices to be tried for murder after the death of the principal accused. To the fury of the new rector at Oddingley the news of the farmers' acquital was greeted by the ringing of his own church bells. The new barn built at Netherwood Farm bore a stone with the discreet inscription '1806—1830'.

Much less gory were the misadventures of the Rev. John Jackson at Ledbury who in 1869 found himself accused of fathering illegitimate children. After being suspended for two years while an investigation took place, Jackson was exonerated. A group of parishoners refused to accept his innocence and set up an alternative church in a hut known as the tin tabernacle in the town's New Street. They even refused to allow themselves to be buried at Ledbury and provided for their funerals to take place at Eastnor until Jackson died in 1891. A pulpit which Jackson himself carved over a period of seven years is still to be seen in the church. A song on the subject of these events entitled *The Ledbury Parson* continued to circulate for the best part of a century:

> In Ledbury Town in Herefordshire
> They rucked up a row with the parson there.
> This pious gentleman they all say
> Was far too fond of going astray.
>
> (Chorus)
> And if going astray should be your plan,
> Just think of the Ledbury clergyman.

Customs

As well as the normal seasonal celebrations churches sometimes have (or had) their own traditional observances. The Nanfan Sermon was preached every February at Berrow Church until 1986. It has been suggested that a woman whose lover was killed in a duel by her brother left £2 a year for the vicar to preach against duelling. In fact, though, the first Nanfan Sermon (endowed by Sir John Nanfan of Birtsmorton Court) was preached in 1745 about a century after the supposed duel occurred.

On Plough Sunday (nearest to 6 January) ploughs used to be blessed in churches. Places where this happened include Kimbolton and nearby Leominster, where a plough was kept in the Priory Church. On the nearest Sunday to Candlemas Day (2 February) small loaves known as Garrold's Bread are still blessed in the church at Aston Ingham and distributed to

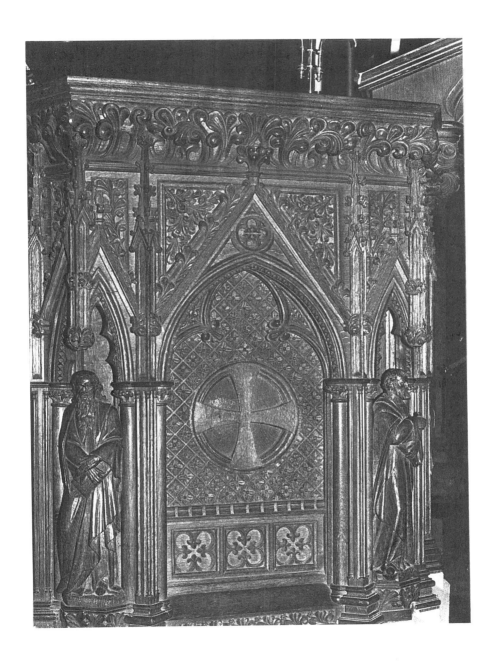

Jackson's Pulpit in Ledbury Church

parishoners under the terms of a bequest made in 1859 by Richard Garrold. Now lost is another ceremony which took place on the same day at Tenbury where figures of the Virgin Mary were removed from the church and snowdrops scattered over the empty spaces. Rings of the flowers—alternatively known as Christ's flowers, Candlemas Bells or Fair Maids of February—were grown in the churchyard for the purpose. It was thought unlucky to pick them for any other reason.

Richard de la Wyche was born at Droitwich, the son of a yeoman farmer. He was 'a brisk young fellow that would ride over hedge and ditch, and at length became a very devout man'; indeed, he was canonised as St. Richard of Chichester. At some point in his lifetime (1197-1253) the salt springs failed at Droitwich and he miraculously restored them. There is a chapel dedicated to him in St. Andrew's Church, Droitwich. The townspeople used to hold a celebration on 3 April which was described by John Aubrey:

This custome is yearly observed at Droitwich, in Worcestershire, where, on the day of St. Richard, they keep holyday, and dresse the wells with greene boughs and flowers. One yeare, in the Presbyterian time, it was discontinued in the civil warres, and after that the Springe shranke up, or dried for some time; so afterwards they revived their annual custome, notwithstanding the power of the parliament and soldiers, and the salt water returned again, and still continues.

On Palm Sunday (the week before Easter) pax cakes are given out after morning service by the vicar at Hentland, King's Caple and Sellack, three villages near Ross-on-Wye. The cakes now take the form of a wafer stamped with the likeness of a paschal lamb and the words 'Peace and Good Neighbourhood'. The same legend, as we have seen, is inscribed on bells at many churches in the two counties. The custom at the villages is claimed to stem from a bequest made in 1570 by Lady Scudamore.

People once decked the graves of their deceased relatives with flowers on Palm Sunday. The custom later moved to Easter Saturday, and was current at Ross and Hereford until at least the mid-1970's.

At Easter women were expected to wear a new hat to church. Failure to do so would ensure that a bird deposited its droppings on the old one. The chocolate eggs of today are merely sweets, but real eggs, an emblem of fertility, were once donated to the church at Easter. Some small ground rents were paid to churches in this form. At Middleton-on-the-Hill, for example, six eggs were supplied every three years.

Forty days after Easter comes Ascension Day, and this is preceded by the four days—Sunday to Wednesday—of Rogationtide. From the eighth

Beating the Bounds, an early photograph

century onwards blessings were asked at Rogationtide (the Latin *rogare*, means to ask) on the coming corn harvest and the beating of bounds—otherwise called processioning or bannering—took place. The parson would lead his parishoners round their boundaries, taking up his station to read from the Bible by strategic trees which came to be called Gospel Oak (for example, where the parishes of Kingsland, Lucton, Aymestrey and Shobdon meet) or Gospel Yew (Bosbury, Castle Frome and Canon Frome). Sometimes the processions carried branches of trees which were stuck in the ground and occasionally took root. Other landmarks were stones (called liberty, or mere-stones), wells, and even public houses: the Virgin Tavern in Tolladine Road at Worcester was a marker for Claines and St. Martin's parishes.

Boys were beaten, bumped or ducked, or given buns or pennies for which to scramble, all to impress the boundaries on their minds so that they could testify to them for the rest of their lives if the need arose. For adults eating and drinking were important parts of the proceedings, as we know from many records which have survived.

In the sixteenth century 'ye vickar of Eckington called Sr James Colwall did in ye company of most of his parishoners use in ye Rogation week to goe ye perambulation of ye Parish ... and did use to say a gospel at one Thomas Taylors gate in woolashill ... and there commonly they had a drincking'. We read that at Bromsgrove in 1573 the bellman was expected to 'waite on the Vicker or Curate in the Rogashun weeke to goe about ye Borders of ye Parish'. Over a century later at Worcester these details were given:

Holy Thursday, may 5, 1692, the minister, churchwardens and p'ishioners of ye p'ish of St Nicholas did goe ye perambulacon, and did remarke ye p'ticular places and bounds of ye said p'ish, viz., from the church to Mr Stirrop's parlour window in Angel Lane, over against a stone in Mr Savage's wall, from thence back again round by the Cross to Mrs Powell's house, widd., now inhabited by Nichs. Nash, mercer, at the hithermost part of the shop where the ground-sill of the house will show an old passage or dove case, at which place there was formerly an entry, and the p'ishioners in ye yeares '61 2 3 and 4 did passe throwe ye said entry, at which time one Mrs Cooksey lived there, to Mr Huntbache's, farther parte of ye house, then to that parte of ye house next the Crosse, being the backe parts of the White Harte, then down to the Trinity to a marke in the wall neare ye old goale, from thence throwe to Mr Blurton's garden, then to the joynt in Mr Blurton's malthouse, then up Sansome Field from that joynt, and soe throw to ye liberty post, then downe ye Salt Lane to the stile at St Marten's workhouse and soe back to the church.

Still in Worcester, St. Clement's recorded the expenditure in 1737 of 33s 8d at processioning, for cakes and ale (9s 4d), half a lamb (2s 6d), bacon and a leg of veal (4s 3d), 'pigg' (3s 6d), 32 quarts of ale (8s), bread, greens and dressing dinner (5d), cider (3d) and 'carrying the bush' (1s). St. John's Church in 1818 spent £10 in three days of which 3d was for 'putting up gospel bushes' and the rest for brandy, tobacco, pipes and 'a heavy wet'—a drinking session.

At Kidderminster, where the custom was called bannering, there were often fights between the men of adjoining parishes when they happened to meet on their rounds. One procession at least—in 1818—was peaceful. The town crier led the way, followed by 'javelin men' and a 'band of music'. Then came church dignitaries, followed by the people. The walk covered several miles, taking in Stourport, Wribbenhall, Trimpley, Shatterford and Wolverley. The party halted eleven times to hear readings from the gospel. A bough planting ceremony was carried out at the centre of the bridges at Mitton, Stourport and Bewdley; refreshments were taken at the Black Boy in Wribbenhall and two other places. The notables took dinner at the Lion at the end of the journey.

Such perambulations continued at Hereford until 1890, where proceedings began with a trip down the Wye in boats to the Franchise Stone, then across fields to another stone, and from there along Holy Well Gutter to the Cock at Tupsley. Next the walkers went to Baynton Wood, Lugg Meadows, Lugg Bridge, where an omnibus took them to Holmer, Three Elms and a particular cottage at Stretton Sugwas. The first day's march

Timothy Sarsons, the Boy Bishop for 1991

ended at the river bank opposite the stone on the Hunderton side. On the second day the party set off from the stone near the river to another near Hunderton fold-yard, and then on to St. John's parish boundary marker. The ceremony ended at its starting point by the Wye opposite the Whalebone Inn at Eign. The total distance covered was 17 and a quarter miles.

Among the places where boundaries are still beaten are Alvechurch and Leysters, though other parishes are showing an interest in reviving the custom.

Crabbing the parson, too, might have its attractions. This used to happen at St. Kenelm's Church, Clent, on Wake Sunday but was discontinued because the pelting grew too vigorous, and sticks and stones were thrown along with the crab apples.

In Hereford Cathedral the ceremony of the Boy Bishop, which dates back to mediaeval times, is held during a special service on the nearest Saturday to St. Nicholas' Day (6 December). The custom is intended as a special celebration of St. Nicholas, the patron saint of children (and also of sailors, unmarried women, merchants, pawnbrokers, apothecaries and perfumiers). After receiving the real bishop's blessing the boy he has chosen from among the choristers, dressed in full episcopal rig, replaces him on his throne as the choir sings 'He hath put down the mighty from their seat'. Hereford is one of a very few places where this ceremony survives. The Boy Bishop remains in office, taking part in all services—except, of course, those requiring an ordained priest—until Holy Innocents' Day or Childermas (28 December). Because of its associations this day was deemed especially inauspicious. No work was started on it, nor new clothes worn for the first time. At Norton, near Evesham, a muffled peal was rung to commemorate the slaughter of the innocents by Herod, then the bells were unmuffled to celebrate the deliverance of Christ.

At Elmley Castle bellringers still maintain the custom, which originated in 1600, of saying a carol at the churchyard gate after ringing the old year out and the new year in.

IV
LIVES

As they always will be the beginning and end of life are marked by rites of passage and attended by many beliefs. Within the poles of existence lies the magnetic field of relationships between the sexes, another fruitful source of traditions. A great many methods of divination—now almost wholly abandoned—were employed by young women in an effort to discover the identity of their future partners. Marriage, still a major time for family celebration, was and is surrounded by customs. The poor man's practice of wife selling has long been superseeded by relatively easy procedures for legal divorce, not to speak of the widespread current habit of couples' living together or separating without benefit of clergy or legal process. Certain rituals of communal disapproval of individual morality, such as 'colestaff' or 'skimmington', have also disappeared though they might be overdue for revival.

Birth

Until at least the 1930's people in Stourport—and no doubt elsewhere, too—believed it unlucky for a woman to wash her feet during pregnancy. In Herefordshire there was a notion that the father of a child suffered as much during its gestation and birth as the mother. Thus, if a woman refused to identify the father of an illegitimate child people would watch to see which young man was taken ill at the time of her delivery.

It was considered unlucky—tempting fate, perhaps—to bring a child's cradle into the house before the birth. A cradle previously there would be stored elsewhere from the beginning of the pregnancy. A new cradle was unlucky in any case, so an old one would be handed down from generation to generation, usually on the male side. One farm at Tenbury Wells was let complete with a cradle passed on with the tenancy. As cradles fell out of use the superstitions associated with them passed to cots, and even prams.

To help a woman in labour sheep's lights were tied with string to her hands and feet, or a roasted mouse was laid on her stomach. To help ease the pain of childbirth women, until the early twentieth century, bought a sheet entitled *Our Saviour's Letter* to hang over the bed. More recently, at Broadwas-on-Teme in 1960 a midwife refused to allow a young woman to remove her shoes until after her child was born. The reasons remain obscure.

In the days of open fires—at least until the 1960's, to my personal knowledge—midwives would burn the afterbirth. Some believed that the number of times it popped would denote the number of children the mother would subsequently have. There was a strange notion in certain places that if a woman died in childbirth the clergyman could demand that the infant be christened over its mother's coffin.

It was customary for new babies to be given something silver, such as a sixpence: 'a tanner for the baby'. Some households put a bowl out for just such contributions from visitors after a birth. The first time a new baby is carried from the room in which it has been born it must be taken upstairs rather than down if it is to rise in the world. When Stanley Baldwin, a future prime minister, was born at Bewdley in 1867 his nurse was careful to follow this ritual. If no higher room existed someone would clamber on to a chair with the baby. Lest it grow up light-fingered the child would not have its nails cut, though they might be bitten short. There were different beliefs as to how long this should go on: only at the first trimming; until christening; for one year.

An early baptism was considered essential for a child's future well-being. An infant dying unbaptised would, according to an ancient belief, become a peewit—which might explain the bird's mournful cries. At the touch of the holy water at baptism it was lucky for the child to cry since this showed the departure of an evil spirit. Some churches—Holt, for example—would leave the north or devil's door open during the ceremony so that an evil spirit could depart from the building after quitting the child.

If children of different sexes were being baptised at the same ceremony girls had to precede boys. A woman who with seeming rudeness pushed past parents with boys so as to ensure that her baby girl was christened first offered this explanation:

You see, sir, the parson bain't a married man, and consequentially is disfamiliar with children, or he'd a never put the litle girl to be christened after the boys. And though it sadly flustered me, sir, to put myself afore my betters in the way I was forced to do, yet, sir, it was a doing of a kindness to them two little boys, in me a setting of my girl afore 'em. Why? Well, sir, I har astonished as you don't know. Why, sir, if them little boys had been christened afore the little girl, they'd have had her soft chin, and she'd have had their hairy beards—the poor little innocent. But thank goodness I've kep' her from that misfortin'.

Finding a husband

Both sexes must have been concerned about choosing a partner but women resorted to an extraordinary number of ways of trying to find out not only the identity of a future husband but how long they had to wait for him. A piece of wedding cake or a sprig of yarrow put under the pillow at night would induce a dream of one's husband-to-be. So—but no doubt rather uncomfortably—would a breastbone, knife, fork and plate under the bolster; or a pair of new shoes and stockings worn through the night. A flowering branch of hawthorn could also be put under the pillow; or a woman could place her crossed shoes there (on a Friday) and recite:

> I put my left shoe over my right
> In hopes this night I may see
> The man that shall my husband be
> In his apparel and in his array
> And in the clothes he wears every day;
> What he does and what he wears
> And what he'll do all days and years,
> Whether I sleep or whether I wake
> I hope to hear my true love speak.

A letter from her love could be pinned in nine folds and put next to the heart before she went to bed. Then if she dreamed of gold and jewels he was sincere, otherwise not. Another test for sincerity was to take an apple pip, name the sweetheart, then put the pip on the fire. A bursting noise showed love; silent combustion meant its absence. Alternatively:

> If you love me bounce and fly;
> If you hate me lie and die.

Another test was to stick on the cheek as many pips as there were suitors, and to name them. The pip which fell off last would show the truest aspirant. A much more long-drawn process was to count up all the white horses seen until reaching the hundredth. After that the first man to whom the woman spoke—and this did give some room for manoeuvre—would be the one she married.

The moon also featured in some rituals. A woman would go into the garden at the time of the first new moon of the year and say:

> New moon, new moon, tell unto me
> Which of these three is my husband to be.

Then she would name three men, curtseying each time. When next she saw them she had to notice whether they faced towards her or away. The one who happened to face her would be her husband. If they all faced she would probably have gone through the procedure a second time. Another appeal ran:

> New moon, new moon in the bright firmament,
> If {name} is my true love to be,
> Let the next time I see him
> His face be turned towards me.

A woman could also look through a silk handkerchief or a piece of frosted glass at the reflection of a new moon in a bucket of water. As many moons as she saw would be the number of months before she married. Timing could also be worked out by taking a ring and hanging it on a hair of one's own, then holding it over a glass of water. The number of times the ring knocked against the side of the glass would show the number of years before the wedding.

Further opportunities for divination arose on particular days during the course of the year. On St. Agnes' Eve (20 January) or All Hallow's Eve (30 October) women made and baked over the fire in complete silence a simple cake of flour, salt and water, called a Dumb Cake. If they then ate it or slept with it below the pillow they would dream of their future husband.

At midnight on Midsummer Eve (23 June) a young woman could go backwards into the garden, then move backwards round it, scattering hempseed with the right hand and intoning:

> Hempseed I sow;
> Hempseed is to mow;
> And the man that my husband is to be,
> Let him follow after and mow.

A vision of the future husband, scythe in hand, would then appear. On the same day a woman could take two seedlings of the flowers called Orphine or Midsummer Men (*sedum telephium*) and plant them in the house thatch, saying as she did so her own name and that of her sweetheart. If the flowers flourished a wedding would ensue; if not, the lovers would part. The same flowers were used for medicinal purposes. The Welsh herbal of the Physicians of Myddfai recommended it against fever, sterility in women and over-profuse menstruation; in English cottage gardens it was grown as a 'gash herb' for immediate application to a wound.

At Hallowe'en women were advised:

> If you'd see the man you're to wed
> Touch with a lemon the posts of your bed.

They might also stand at midnight with lighted candle in front of a mirror, where the future husband's image would appear. Two days later, at All Saints (1 November) a woman could sit at the window at midnight with a ball of new worsted thread. She took hold of one end of the yarn and threw out the ball with the words: 'Who holds?' The future husband would pick up the ball, say his name, then disappear.

On Christmas Eve three, five or seven women could meet for yet another ritual. Each took a sprig of rosemary—the herb of remembrance—and put it in a bowl of water in the centre of the room. A line stretched across held a white garment belonging to each. All sat in silence till midnight when the equivalent number of men arrived, each taking a rosemary sprig and announcing his own name followed by that of his sweetheart.

On Christmas Day if a woman wore a rose plucked the previous Midsummer Eve a single man who took it would marry her. Objects put in Christmas puddings were employed for divination until at least 1986 in Malvern. A portion found to contain a silver ring showed the recipient would marry within the year; a bone button—known as the bachelor's button—carried the message that the finder would remain single.

A Dumb Cake, as mentioned above, was also made on New Year's Eve and eaten by a group of women. One of them next put on a chemise—the use of the term indicates the period when the practice was current—on a chair in front of the fire, inside out, and sprinkled it with water from a sprig of rosemary. A silent vigil was maintained until midnight, when the form of the husband of any of the women to be married in the ensuing year would appear by the fire and turn the chemise.

By contrast with such acute anxiety about a future husband the approach of men to their choice of partner was laconic and down to earth: 'Boy, you take a good look round the meadow before you find the gate'. Such good sense was echoed by at least one woman, who said 'There's more to marriage than four bare legs in a bed'.

Whereas cradles—and also grandfather clocks—were passed down the male side of families, Welsh dressers and dower chests firmly belonged to the female line. The chests, often centuries old, were used to accumulate household linen long before a woman had chosen a partner. Once she had done so collecting for the chest or bottom drawer went on apace.

Marriage

The reading of banns in churches attracted different beliefs in different places. Some thought it unlucky for either party to hear all three readings; some for the couple to hear any readings together; some for the woman to hear any. Similarly, certain days—Wednesday or Friday, for example—were considered unlucky by some for weddings. For marriage, as for birth, the month of May was thought unlucky: 'Marry in May, repent for aye'. Some also avoided the whole of Lent and also the week of Easter.

The old notion that the bride should wear something old, something new, something borrowed, something blue, is still widely held. The bride should not see her reflection in the mirror on her wedding morning once she is fully dressed for the ceremony; nor should she turn back on any account once she has set off from home for the church. It is also unlucky for the bride and groom to leave by a back door after their reception. That they should not see each other on their wedding day until they meet in church is also widely accepted, even by couples who have been living together for some years before deciding to marry.

Some weddings used to be timed to begin at five minutes past the hour so that the clock should not strike during the service, thus avoiding another bad omen. Ringers might predict the number of children to be born to a couple by the number of strokes of the great bell after the final peal for the wedding.

At Peterchurch a groom who omitted to pay the ringers was censured by their ringing the bells backwards as a kind of curse. Another instance of this practice was noted at Eckington in 1714. The ringers were sent three shillings for drink after ringing for a celebration 'but thinking that not sufficient they declar'd they would ring the bells backward. Accordingly did, and allarum'd thereby the whole neighbourhood'. It was a very bad sign if a ringer overthrew a bell when ringing a wedding peal or if a bellrope broke.

At Hanbury, and probably elsewhere, if a younger daughter married before an elder, the elder was made to dance in a pig trough on the day of her junior's wedding, which must have been a great humiliation. Mothers made sure that a bride always carried in her bouquet some myrtle, an emblem of peace, love and happiness. One song says:

In the middle of the ocean there shall grow a myrtle tree
Before I ever prove false to her, the girl that loves me.

A groom at Cusop was greeted by a different plant as he emerged from church with his bride on his arm. A woman he had jilted threw a handful of rue at him, with the words 'May you rue this day as long as you live'.

The better-disposed threw things with happier associations. 'Our dear little bride', wrote Kilvert in 1874, 'went off with her husband happy and radiant amid blinding showers of rice and old shoes'. Rice stood for plenty, and the old shoes symbolised the transfer of authority over the woman from the father to the husband. The latter notion at least would be indignantly rejected by today's brides, and the shoes tied to honeymoon cars are just an expression of good luck wishes.

Couples are often met at the church door by a guard of honour. For huntsmen a pack of hounds is sometimes whipped in. At Dorstone salutes to newly-weds were once fired on the blacksmith's anvil. Gunpowder charges in a hole in the base were set off by a fuse, causing the anvil to jump and a loud report to be heard. In the same village maroons which normally warned of fog were placed on the railways and fired by trains taking couples on honeymoon.

East of Worcester a group of villages including Abberton, Flyford Flavel, Naunton Beauchamp and Wick kept the custom of firing guns to give a nocturnal salute outside the house of a newly-married pair—this was in the mid-nineteenth century. Unfortunately:

some parties at Wick were not long ago summoned before the magistrates for having participated in one of these popping bouts, but the indignation of the district was greatly aroused by their being mulcted in certain expenses and ordered to discontinue the practice, for it is believed to be nearly as "old as Adam", and as indispensable a ceremony as the marriage vow itself.

Another case was reported by the *Worcester Herald* in March 1845:

From time immemorial the custom has been ... to rejoice and be glad at a wedding, and ... to ring merry peals upon the church bells. ... But there are parishes and places where ... their churches never had bells. Among those unhappy districts may be reckoned Pensham, Pinvin, and other places in that neighbourhood, and to make up for the want of a merry 'ding dong', all the male residents, from the newly-breeched urchin to the ancient sire, tottering on the grave, who could command a firelock ... have assembled round the bridegroom's house, and kept up an irregular volley of blank cartridges. ... On Tuesday last, one George Gould was summoned before the magistrates of Pershore ... for shooting at the wedding of Miss

Bright, of Pensham, and in so doing, damaged the door of Mrs Bright, her mother, in whose house the marriage feast was given. This serious offence was said to have been committed on Sunday evening se'ennight, and, in extenuation, George pleaded ancient usage and the custom of his forefathers. His plea did not avail him, as the right to blow holes in other people's doors, although they may have been unfortunate enough to get married, was not to be found in the common, or statute law. His offence, however, did not appear to be deemed a very heinious {sic} one, as he was let off on paying a fine of 6d with 6d damage and 6s 6d costs.

Before Lord Hardwicke's Marriage Act came into force in 1754—it was this act which made the reading of banns a legal requirement—couples could be married 'by consent', with few formalities. St. Michael's Church at Worcester no longer exists (it stood close by the cathedral, to the north-east) but during the second half of the seventeenth century it enjoyed a reputation for providing quick marriages. The registers have entries for couples all over the Worcester diocese and as far afield as Westminster. Few questions seem to have been asked by Rev. Jospeh Severn at Birlingham, near Pershore. During the first 45 years of the eighteenth century 282 couples—mostly from outside the parish, and some even from Scotland—were married in his tiny church.

An unusual twist to the ritual was reported by the *Worcester Journal* in 1775:

A widow, being married again, to exempt her future husband for payment of any debts she might have contracted, went into one of the pews and stript herself of all her cloths {sic} except her shift, in which only she went to the altar, and was married, much to the astonishment of the Parson, Clerk, etc.

The notion of a woman's avoiding debt in this way occasionally recurs in accounts of another ceremony, the sale of a wife. As recently as the 1930's a man told how his mother had witnessed such a sale made for a few shillings at Bromyard market. A dozen or so further cases were reported between 1766 and 1876 from Bredon, Hereford, Leominster, Stourbridge, Stourport and Worcester.

The sales were a form of divorce which although not legal was firmly believed so by ordinary people. On 12 May 1784 James Grubb, 'bachelor', and Ann Hand, 'widow', were married at All Saints' Church. Worcester. They made their marks in the register, and James Hand was one of their witnesses. Rev. Harrison of Crowle officiated, in the absence of the rector of All Saints', William Cleveland. On inspecting the register Cleveland later added a note : 'Invalid ... Ann Hand proves to be the wife of James Hand the witness ... He sold her'.

In 1857 this document was solemnly drawn up:

Thomas Middleton delivered up his wife Mary Middleton to Philip Rostins for one shilling and a quart of ale; and parted wholly and solely for life, never to trouble one another.

Witness. Thomas X Middleton, his mark
Witness. Mary Middleton, his wife
Witness. Philip X Rostins, his mark
Witness. S.H. Stone, Crown Inn, Friar Street

As late as 1881 a woman produced in a police court at Worcester a stamped receipt for 25 shillings to prove that she was an honest woman, having been sold, and therefore divorced and re-married.

A 90 year old woman who wrote to the *Hereford Times* in April and May 1876 had personal knowledge of a number of cases. 'I have seen several wives bought and sold in the market', she claimed. 'One man who bought ... lived in Price's Hospital, and that was the woman who carried the bloody loaf in the bread riots {of 1800}'. 'Nonagenarian' went on to describe a ceremony in Hereford in detail:

I must recall to your memory my statement as to my being playfellow to Mona Delnotte Coates, for it was while walking out with her and her attendant that I first saw a man selling his wife. We were going from the Barton to the other side of the town, and necessarily had to pass the bottom of the pig market. Here we saw a crowd. The girl was desirous of knowing what was the matter, so she elbowed her way through the people, and was followed by the children to the open space in the centre. There stood a woman with her hat in her hand. All classes of women wore hats very much like those worn now, only as artificial flowers were then very dear, they were covered all over the tops with massive bows, and sometimes had a plume of feathers. The woman's hat was a very smart one. She stood looking down. At first I thought she was admiring her own red cloak, but as she stood so still my eye wandered over to see what was amiss; and I shall never forget how surprised I felt when I observed she had a rope about her neck, and that a man was holding one end of it. 'What has she done?' we both cried out, for I believed she was going to be hanged. 'Oh', said a bystander, 'she has done no good, depend upon it, or else he wouldn't want to sell her'. Just then there was a loud laugh and a man shouted: 'Well done, Jack, that is eleven pence more than I would give; it's too much, boy, too much'. But Jack stood firm. 'No', said he. 'I'll give a shilling, no more, and he ought to be thankful to be rid of her at any price'. 'Well', said the man, 'I'll take it, though her looks ought to bring more than that'. 'Keep her, master, keep her for her good looks', shouted the laughing bystanders. 'No', said he. 'good looks won't put the victuals on the table for me without willing hands'. 'Well', said Jack, 'here's the shilling, and I warn't I'll make her put the victuals on the table for me, and help to get it first; be you willing, missis, to leave him and take me for better or worse?' 'I be willing', said she. 'And be you willing to sell her for what I bid, master?' 'I be', said he, 'and will give you the rope into the bargain'. So Jack gave the man his shilling, and the man put the rope into Jack's hand, and Jack walked off up the pig market leading his newly bought wife by the halter.

The writer knew the couple subsequently, and reported that the woman was 'a bit of a mag {scold} but he conquered her', and that she worked hard to help him in his trade of weaving. They had one son. 'Nonagenarian' went on to mention another woman sold in a similar fashion, this time in the butter market, and then in contradiction of the view that such events invariably involved consenting parties observed: 'Several years after-wards a much more dreadful sale took place in Hereford for the individuals were very unwilling to be sold, and upon their bended knees bitterly cried and entreated not to be sold.' The outcome was not recorded.

A sanction directed not merely against wives but women in general was the 'scold's bridle', of which examples have been preserved in both the Hereford and Worcester Museums. A spell in the iron gag with a framework

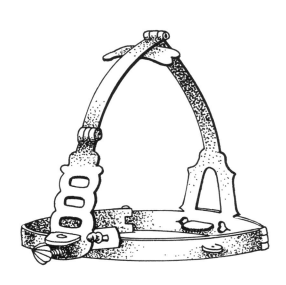

Scold's Bridle

Ducking stool, Leominster Priory

which clamped round the head was inflicted on turbulent women such as Margaret Bache who appears in the Worcestershire County records as a common scold and source of strife among her neighbours. In addition she had insulted her mother-in-law at Bromsgrove, and been excommunicated for other unspecified offences.

A more serious punishment was the gum or ducking stool which the magistrates could order not only for unduly sharp-tongued women but for tradesmen who gave short weight or sold adulterated food. It was used both at Hereford and Worcester, where the records have entries on 'making the gome stool' (1599) and on 'the money for whipping of one Rogers and for carrying of several women upon the gum stool' (1623). After being paraded through the streets, offenders were taken down a thoroughfare variously known as Cucken, Cooken or Cooking Street (called Copenhagen Street since Nelson's visit in 1802) to the Severn at the slip by the old Wherry Inn.

At Bromyard until the sixteenth century the grimstool or gumstool was kept in Church Lane. At Upton-on-Severn the stinking water of Gum Stool Pond at the bottom of New Street was preferred to the river for duckings. The nearby Gum Stool Cottages were demolished only in 1882. The Leominster stool, a formidable structure originally used in Worcester, has survived and is kept in the Priory Church. The device, widely used from the fifteenth to the seventeenth centuries, is frequently mentioned in the town records, often as being in need of repair. The last ducking in Leominster—and probably in England—took place in 1809, when Jenny Pipes was paraded before being lowered into the Lugg. The stool was wheeled out again with Sarah Leake in 1817 but she escaped ducking because the river was too low.

A sign of communal rather than judicial disapproval involved parading originally people and later effigies on poles, to the accompaniment of rough music. As early as 1572/3 an instance from Lindridge, east of Tenbury Wells, appears in the records as 'colestaffe riding'. In 1587 at Shrovetide a man was carried on a 'colestaffe' at Cradley. At Upper Mitton in 1613 the procedure involved a curate and the rough music was supplied by a horn, fiddles and beating 'upon a fryinge panne'. The reason for the procedure is not given in these cases but at Worcester the community's disapprobation was aroused in about 1800 by a wife's beating her husband. Here, a man dressed as a woman rode on horseback behind the stuffed figure of another man and hit it upon the head with a ladle.

By this time the name given to the procedure was 'skimmington', and a description was offered in 1893:

a rough play got up for the annoyance of unpopular individuals. It usually consists of a procession, in which effigies of the objectionable persons are carried through the village accompanied by beating of tin kettles and other discordant noises. Under particular circumstances, certain articles of wearing apparel are carried on sticks, after the manner of flags or banners. The performance concludes with the burning of the effigies.

The writer, Jesse Salisbury, adds that Samuel Butler gives a description of such a performance in his poem *Hudibras*. Butler, the son of a farmer, was born in 1612 at Strensham where there is a memorial to him in the church. Local tradition holds that he wrote part of *Hudibras* at the Ketch Inn, Worcester.

Salisbury also says that 'a skimmington performance took place at Little Comberton at the beginning of 1893. Mrs. Leather, writing in 1912, reported—without giving details—cases at Leominster and Weobley Marsh 'within the last twenty years' and at Walterstone 'a few years since'. One wonders whether this was the last skimmington in the two counties.

Death

A host of signs were thought to give warning of imminent death, and many of these are given in chapter 5. Parishioners at Bredwardine thought that Kilvert's death in 1879 was foreshadowed by an omen, that of a bell at the church which rang with a 'heavy sound'. Families would interpret as other harbingers events such as the fall of an old tree.

Those wishing for precise prediction could take ivy leaves, write on them the names of members of their family, and steep them in water overnight at Hallowe'en. Next morning the leaves corresponding with those members of the family who were to die during the ensuing year would bear the mark of a coffin. Some thought that if one listened on the same night at the door of the church the devil would be heard reading inside a list of the names of those due to die within twelve months. At Kington, close to the Welsh border, people once believed in the corpse candle, a ghostly light seen leaving a house where a death would occur, then moving to the churchyard and hovering where the grave would be dug.

The passing of a person close to death would be assisted by removing the pillow from beneath the head. All doors would be unlocked and opened so that the soul's departure would not be hindered. At Broadway, and no doubt elsewhere, a corpse lying unburied over a Sunday was thought to bring about another death a week later.

Bees had to be told of family events such as births, marriages and deaths. 'This is observed even today', says Mr. Stanley Yapp of Tenbury Wells. 'Many people are reluctant to say they do, but I know of a case where this happened in 1980'. If the man of the house died his widow would 'tang' (rap) the hive three times with a front door key—a back door key would not do—and address the bees in one of several ways:

Bees, bees, my husband is dead. Will you stay and work for me?

or:

Your master's dead but don't you go. Your mistress will be a good mistress to you.

or:

Bees, bees, your master's dead. You be gwain to have a new master.

It was widely believed that if the ceremony were omitted the bees would either die or leave. The hive would sometimes be dressed with black crepe, and turned round as the corpse left the house.

The sins of the departed could be assumed by a kind of scapegoat, the sin eater. John Aubrey—who owned estates in Herefordshire at Burleton and Stretford—wrote the classic account of this practice in the seventeenth century:

In the County of Hereford was an old Custome at Funeralls to have poor people, who were to take upon them all the sinnes of the party deceased. One of them I remember lived in a cottage on Rosse high-way. He was a long leane, ugly, lamentable poor raskel. The Manner was that when the Corps was brought out of the house and layd on the Biere, a Loafe of bread was brought out and delivered to the Sinne-eater over the corps, as also a Mazer-bowle of maple full of beer, which he was to drinke up, and sixpence in money, in consideration whereof he took upon him ipso facto {by the same token} all the Sinnes of the Defunct, and freed him (or her) from walking after they were dead ...

This Custome (though rarely used in our dayes) yet by some people was continued even in the strictest time of the Presbyterian government; as at Dynder {Dinedor}, volens nolens {willy-nilly} the Parson of the Parish, the relations of the woman deceased there had this ceremonie punctually performed according to her Will; and also the like was done at the City of Hereford in these times, when a woman kept for many years before her death a Mazard-bowle for the Sinne-eater; and the like in other places in this Countie.

Aubrey may or may not have known, but one of the other places was Ross itself. A young gardener, Roger Mortimer, who worked at Alton Court half a mile south-east of the town in the seventeenth century, fell in love with his employer's second daughter, the beautiful Clara Markey. She reciprocated, but they were fully aware of the social gulf between them and therefore kept their feelings secret. To their dismay the time came when Clara's father told her that he arranged for her to marry a young man from the well-to-do Rudhall family. (Monuments to both Markeys and Rudhalls can still be seen in Ross Church).

Mortimer was so distraught that an old woman called Nancy Carter was accused of bewitching him. Straws in the shape of a cross were strewn after her and pins plunged into her in attempts to lift the imagined spell. (Drawing a witch's blood was thought to remove her powers). Then Mortimer's hat was discovered lodged against the central pier of Wilton Bridge, and searchers found his body upstream, near The Acres. The body was carried to the Welsh Harp Inn, Alton Street, and Jack 'the Scape' Clements who lived in Walford Road was hired as sin eater. A quart of beer and sixpence were passed over the corpse to him, and he stated: 'I take all the consequences and so I has all the beer'.

After sunset the body was taken up the road and buried without ceremony other than the driving of a stake through the heart, so as 'to be sure he would not walk, and bite people in their beds'. That was how Corpse Cross (now Copse Cross) acquired its name, though Mrs. Leather suggests it is a corruption of Corpus Christi Cross. (The bodies of those who had committed suicide were buried there in similar fashion until 1823, when the law ended the practice).

Clara's marriage was due only a few days after the burial. In Ross Church when the parson enquired whether she would take Rudhall as a husband she uttered a scream, then fainted. She was taken home unconscious, but half an hour later she was found wandering in a daze, seeking where Mortimer had been buried at the crossroads on Alton Road. Her family led her home, but every time she could escape their vigilance she would slip away to pace slowly up and down the lane leading to Corpse Cross. Eventually she was given her head, and made her lonely walk for decades until she herself died. The lane is still called Old Maid's Walk.

In the twentieth century Mary Webb inserted a fictional sin-eating passage into her novel *Precious Bane* (1924) set in Shropshire. There is no evidence from that period in Shropshire, but Mrs. Leather mentions a Herefordshire relic of the custom in the drinking of port wine and the eating of biscuits at Craswall and Walterstone in the room where a body lies. In 1926 the bishop of Hereford, Dr. Linton Smith, reported being told by a woman from the north of the county that when her child died 'the nurse pressed her to lay a piece of bread on the breast of the dead body'. He considered this to be another survival of 'sin-bread'.

Before a funeral procession left the house it was customary for the deceased's will to be read or to be passed over the coffin to the legatee. Some country solicitors still follow this procedure.

Coffins were sometimes carried long distances by relays of bearers, and it was not done to refuse a request to act as a bearer. Whether the route were long or short householders kept their curtains drawn along it until the coffin had passed. This was either a mark of respect or because it was unlucky to see a funeral procession through glass, or a combination of the two. When a coffin had to be carried from an isolated house across cultivated fields it was believed that a right of way would be created unless some payment, if only a few pence, were exacted by the landowner. Alternatively, a detour could be made to avoid private ground. 'One of these "corpse ways" as they were called', wrote Bill Gwilliam in 1991, 'is the Burial Way from Ham Green to Feckenham Church. It is an extremely primitive track, in most parts overgrown and impassable for vehicles. It has twists and turns and makes a final wide curve to reach its destination by the side of Feckenham Church'.

Until 1864 people who died at Far Forest had to be buried at Ribbesford, three miles off. The bearers were in the habit of refreshing themselves on the way at eleven inns or alehouses: the Wheatsheaf, Plough, Blue Ball, Green Dragon, Royal Forester, New Inn, Mopsons

Cross, Duke William, Tower Farm, Running Horse, Rose and Crown.

At Ross mourners sang psalms before the corpse on its journey from house to church. In former times an effigy of the deceased was carried before the coffin, and this practice was followed at Much Marcle until 1878. One effigy, that of the fourteenth century reeve, Sir Hugh Helyon, is still kept in the church there. Another, that of a priest dating from about 1300, is at Clifford; it resembles in turn the effigy of Bishop Aquablanca (died 1268) at Hereford Cathedral.

Richard Parry, the nineteenth century historian of Kington, wrote that 'When a funeral procession arrived at a cross road, it was the custom ... to put down the corpse for a few moments, and for the mourners and others to stand still'. Many miles away and almost a hundred years later, the bearers at Broadwas-on-Teme still put down the coffin in the middle of a lane leading to the church, formed a circle, and bowed 'most reverentially'. At Brilley the coffin was carried three times round the Funeral Stone (which has now gone) by the churchyard gate before passing through. The manoeuvre was thought to ensure that the devil could not take the soul of the deceased. The same notion probably lay behind the Pembridge custom of taking a roundabout route with the coffin, then going right round the churchyard 'the way of the sun'. Funerals at Malvern Link halted at the crossroads just below the station for the bearers to put the coffin on the ground and change places. At least one undertaker tried to stop this, but the bearers insisted.

At Ocle Pychard and elsewhere in North Herefordshire all the church bells are chimed when the funeral procession approaches. This is called 'ringing home' or 'welcoming home' the deceased.

*Effigy of
Sir Hugh Helyon*

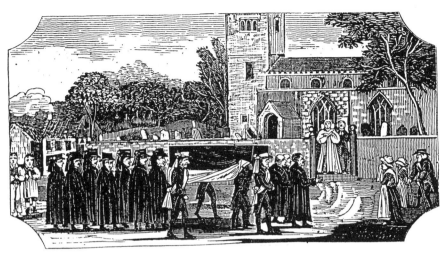

Engraving of a funeral from a ballad sheet

If at all possible bearers would avoid entering church or churchyard on the north side. At Leysters, for example, funerals always entered the churchyard by the east gate and paused at a funeral stone from which the cortège would be read into the church by the vicar. The north or devil's side, reserved for suicides and strangers, was unacceptable for burials. Since the usual door for access was on the south side the dead buried there would receive the prayers of the living as they passed the graves and read the inscriptions. People were buried on an east-west alignment, looking towards the east from whence the resurrection would come.

Orleton in Herefordshire was for some reason thought to be the place where the resurrection would begin on the Day of Judgement. People from all over England arranged to be buried there, thinking they would be the first to rise from their graves.

By a cruel irony the name of resurrectionists was given to those who stole newly-buried bodies for dissection. In 1831 two bodies taken from St. Mary's Churchyard at Hanley Castle were found in packing cases at the Anchor Inn, Upton, and restored to their graves. The following year at Hereford two men were arrested for stealing the body of an army veteran, William Hardman—it was found in a hamper opened at the local coach-office. The men appeared before the mayor, and as they were on their way to gaol 'they were followed by an immense crowd, and assailed with the most vociferous expressions of disgust and contempt'. Long after the Anatomy Act of 1832 legalised and regularised the supply of corpses for dissection, stories continued to be told of the hated resurrection men.

In the Golden Valley a premature rising in the form of a ghost was averted when the need was felt by burying a corpse face down. One man who lived near Tenbury gave instructions that he was not to be buried in the same churchyard as his late wife, on the grounds that he 'had enough of her in her lifetime'. He was duly interred elsewhere, and left a generous donation for the church bells to be rung once a year in his memory.

At Feckenham when a single woman died it was usual to carry a garland—Shakespeare called it 'virgin's crants'—before her coffin to the church and hang it there. The custom was continued at Holt until the 1930's. Shakespeare's 'rosemary for remembrance' is still planted on graves as a token that the dead are not forgotten.

V
SUPERSTITIONS

When life is precarious superstitions abound. Even in today's relatively secure society few people will claim to be completely without some little taboo or odd belief. Few of such superstitions are peculiar to particular places and many have national and even international currency. An exception which may prove the rule is apparently specific to the village of Mathon, where there is a belief that if part of a particular field is inadvertently left unsown a death in the farmer's family will follow within a year.

Explanation for superstitions is often hard to find. The word literally means 'standing over something in awe or amazement', and it has overtones of mystery and fear. Touching wood to avert ill-luck may date back to the practice of touching a fragment thought to come from Christ's cross. Alternatively, pre-Christian religions venerated trees so the superstition may go back to very early times. Whatever the truth of this may be, the feeling that possible misfortune needs to be warded off can easily well up. In August 1991 chain letters from Venezuela started to arrive in Ledbury. They promised good fortune if the recipients sent copies of the letter to twenty people within four days, death and disaster otherwise. Those who complied would receive sums of money out of the blue, or offers of jobs. One man who had broken the chain—so it was alleged—died nine days later; another lost his wife. Police advised people to tear up the letters, and offered to do so themselves for anyone too frightened to do so.

Folk medicine, especially the herbal variety, seems to be enjoying a new lease of life, though some of the wilder remedies for such things as whooping cough are unlikely to return. Nevertheless, within living memory a charm was used at Dorstone to ensure that when a tree was cut down it fell in the right place.

Weather lore is facing stiff competition from scientific meteorology but still has much to offer. A great deal of wisdom and humour is encapsulated in traditional rhymes and sayings. One writer—John Noake—dismissed all superstitions as 'fooleries' but many would reject such a peremptory judgement.

Sayings
Practical wisdom found expression in a host of semi-proverbial axioms such as: 'an ounce of help is worth a wagon load of pity'; 'a good

contriver is better than an early riser'; 'dilly-dally brings night as soon as hurry-scurry'; 'and I was born too near a 'ood (wood) to be frightened by owls'. There is wry humour in such comments as 'a good man round a barrel but no cooper' and (applied to a woman with a boorish husband) 'Her'll never want for bacon; her's allus got a hog in the house'. In the same vein are 'The wind be that lazy it fair goes through yer' and 'I be that 'ungry me stomach thinks me throat be cut'.

Set comparisons were much appreciated. 'As big a fool as Jack Havod' has now died out. The reference was to the last jester kept in the household of a Mr. Bartlett, a country gentleman from Castlemorton. However, 'as busy as an ant' can still be heard, together with 'as fat (or slick, or smooth) as an oont' (mole), 'as sour as varges' (crab vinegar) and 'as useless as a sundial in a cellar'. A child grows 'like a hop-vine' and a grating voice is 'like a humble bee in a churn'. 'As long as the oak and ash grow' means always; 'as well sip up Severn and swallow Malvern' points to the impossible; and 'as sure as God's in Gloucestershire' indicates certainty. The last expression is said to have arisen because of the large number of religious houses once found in that county.

Signs

A large number of omens forewarned of possible misfortune. As recently as 1991 some nurses at Bosbury told me that a series of creases making the shape of a coffin in a newly laundered sheet were a sign of death. A similar portent was created if a person brought the first snowdrops of the season into the house, opened an umbrella there, shouldered a spade or dropped scissors so that they fell on one point. (To fall on the two together indicated a wedding).

Other tell-tale objects presaging misfortune were a clock falling, a church bell being rung as the clock strikes, a winding sheet—that is, an unburnt wavelet of wax curling away from the flame—on a candle, or a wick glowing long after it is extinguished, or a long run in black suits during a game of cards. Signs of death indicated by plants included the blooming of an apple tree twice a year or its bearing fruit and blossom at the same time, the dying off or shrivelling of a gooseberry or currant bush while it is fruiting, the death of ivy on a house, and the appearance of a rose with leaves between the petals. Certain animal behaviour was seen in a similar light—the howling of a dog, the coughing of a cat, rats' nibbling furniture, the entry to a house of a mole, frog or toad, the flight of a white bird against a window or the tapping of any bird at a pane.

The actions of birds were carefully watched. The flight of a bird over a sickbed signalled the death of its occupant. A robin's entering a house gave the same warning, though a bee's incursion meant a visit from a stranger. (So did a cock crowing in an open doorway, or a lid accidentally left off the teapot). Otherwise the robin was a lucky bird. As was the wren:

> Malisons, malisons, more than ten,
> Who kills the Queen of Heaven's wren.

It was considered unlucky to destroy a swallow's nest or kill an owl. The latter was favoured because it flew out of the oak tree not when Charles II hid in it but when searchers arrived, thus causing them to miss the fugitive. To see a raven was a bad sign. Magpies varied:

> One for sorrow, two for mirth;
> Three for a wedding, four for a birth.

Two crows meant a wedding, and one a funeral, though a Worcester man thought the latter could be avoided by saying aloud the word 'break' on sight of the crow. The Seven Whistlers passing overhead at night portended disaster. There is uncertainty as to what these birds were, and this perhaps increases the fear. One possibility is the swift, known in Herefordshire as 'the devil screamer'.

Despite its unpleasant habits the cuckoo does not bring ill luck. Some believed, though, that whatever one was doing on first hearing it would be one's main occupation through the ensuing year. Rain is predicted by the call of the stormcock (another name for the green woodpecker or yaffle), the bray of the donkey and the closing during daylight of the scarlet pimpernel.

A very long list of actions or omissions brings bad luck or unpleasant consequences. Kicking fungi leads to seven years' bad luck. The results of picking herb robert (*geranium robertarium*) are shown in its local name Death-come-quickly. Ill luck comes of taking into the house snowdrops before 1 May, or mistletoe or holly before Christmas. Elder wood should not be burnt at all, and no wood should be burnt green: 'Burn green, sorrow soon seen' except for pear: 'Pear dry, pear green, makes a fire fit for a queen'. Red and white flowers in the same bunch are considered unlucky, especially in hospitals, where they may point to blood on the sheets. Parsley should not be transplanted: 'Well, if you plants parsley you plants the Old Man'. The willow is cursed since the Virgin Mary whipped her son with it and caused him to say, in the words of the *Bitter Withy* (see also chapter 9):

> Cursed be the sally tree which maketh me to smart;
> The sally tree shall be the first to perish at the heart.

How cricketers escape from this injunction is not clear, but there was a time when no countryman would hit an animal with a stick of willow.

A hare running down a village street showed that there would be a fire. A weasel crossing one's path was unlucky; so was the first lamb or colt of the season if it were seen facing away. Killing a ladybird was also unlucky, and so with many other things which people carelessly did or left undone.

Salt was a precious commodity, and also a symbol for immortality. Spilling it was decidedly unlucky: in Leonardo da Vinci's painting of the Last Supper Judas is shown over turning the salt, but the superstition may pre-date the picture. Returning borrowed salt was unlucky; so was putting salt on someone else's food, rather than simply passing it. Still at table, crossing knives led to a quarrel, but this could be averted if the lower of the two were withdrawn, and these words said: 'Blessed are the peacemakers'. Putting new shoes on the table is still considered unlucky by many.

A quarrel can again be caused when two people wash in the same water, unless the second spits in it first. Giving knives or scissors as a present leads to the end of a friendship unless something is given in exchange. However, the gift of a pin should not be repaid, even with thanks. A light should not be given at Christmas or the New Year, and being one of a party of thirteen was especially unlucky at Christmas.

Throwing out soapsuds on Holy Thursday (the Thursday before Easter) was unlucky, and hanging out clothes to dry on the same day would ensure that there would be a death in the family, with the corpse laid out in one of the items on the line. Good Friday was thought to be a special day for planting since this was 'the only day the devil has no right to the ground'. However, to leave soapsuds in a boiler over Good Friday will lead to a death in the house, and washing on the day brings bad luck for twelve months. At Weobley there was a belief that nothing should be poured down the sink until after 3p.m. on Good Friday since the gutters of Jerusalem were running with Christ's blood till that time.

The phases of the moon were carefully watched, since planting had to be done as it waxed, and also the killing of animals and even the cutting of hair:

> Crop your head in the moon's wax,
> Ne'er cut it in the wane;
> And then of a bald head
> You shall never complain.

Pointing at a new moon (and also a rainbow) is unlucky; so is to see it first through glass. When it is seen in the open people should turn the money in their pockets and wish for a lucky month.

Certain days were unlucky, especially Friday—the day of the crucifixion—when fresh work should not be undertaken nor a journey begun nor a mattress turned. Cutting nails on a Sunday—a Friday in some versions—was to be avoided:

> Better had he never been born
> Than pare his nails on a Sunday morn.

Further ill luck came from saying goodbye over a stile or at a cross-roads; treading on a piece of iron; meeting or passing someone on the stairs; going back over the doorstep for something forgotten (unless a person sits down and counts to ten to break the spell); passing beneath a ladder (unless bad luck is averted by crossing the fingers and thumbs); and even meeting a squinting woman (unless one speaks to her). When a fire was lit the devil was shamed when logs were crossed, and a useful tip was:

> One log can't burn.
> Two logs won't burn.
> Three logs make a fire.

Very few things seemed to bring good luck. A black cat crossing one's path is still very well known, but a fox's doing so at night is also lucky. Some farmers thought white cows lucky; others, a flock of sheep or a load of hay encountered on a journey. Certain omens were inescapable. A burning face indicates that someone is talking about the person. A shudder shows that someone is walking over the spot where one's grave is to be. An itchy foot will soon be treading strange ground; an itching ear portends news from the living; a nose, bad news or that 'You will be kissed, cursed or vexed, or shake hands with a fool'. When rosemary flourishes in a garden, the mistress is master. So too if the lavender does well, or the sage thrives.

Charms

Horseshoes nailed to doors or fixed over bedsteads performed the double function of keeping away witches and bringing good luck. Some favoured the points up, others down. The former is associated with the horned moon, the latter with the Greek omega.

147

The Severn Naturalist
Club met at the site of
the old Sorb to the number
of ladies and gentlemen
where they sang a requiem
lamenting the destruction
of the old tree so long an
object of veneration.

Burnt down by some
worthless miscreant in
April 1862
There is one tree now
growing at Upper Arely
reared by Earl Mountnorris

It would now have
been in a flourishing
state notwithstanding
its great age had it not
have been so barbarously
mutilated by ignorant
visitors cutting of branches
and portions of the bark
to cut their names.

Sorbus domestica, Lin
Pyrus domestica, Hooker
In Bawdley Forest
as it appeared 1851

The Whitty Pear

110

Rowan—otherwise known as witty, wittan or wittern—also provided protection against witches, both as a living tree and as detached pieces. Parson Kilvert found Hannah Preece's cottage on Monnington Common hung with rowan and birch twigs which serves 'to keep the old witch out' and were renewed annually on May Eve.

First recorded in 1678, the Whitty Tree (*pyrus domesticus*) stood in the Wyre Forest until 1862 when it was burnt down by vandals. Its small, hard, pear-shaped fruits were much prized for their perceived value as witch repellents. (See also chapter 7).

Many villages once had a healer or charmer. Nanny Haines of Feckenham had the gift of second sight, and could foretell the future. The astrologer, herbalist and magician, Culpeper, is reputed to have lived at Astwood Court, Astwood Bank, in the sixteenth century. Useful herbs can still be found in the meadow adjoining the farm, and in a nearby field a circular depression where spirits came to do Culpeper's bidding is called Spirity Pit. At Upton-on-Severn a bonesetter called Beale had a great reputation in the early eighteenth century.

One family of bonesetters, the Lloyds, practised on the Herefordshire-Radnorshire border for some two hundred years up to the 1970's (though latterly only on animals). Relatives still live in Kington and Eardisley. The story of one eighteenth century member, Silver John, is told in chapter 10. Hugh, who was perhaps John's brother, is buried at Michaelchurch-on-Arrow, where a plaque in the church reproduces his epitaph:

> A talent rare by him possessed
> T'adjust the bones of the distressed;
> When ever called he ne'er refused
> But cheerfully his talent used.
> But now he lies beneath this tomb,
> Till Jesus comes t'adjust his own.

Bonesetting is currently enjoying a new lease of life, but those now engaged in the art call themselves chiropractors or osteopaths.

Fladbury was noted for its female charmers, Weobley for its charmers and herbalists. Mrs. Leather obtained a manuscript dated 1804 in which John E. of Weobley recorded charms against toothache, burns, ague, sprains, cuts, the bite of a mad dog, thorn wounds and spells. As recently as the 1930's Lizzie Watkins of Dorstone was both feared and respected as a folk doctor and herbalist. Amongst her charms were those for toothache and warts, muttering words which have not been recorded, and were probably not meant to be. Other charms have been documented elsewhere:

Burns

There were two angels came from the north.
One brought frost and the other brought fire.
In, frost. Out, fire.
In the name of the Father, Son and Holy Ghost. (Mathon)

Bleeding

Jesus was born in Bethlehem,
Baptised in the River Jordan;
The water was wild and wood,
But he was just and good.
God spake, and the water stood,
And so shall now thy blood. (Worcestershire)

Nettle Sting

Apply a dock-leaf and say:

'Ettle, 'ettle, 'ittle dock,
Dock sh'll 'ave a golden smock,
'Ettle shaunt 'ave nerrun. (South-east Worcestershire)

Toothache

The following was written on a small piece of paper and sealed with pitch: Crist met with Peter and saide unto him Peter what is the mater with the. Peter saide lorde I am tormented with the pains in the tooth the worme shall die and Thou shalt live and thow that shalt have this in wrightin or in memory shall never have the Paine in the tooth the worme shall Die and thou shalt live and thou shalt have this in memory or wrightin shall never have the paine in the tooth. Therefore believe in the lorde youre God. (Craswall, 1886)

Whooping Cough

A sufferer would be taken to the miller, who would set his mill going and say: 'In the name of the Father, Son and Holy Ghost I grind away this disease'. (Worcestershire)

The notion that such charms could have therapeutic powers seems ludicrous but apparently they often worked on the principle, no doubt, of faith healing. They embody a curious mixture of magical practice and religious faith, and must at times have been last ditch attempts at finding a cure when proper medical treatment was wanting.

Desperate Remedies

Certain substances were thought to have particular powers. Iron retained from primitive times a reputation for efficacity against witchcraft. The gold of a wedding ring blessed during the marriage ceremony could cure certain ailments (see below). Lead stolen from a church roof was doubly effective—for many years a cross made of lead taken from Cusop Church hung in the neighbouring Blackhill Farm, where it was thought to give protection against fire and lightning. Water left over in a font after a baptism was eagerly sought for its curative properties. The ceremony of baptism itself was considered a helpful step for a weakly or fractious infant, and consecrated wine was regarded as a useful medicine.

Personal amulets were widely carried. A double hazel nut or a potato carried in the pocket could ward off ill luck. A bloodstone gave protection against bleeding. The touch of some people, from dead man to living monarch, could also have therapeutic effects.

The principles involved in folk medicine range from faith healing to the use of substances now known to be chemically beneficial, such as cobwebs to staunch bleeding. They include would-be magical transference of disease to other people, animals, or objects. Some of the remedies, though, could have exacerbated rather than allayed disease. For example, a suggested cure for rabies caused by a mad dog was to write a few words on a piece of cheese and give it to the animal to eat.

Ague

Go to a tree grafter. Tell him what is the matter and then go away. When you are at home he will cut the first branch of a maiden ash and you will be cured. (The same technique was used for rupture). At Stourport the grafter said these words: 'Ague, farewell, till we meet in hell'.

Baldness

Wear a cowpat on the head in bed. Wear a cap made of ivy leaves.

Cholera

Eat grated crumbs from bread baked on a Good Friday and kept till the following Good Friday. At Bredwardine, Much Marcle and elsewhere, small loaves of two to three inches in diameter were cooked on Good Friday to be saved, then ground to powder and mixed with hot water to be given for a variety of common ailments.

113

Cramp

Wear an eelskin garter below the knee. Wear a ring made from a coffin hinge or a consecrated shilling. There is a record of a mid-seventeenth century goldsmith in Hereford who was brought such coins 'by Papists' to have cramp rings made. Alternatively, be christened or confirmed, as appropriate (also a cure for fits).

Dog bite

Pluck three hairs from the dog's tail and swallow them.

Fits

Drink an infusion made from mistletoe growing on hawthorn. Wear on the finger or on string round the neck a ring made from sacrament silver— a coin given in collection at church, and blessed by clergymen. Parsons were frequently asked for 'sacrament shillings' for this purpose, and the remedy was widely employed.

Jaundice

Take the inner rind of elder bark boiled in milk.

Rheumatism

Carry a piece of alder wood in a pocket. Lay a hop pillow under the bed. (The latter remedy was prescribed for George III by a doctor at Reading).

Rupture

Slit a sapling; walk between the halves, then tie them up. The ash was chosen at Broxwood, Thruxton and Walterstone; the willow at Eardisland.

Scrofula

Be touched by a king. In 1687 James II visited Worcester Cathedral for the purpose of touching sufferers. On other occasions people were given money to allow them to travel to London for the same purpose. In 1711, for example, the churchwardens of St. Nicholas Church, Worcester, paid 11 shillings 'for carrying of Walker to London to be touched'.

Shingles

Apply grease from the bearings of a church bell.

Sore eyes

Apply water from a holy well, or rainwater caught and bottled on Ascension Day.

Sore feet

Put silverweed (*potentilla anserina*, locally known as Traveller's Ease) in the shoes.

Stitch after running

Fix crosses to shoes.

Stye

Rub with wedding ring.

Teething

Hang bag of woodlice round baby's neck.

Toothache

Wear oont's (mole's) feet in bag round neck; or, also round the neck, a spider in a nutshell. Carry the gall of a wild rose.

Viper bite

Wrap affected part in a skin taken warm and reeking from a sheep. Or kill the snake, then make a paste of its liver and eat it. Adder skins were used to cure wounds made by thorns.

Warts

These are all different possibilities. Put a small pin in the earth to rust. Steal a piece of beef and bury it. Rub the warts with a black slug, then impale it on a thorn. Gather some ripe ears of wheat and cross the wart with them several times; then put the corn into a packet and drop it where three roads meet. Cut as many notches in a stick as there are warts, and drop it where four roads meet. Secretly pinch out of a loaf of bread as many pieces as there are warts and bury them. Cut as many notches as there are warts in two sticks; lay them crosswise in the road, and the warts will be taken by whoever picks up the sticks. Make the sign of the cross and repeat *Gloria Patri* (Glory be to the Father)—though this can be done only by someone with the gift of charming. Sell them. (I met in 1990 a Bromyard doctor who said that he had often bought warts from patients). Two cases from the 1960's are supplied by Lavender Jones: 'Miss Phyllis Turner, aged about 64, told me that when a child she and her mother were walking down Hospital Lane, Powick, when she saw a small parcel under the hedge which she picked up and opened. It contained a piece of burnt wood. Her mother smacked it out of her hand to the ground. It was a wart cure and had been put there to remove someone's warts. Phyllis Turner by touching it had transferred the warts to her own hands. She said she subsequently had several warts. Mrs. Leeke of Powick told me that her daughter Peggy had warts on her hand. Mrs. Leeke put a grain of wheat for each wart into an envelope and took it to Worcester and dropped it at the Five Ways. This is an inn on the corner of Angel Street and the Butts where five roads converge. All the warts disappeared. It is essential that the person losing the warts should not turn round or look back after losing them'.

Wen
Arrange for the wen, a lump or protuberance on the body, to be touched by the hand of a dead man.

Whooping Cough
Here again there are many different options. Eat bread and butter which has been placed in a dead man's hand. Take a pie dish to the River Rea—this is mainly from Mamble; catch a trout and drown it in cider, then fry the fish; the patient eats the fish and drinks the cider. Take twenty hairs from the nape of the patient's neck (or seven from the tail of a white horse) and put them between slices of bread and butter; give this sandwich to the first strange dog which passes, and say the Lord's Prayer; the dog will carry away the disease. Hold a frog in the mouth of the patient and cause him to breathe into its mouth; the frog will take away the disease. Inhale the breath of a piebald horse. Pass the patient nine mornings running under the arch made by a bramble rooted at both ends; say the Lord's Prayer, eat some bread and butter, and give some to a bird or animal. Cause the patient to drink from a sacramental cup or eat from a bowl of ivy wood. Tie a string with nine knots round the neck. Find a married couple called Mary and Joseph and send them an unsolicited gift or ask the wife to lay her hands on the patient (the latter was recorded from Abbot's Morton in 1932). Find a woman successively married to two men of the same surname but of different families; ask her to cut bread and butter and give it to the patient. Find a woman with a second husband whose surname is the same as her maiden name; anything she suggests will produce a cure, though in practice bread and butter with sugar was usually recommended.

Weather Lore
Before the days of scientific weather forecasting people amassed a whole host of predictions, some general, some particular, which were the fruit of generations of knowledge. Many provide sound advice, particularly when

116

The moon upside down, from a misericord at Ripple

they describe the sky itself, though none works all the time. For example, 'Rain before seven, dry before eleven' often proves true because most frontal rain bands last only a few hours; however, we can all remember occasions when rain has continued for a whole day or even longer. To take a different instance, the traditional view (see below) that January is the 'blackest' month is confirmed by scientific evidence that it is indeed, on average, the coldest month of the year in most places in the British Isles. On the other hand, the calendar changes of 1752 and also variations in climate such as the global warming we are beginning to experience affect the accuracy of any weather lore of long standing. The easiest traditional observations to dismiss are those connected with miracle-working saints such as Swithin (for whom, see below). Weather lore was often cast into rhyme to make it easily memorable.

The moon was believed to be a very useful indicator. For example, the appearance of a new moon on a Saturday would bring twenty days of wind and rain. Put another way:

> If the moon on a Saturday be new or full,
> There always was rain and there always wull.

On the other hand, 'Sunday's Moon comes too soon', that is, a new moon on a Sunday brings ill fortune. A moon on its back brings dry weather: 'Moon on its back holds water in its lap' but if the points are downward rain is indicated.

We are still preoccupied with rain, both in timing and in quantity, and there are probably more traditional sayings on this subject than any other. 'When the sun sets in a muddy mist, be sure that rain's at hand', is how one expression puts it. A local variant of the old shepherd's rhyme goes: 'A rainbow at night is the shepherd's delight'. A more elaborate verse runs:

> When the reds are out at night it's the shepherd's delight,
> But when out in the morning it's all day storming.

Particular landmarks feature in some predictive rhymes. One verse is still widely known:

> When Bredon Hill puts on his hat
> Ye men of the vale beware of that.
> When Bredon Hill doth clear appear
> Ye men of the vale have nought to fear.

Others must have been familiar to perhaps only a few hundred people. 'A mist round the tower, It'll rain an hour' refers to the folly built on the hill above Broadway. Several signs of rain were known at Weobley. Jackdaws circling the church spire gave one. Another was when the wind blew in 'Weobley hole'. A third concerned a high, tree-covered hill:

> When Lady Lift puts on her shift
> She fears a downright rain,
> But when she doffs it you will find
> The rain is o'er, and still the wind,
> And Phoebus shines again.

Farmers with land by the Severn watched the tide:

> If it raineth when it doth flow,
> Then take your ox and go to plough;
> But if it raineth when it doth ebb,
> Unyoke your ox and go to bed.

Oxen ploughing, 1803

The last time oxen were used in Worcestershire as draught animals was during the 1920's, so the rhyme may not have been heard for some years.

Still current, though, is the belief that the appearance of black beetles points to rain—and if they are killed it will be all the wetter. A cock's crow can also be significant:

> A cock crowing on going to bed,
> Sign he'll get up with a dropping {dripping} head.

The well known rhyme about the oak and ash is often thought to mean that we shall have rain either way, but a local variant makes clear this this is not so:

> If the oak be out before the ash
> There'll only be a little splash;
> If the ash be out before the oak
> Then there'll be a regular soak.

Another sign from a tree relates not to weather but to fishing:

> When the bud of the orl {alder} is as big as a trout's eye,
> Then that fish is in season in the River Wye.

Among the many ways of predicting rain in the vale of Evesham were these: clouds passing rapidly; a remarkably clear atmosphere; swallows flying near the ground; restless sheep; cows herding together; donkeys constantly braying; bees remaining close to the hive; frogs croaking and coming out onto the road; a smoky chimney; a taut clothes line; the closing of their petals by crowsfoot, speedwell, wood sorrel, scarlet pimpernel, anenome or stitchwort; damp bricks in a yard or path.

The best of the weather lore derived from a careful reading of the sky and the winds. 'Cruddledy {curdled} sky, cruddledy sky, not long wet, not long dry', says one forecast. Others predict 'Cloudy mornings turn to clear evenings' and 'Dew before midnight, next day will be bright'. The wind features in 'The weather's always ill when the wind's not still' and 'When the wind is in the east, there it will be for some days at least'. As winter approaches 'A storm of hail brings frost in its tail'. Even onions can provide predictions:

> Onion skins very thin,
> A mild winter coming in.
> Onion skins thick and tough,
> Coming winter wild and rough.

Most months of the year have their own lore. People were reluctant to settle bills on 1 January since they believed: 'Pay away money on New Year's Day, all the year through you'll have money to pay'. The same day had a rhyme about the lengthening of light:

> At New Year's tide a cock's stride;
> By Twelfth-tide another beside.

At Upton Bishop the second line was varied to 'Candlemas an hour's tide'. Twelfth-tide, or 6 January, was also known after the change of calendar in 1752 as Old Christmas Day; on this occasion one should rejoice if the sun shines through the branches of the apple trees.

On the whole January was not a popular month. 'As the days lengthen the cold strengthens' can still be heard, though perhaps not 'The blackest month of all the year, it is the month of Janiveer'. A mild January was thought to bring a cold May, though it was considered good time for planting at least one crop: 'Who in January sows oats, gets gold and groats'.

The weather on Candlemas Day (2 February) seems to have been very carefully watched for its predictive qualities. If the wind was in the west at midday it was thought to portend a good year for fruit. Wherever the wind was, especially in the east, there it would 'abide till the second of May'. Still at Candlemas, geese should begin laying. A farmer should still have half his straw and half his hay because a good deal of the winter might still be to come. 'Never come Lent, never come winter' means that one cannot rely that winter is over till Lent is past. If the birds sang before Candlemas (or alternatively, on Candlemas Day) they would cry before May. The message is given with greater clarity in this verse:

> If Candlemas Day be dark and black
> It will carry cold winter away on its back,
> But if Candlemas Day be bright and clear
> The half of winter's to come this year.

'A February spring is worth nothing' seems another way of expressing the second couplet. 'February grass wipes March's arse' is taken to mean that a flush of grass in a mild February is always checked by bad weather in March. More optimistically, 'Much February snow a fine summer doth show'.

'Never come March, never come winter' was an expression used until at least the 1960's at Much Marcle. The feeling that winter is not yet over is also reflected in:

> March will search and April try
> But May will tell if you live or die.

The winds of this month were regarded as significant:

> If the wind is in the east at noon on St. Benedict's Day {21 March},
> It will neither chop nor change till the end of May.

One rhyme was peculiar to the people of Ledbury:

> If the March wind blows to Ross {that is from the north-east}
> The fruit crop will be a loss.
> If the March wind blows to Worcester {that is from the south-west}
> All fruit will hang in clusters.

A general comment on fruit growing runs:

> March dust on the apple leaf
> Brings all kind of fruit to grief.

In other words, a wet March does good; but opinions differ, for another saying claims 'A peck of March dust is worth a king's ransom'. One more rhyme to complete March's story:

> If the apple trees bloom in March
> For barrels of cider you need not sarch;
> If the apple trees bloom in May
> You can eat apple dumplings every day.

The theme of cider making was taken up in April:

> When apple trees are in blossom in April and before May
> You can put all your barrels away,
> But if they blossom at the end of May and the beginning of June
> You can get all your barrels in tune.

Other sayings for the month include 'A cold April, the barn will fill' and 'If it thunder on All Fools' Day, it brings good crops of grass and hay'. However, 'April oats and August hay, weeds the farmer's living away'; the implication here is that the oats are planted and the hay gathered too late. A parallel rhyme runs 'Cuckoo oats and orchard hay, make a farmer run away', the oats having been sown too late, the hay being too difficult to cut.

The cuckoo in Worcestershire was thought never to be heard before Tenbury Fair (20 April) or after Pershore Fair (26 June). Of the latter it is said: 'The cuckoo guz ter Parsha Fair, and then 'er 'ops it off from there'. In Herefordshire she came to the cattle fair once held on 23 April at the Boot Inn, Orleton; there she bought a horse, and went to Bron Fair (Brampton Bryan) to sell him. No doubt the coincidences of the cuckoo's coming and going with these events led to the belief. Incidentally, the expression 'gone to Bron Fair' was used of peas and other crops which looked weakly.

'Easter come early, Easter come late, it's sure to make the old cow quake' gives warning that bad weather is still to be expected at this time of year. Another prediction seems to show that plenty will grow but little will be gathered in:

> If the sun shines through the trees on Easter Day
> We shall have a good year of grass and a poor one of hay.

The same is said of Christmas Day and also—with regard to hops—of Good Friday.

'A cold May is kind' recalls the rhyme about the benefit of a cold April. On the other hand, 'A May wet was never kind yet'; but there are, as always, other views: 'A wet and windy May, and the barns are full of hay' or 'A warm and dappeldy May, the barns are full of hay'.

To ensure successive crops runner beans should be planted on May Eve and June Eve. In South Herefordshire the people believed in planting swedes at the time of Coleford Fair (9 June). The classic formula for bean planting is:

> When elmen leaves are big as a shilling,
> Plant kidney beans if to plant 'em you're willing.
> When elmen leaves are as big as a farden,
> Plant kidney beans in your garden.
> When elmen leaves are as big as a penny,
> Plant kidney beans if you mean to have any.

Apart from the lack of elm leaves to observe, this rhyme is now surely doomed to fall out of use through the disappearance of the farthing and the old penny.

The rhyme about the value of swarms of bees in diferent months remains very well known, but the one about thistles is less so:

> Cut thistles in May,
> They grow in a day.
> Cut them in June,
> That is too soon.
> Cut them in July,
> Then they will die.

The weather in May and June was rightly seen to have its effect on the coming harvest. 'Mist in May and heat in June will bring the harvest very soon', was one prediction. Contrariwise, another said 'A dry May and a dripping June always brings things in tune'. St. Barnabas Day (11 June) signalled the beginning of haymaking. 'On Saint Barnabas put the scythe to grass'. If the cuckoo were heard after Pershore Fair (26 June) she had failed to buy a horse on which to ride away—merely another way of saying she was staying longer than expected. Rain was expected on that day to christen the apples, though some areas applied this belief to St. Peter's Day (29 June).

Many country people still hold to the opinion that if rain falls on St. Swithin's Day (15 July) it will continue for forty days. The belief has over a thousand years of history behind it, but no weight of metereological evidence. When Swithin died in 862 he left instructions that he was to be buried outside the west door of the Old Minster at Winchester. This was done, but about a hundred years later a decision was taken to move his remains inside the cathedral. On the day in question—15 July 971—miraculous cures were effected and heavy rain began to fall and lasted for forty days.

The period from August to November seems less rich in weather lore, perhaps because after harvest at least the weather was not so important. Michaelmas (29 September) occasioned the wry reflection that plentiful supplies of apples would not last for ever:

> At Michaelmas or a little before,
> Half the apple's thrown away with the core.
> At Christmas time or a little bit arter
> If it's as sour as a crab,
> It's 'Thank you, master'.

In October farmers put rams to their ewes: 'At St. Luke's Day {18 October} let tups have play'. In November signs of winter started to be seen:

> Ice in November to hold a duck,
> There follows a winter of slush and muck.

However, if the first snow of the season hung in the trees it was thought to show that the following year would be good for fruit. A similar sign was that if the sun shone through the orchard on Christmas Day a good year for apples would ensue. The same weather unfortunately predicted many fires in the year. Other signs were: 'Hours of sun on Christmas Day, so many frosts in the month of May' and 'If Christmas Day be bright and clear, there'll be two winters in the year'.

The day on which Christmas fell had its significance:

> If Christmas on a Thursday be
> A windy winter you shall see:
> Windy days in every week,
> Winter weather strong and thick;
> Summer shall be good and dry,
> Corn and wheat shall multiply.

An alternative was that if Christmas Day fell on a Sunday the following summer would be hot. Finally, and somewhat lugubriously, 'A green Christmas means a full churchyard'.

VI
THE SUPERNATURAL

The supernatural has been a very long time a-dying. Although fairies are now largely confined to children's books and films, belief in them among adults lingered until the earlier part of this century. Similarly, the physical presence of the devil was accepted by many until well within living memory. Fears of witches (chapter 7) and the Wild Hunt—spirits of the restless dead riding through the sky and presaging calamity—may now have vanished, but the notion that in some circumstances the spirits of the dead return to their erstwhile surroundings is undoubtedly persistent. The perturbation in life—violence, injustice, sin of omission or commission—which causes ghosts to walk is sometimes well documented, sometimes mysterious.

Fairies

The novelist, Mary Martha Sherwood, was born in 1775. As a child she was shown fairy rings in the woods near Stanford-on-Teme. A century later another writer, John Masefield, was being shown similar rings on a hill near Ledbury—he does not say which. Until at least the 1920's small clay pipes found by people digging their gardens were called 'fairy pipes'. Roman coins unearthed at Bolitree (Ariconium) were known as 'fairies' money'. The same was true of Kenchester (Magna Castra), where in the time of Leland ruins included 'The King of the Fairies' Chair'. The little people were thought to dance round it on moonlit nights.

Place names referring to Puck, Hob or Dob—all beneficient and occasionally mischievous spirits—are widespread. They include Hob's Hole (Offenham), Hob Moor (Chaddesley Corbett), Little Dobbin's Hill (Berrow), Dobbin's Meadow (Mathon), Puck Meadow (Hallow), Puck Hill (Himbleton), Puck Croft and Pixies' Ham (Powick), Puck's Piece (Abbot's Lench) and Cob's Piece (Dodderhill).

At Alfrick people said they were waylaid by Puck and led into ditches. The same applied in Pokehouse Wood at Aymestrey, where a man bequeathed money to provide for a bell to guide benighted travellers (see chapter 3).

People tried hard to befriend the fairies. A labourer at Upton Snodsbury heard one of the little creatures crying over a broken seat. He mended it, and the fairy fed him in return on biscuits and wine. Everything he did

125

afterwards turned out well, and he prospered. A similar tale was told at Alfrick, where a man and a boy were ploughing when they heard lamentations coming from a copse. They went over, and found a fairy grieving over a lost pickaxe. They managed to find it, and were rewarded by bread, cheese and cider. The man ate and drank but the boy was too frightened to do so. Another example of fairy benevolence was the belief in Lulsley that if a woman broke her peel—the flat tool used for moving bread into and out of the oven—the fairies would mend it if she left it in a cave by Osebury Rock, near the River Teme.

On the other hand, as with the ploughing boy, the fairies could inspire fear. They were able to spoil butter, to steal babies and substitute changelings, to inveigle people into accompanying them for what seems a few minutes or hours and turned out to be years. They rode borrowed horses on moonlit nights, the evidence for which was that the animals would be found first thing in the morning dishevelled and sweating in their stables.

Until the twentieth century stories were told such as this, related to Mrs. Leather in 1910 by a seventy-five year old woman from Wigmore:

She said it happened to her mother's first cousin ..., a girl about eighteen, {who} was very fond of dancing: she insisted on going to all the balls for miles around: whenever there was dancing going on, there was she. Her people told her something would happen to her some day, and one night when she was coming home just by the 'Dancing Gates', near Kington, she heard beautiful music. It was the music of the fairies, and she was caught into the ring. Search was made for her, and she appeared to her friends from time to time, but when they spoke to her she immediately disappeared. Her mother was told (probably by the wise man or woman), that if seen again she must be very quickly seized, without speaking, or she would never come back. So one day, a year after her disappearance, her mother saw her, and took hold of her dress before she could escape. 'Why mother', she said, 'where have you been since yesterday?' The time must have gone merrily with her, for the year had seemed but one day.

The girl was none the worse, however, and they sent her to serve at a small shop in Kington. Before long the fairies came there, and used to steal little things off the counter. Afraid that she might be accused when the things were missed, the girl told her employer. 'How can you see the fairies?' he said, 'They are invisible'. She told him that when she lived with them they used a kind of ointment, and she rubbed a little of it on one eye, to try the effect. She afterwards warned the fairies that their thefts were discovered; they were much puzzled to find themselves visible

126

to her. She was careful not to explain lest they might try to damage the eye with which she could see them.

The Devil

Many people disliked to name the devil or the fairies. They preferred Old Nick, 'the old 'un' or simply 'him' for the one, and 'the little people', 'the pharisees' or 'them' for the others. In former times, though, feelings went well beyond vague unease to downright fear.

A demon—if not the devil himself—is said to have turned up in Hereford Cathedral in about 1290. He was beaten over the head for his trouble, and locked up. The treatment is somewhat curious for a creature supposedly possessing satanic powers, but perhaps reassuring to anyone hearing the story.

Some four centuries later, John Aubrey recorded an amusing incident involving the mathematician, Thomas Allen (who died in 1632):

One time being at Hom Lacy in Herefordshire, at Mr. John Scudamore's (grandfather to the Lord Scudamore) he happened to leave his Watch in the Chamber windowe. (Watches were then rarities). The maydes came in to make the Bed, and hearing a thing in a case cry Tick, Tick, Tick, presently concluded that that was his Devill, and tooke it by the String with the tongues {tongs}, and threw it out of the windowe into the Mote (to drowne the Devill). It so happened that the string hung on a sprig of elder that grew out of the Mote, and this confirmed them 'twas the Devill. So the good old Gentleman gott his Watch again.

In 1647, young Joyce Dovey of Bewdley was thought to have been 'possest with the Devill'. The same notion may have crossed the mind of Rev. George Powell, rector of Dorstone for 47 years until his retirement in 1953, when Lucy Probert of Scar Cottage complained that chairs and tables were thrown round her rooms, and her bed was shaken so that 'it do make my teeth rattle'. Rev. Powell visited the house, prayed and read *Matthew* 4: 23-4: 'And Jesus went all about Galilee, teaching in their synagogues, and preaching the gospel of the kingdom, and healing all manner of sickness and all manner of disease among the people. And his fame went throughout all Syria: and they brought unto him all sick people that were taken with divers diseases and torments, and those which were possessed with devils, and those which were lunatick, and those that had the palsy; and he healed them'. The disturbances at Scar Cottage ceased.

Many place names are associated with the devil. A deep dingle between Dodenham and Martley is called the Devil's Leap. The Devil's Den is the name of a dark wood near Stanford-on-Teme. One spot in the wood is called Hell Hole, and a plant called Devil's Bit (*succisa pratensis*) grows there. This was once used to heal deadly wounds, and when the devil saw how many were being saved he bit off the roots, but the plant appears to grow without any.

The devil attempting a seduction, from a mediaeval woodcut

Stoke Edith Church

Another Devil's Wood is to be found on the north side of Orcop Hill. It is also known as Fairy Ring or Poor Man's Wood, and may have been a grove sacred to the Silures in which human life was sacrificed. A local belief was that if the wood were felled the owner of the Mynde, a mansion at Much Dewchurch, or his heir, would die within the year. A variation is that the prohibition refers only to a certain stump, or merely to wych hazels and wych elms. One wych elm on the Witches' Tump in the grounds of the house is said to mark the spot where a witch was burnt. The wood's evil influence has been blamed for a series of misfortunes stretching over two hundred years up to 1948 at Symons Farm. One explanation for these stories is that before the Reformation a curse was placed on the owners of the Mynde for alienating the wood from the poor of the parish to whom it had been bequeathed. Another is that Poor Man is a euphemism for the devil, whose writ still runs through the wood.

Near Stourbridge is Hell Bank, and at Upton Warren, Hell Patch. Inkberrow has a Devil's Bowling Green, and Leigh, a Devil's Pig Trough. The Devil's Garden is a piece of ground on Stanner Rocks, near Kington, where nothing will grow. In Kington itself a dissolute tailor made a suit for the devil but took fright at the last moment and declined to take any payment. Afterwards he became a model of good behaviour. A friar at Stoke Edith was less fortunate. In a wood he spotted the devil in the guise of a badger, but the badger carried off the friar.

Still at Stoke Edith—which for all its small size seems to be full of traditions—you could see the devil if you walked seven times round the church, then looked through the keyhole. Neighbouring Tarrington had a similar belief; there the ritual included saying the Lord's Prayer backwards. This was the case, too, at Weobley, where one had to walk seven times backwards round each tier of steps on the preaching cross in the churchyard. The feat has been tried many times, but apparently without success. On one occasion at Weobley, though, boys at the school managed to raise the devil by following a formula they found in a book of their master which they consulted in his absence. Having conjured the devil they were unable to get rid of him, but the scandalised schoolmaster did the trick on his return. What he did to the pupils afterwards was not recorded.

At Dorstone a ne'er-do-well called Jack of France happened to look through the keyhole of the church door on the eve of All Souls' Day (1 November). He saw the devil in the pulpit, dressed as a monk, and heard him reading the names of those who were to die in the ensuing year. Jack's name was on the list. He went home, took to his bed, and died.

Such fears are now forgotten, but some still tell children not to pick blackberries after 29 September because on that day the devil spits on them.

The preaching cross outside Weobley Church

The Wild Hunt

The ghostly hunt which rides through the sky on stormy nights is known in most parts of the world. Its appearance—even the mere sound of its riders and hounds—is thought to presage ill, and possibly disaster, for a community.

An early wild hunt story was written by a Herefordshire man, Walter Map, in about 1190. It concerns Herla, a king of the ancient Britons, who was making preparations for his wedding when a pygmy king, mounted on a goat, visited him and asked to be allowed to attend. This was agreed,

131

and Herla accepted an invitation to the pygmy's wedding to be held a year later.

On Herla's wedding day the pygmy returned with richly-dressed attendants who served food and drink in opulent vessels. He left at cock-crow after reminding Herla of their agreement. A year later he came back, and led Herla and his retinue to a cave in a cliff by the Wye. The pygmy's wedding was celebrated with great pomp, and after three days of feasting Herla left, laden with gifts which included a small bloodhound. This had to be carried until it jumped down of its own accord; no one was to dismount until then.

Outside the cave Herla met an old shepherd whom he asked for news of the queen. The man replied that he barely understood the question since his language was Saxon; the only queen of the name given that he knew was the wife of King Herla who had disappeared at the very cliff several centuries earlier.

Forgetting the injunction about the bloodhound, some of Herla's men dismounted and immediately crumbled into dust. Herla warned the rest to stay on horseback till the dog jumped down, but it never did. The cavalcade rode on through the centuries at least until the time of Henry II when it disappeared into the Wye, at last finding repose, and transferring its ceaseless quest to others.

One of the hunt's manifestations experienced in more recent years is the sound of the Seven Whistlers in the night sky (see also chapter 5). To hear all six of these is an ill omen; seven at once would signal the end of the world. No one can identify these birds, which have variously been taken to be swans, wild geese, whimbrels, curlews and swifts.

One phantom huntsman was known as Harry-ca-Nab. He kept his dogs at Halesowen—Hell's Own in popular etymology—and appeared on stormy nights mounted on a winged horse or wild bull to hunt boar across the Lickey Hills. To see this hunt would bring bad luck at best, death at worst.

Another hunter, Callow, frequented the Forest of Feckenham. He seems also to have appeared far from there, near Tenbury, where Callow's Grave is marked on maps. Hideous black dogs have been seen running round the spot at nights, and these also manifest themselves at Callow's Leap at Alfrick, where the hunter jumped down a precipice. The equally shadowy figure of Herne the Hunter also roamed in Feckenham Forest, where he killed a sacred stag belonging to the abbess of Bordesley. Shakespeare was well acquainted with such tales, and his own Forest of Arden was close to Feckenham. Indeed, there is a tradition that while waiting for some trouble to blow over at home Shakespeare spent eight months living in the Drainers' Arms—an inn which was burned down in 1892—at Earl's Common. He certainly mentions Herne in *The Merry Wives of Windsor*, though he transfers him to Windsor Forest.

Yet another ghostly huntsman was Sir Peter Corbet, who died in about 1300. He owned Chaddesley Corbett, together with a great deal of land at Alcester, and held a charter from King Edward I to kill wolves in the royal forests of five counties—Gloucester, Hereford, Worcester, Stafford and Shropshire. His pack of wolf hounds was kept in the Dog Kennels, a great stone pit close to Harvington Moat, and Corbet lived in Harvington Hall, or rather an earlier house on the same site.

An underground passage known as Bumble Hole ran from Dunclent to the hall, passing beneath the moat and ending in a dry well, with a branch joining the Dog Kennels. One night the restless baying of the hounds alerted a huntsman, who fetched Sir Peter. They witnessed a meeting between 'a gentleman from Wolverley'—his name is not given—and Sir Peter's daughter, and heard a further assignation made.

The following night the daughter was forcibly confined to her room, and the hounds were loosed. At the time appointed for the lovers' meeting a terrible uproar was heard, followed by silence. Next morning all that remained of the young man was his hands (which animals are said not to touch) and his feet (which were in his boots). On hearing the news the woman threw herself into the moat and was drowned. Sir Peter, filled too late with remorse, hanged all the dogs and sank their bodies in what came to be called Gallows Pool, a few yards from the pit. After his own death he was doomed to hunt the forest by night, accompanied by a spectral pack.

Ghosts
For reasons which remain mysterious some people seem to have been reluctant to leave their earthly haunts. Long after her death a Mrs. Holland continued to frequent her library at Holland House, Cropthorne. In the same house a grey lady appears, as does a soldier in the dress of a Welsh regiment of the battle of Worcester (1651). On Cropthorne Heath at midnight a funeral procession is sometimes seen. The cortège, known as Old Dutton's Funeral, turns off at a particular gate and vanishes.

Ashton-under-Hill had a white lady who swept screaming along the village street, and also the phantom of a robber-monk called Benedict. The dissolution of the monasteries by Henry VIII may account for some ghostly happenings. Once in the 1920's when the oven at Abbey Farm, Craswall, was under repair the Bevans (who lived at the farm) decided one evening to heat the oven in the nearby abbey ruins. When they returned a little later to see how it was getting on they saw the figures of a man and woman standing before it with hands uplifted, as though warming themselves at the fire. They did no baking that night.

Many houses have their stories. Mrs. Jacqueline Taverner writes of the 1960's:

We lived in the Red House at Spetchley, near Worcester, when my children were small. During the seven years we lived there I saw a woman upstairs, and felt someone help me down from a step ladder in the dining room when there was nobody there. We all experienced something, even my mother when she visited us. Subsequently I met Mrs. Mills, the doctor's wife from Callow End, and she said that during the war Joseph Conrad's son had lived at the house with his wife and family, and they frequently saw a woman on the stairs.

The owner since 1974, Mr. Paul Ryder, has experienced 'various strange phenomena' including the sound of footsteps from an empty bedroom. A frequent visitor, Mrs. Rose-Marie Bradly, writes (1992): 'I have felt a "presence" from the very first time I entered the Red House'. She mentions unaccountable 'feelings all around the house and also from the house to the barn', and adds:

I first noticed whenever I went up and down the stairs someone drew me into ... the dining room. Also I kept having "flashbacks" of a family who I believe to be mother, father and daughter of about 8-10 years old. The child has strawberry blond long curly hair, the father is tall with very dark hair, the mother although I knew was there I couldn't see as clearly.

I also get a very bad vibration up the flight of stairs towards the attic and I hate going in the one attic room. I'm sure some awful thing has happened there as I feel like crying if I go in. The steps to the cellar are also bad. I can go down there but I feel I need to mentally protect myself.

It remains a mystery how over a period of fifty years at least the Red House has stimulated such experience in so many people. The answer may lie in its past—it was a dower house belonging to the Berkeley family, part of the estate at Spetchley Park.

In the attic corridors of Holt Castle a black-clad lady walked at night; whilst a raven materialised in the cellars and put out with its wings any candle that was lit there. The latter story is also told of Leigh Court, put about—it has been suggested—by servants who wished to frighten people away from the supplies of cider and ale kept in the cellar. Until the 1980's at least tales were told at Callow End of Prior's Court ghosts: a grey lady, a cavalier whose body is said to have been walled up in the house, and a butler of the 1920's who continued to welcome visitors long after his death.

At Middleton-on-the-Hill a lady in white is to be seen sitting on Gravenor's Bridge on certain moonlit nights. In the same parish a grey lady walks close to a now derelict house. Not far away, at Bockleton, the shade of Sir Robert de Bockleton rides on certain nights around what was his estate. Another mounted ghost is that of a hard-drinking Georgian squire who still spurs over hedge and ditch on stormy nights at Ashton-under-Hill.

Ralph de Wysham lived at Woodmanton Manor, Clifton-on-Teme, during the fourteenth century. He happened to die under a great yew, and some villagers still feel a strange presence when they pass the tree. Clifton abounds with accounts of phantom horses, a white lady bending over a baby's cot, and soldiers of the Civil War heading down through steep woods to Ham Castle (which was in fact besieged by Parliament).

Echoes of the Civil War also linger at Holywell Cottage which, as the name implies, was built over a holy well, at Henwick. In 1991 Mrs. Sue Spackman commented:

Since we moved here four and half years ago both my husband and I, and one or two of our visitors, have seen the ghosts of a man and sometimes a woman, and on one occasion that of a little girl moving through from the front door to what was once the back door, although the back lobby has now been converted into a cloakroom. My husband until recently has always been very sceptical about ghosts and, whereas I never had any experience of them before, I certainly did not pooh-pooh the idea of their existence. On the occasion of our first sighting we both saw the same man, and our descriptions tallied exactly, and at the same time we experienced a cold feeling with the hair at the back of our necks rising. However, now we are used to them we experience no unpleasant sensations and they seem entirely benevolent, although by inclination I think I would have been a Royalist supporter and they are definitely Puritans by dress, the man in black and the females in grey.

If such ghosts seem ancient it is worth reflecting that villagers at Kenchester have seen Roman soldiers marching past on certain nights. One old lady now deceased insisted that they went through her house at the full moon, and another that they were seen making camp in her garden.

Some villages seem more haunted than others, and Alfrick claims to have the most ghosts in Worcestershire. Its many apparitions include a black dog, a horseman, a wagon and horses, a crow, the persistent sound of a cooper's hammer, and a man, woman and dog walking from the old forge to the church of St. Mary Magdalene.

In Herefordshire similar claims might be made for Hoarwithy. A manuscript of the 1850's mentions a pool at Hoarwithy 'said to be haunted—teams {of horses} used to be frightened there at night or run away—one wagoner had his leg broken in an attempt to stop his team—& I am not sure there was not one killed for similar cause'. The pool was close to where 'the Bierless road falls into the Hereford Road'. In the opinion of a local historian, Heather Hurley, Bierless Road (which no longer exists, though its line can be traced) was a corpse way leading to a burial ground where the corpses of outcasts such as suicides, paupers and vagrants were interred.

Members of Hoarwithy Women's Institute gathered more stories in 1953 when a manuscript history of the village was compiled, many of them connected with the cell (burned down in mediaeval times) of Aconbury nunnery at King's Caple, or possibly St. Dubricius' Church of the Brethren at Llanfrother. Mr. Reg Langford of Red Rail Farm, close to an ancient ford over the Wye, told how on three occasions—once in the company of two other men—he had seen a cowled lady, dressed in white, who emerged from a wood, walked a litle way into a field, and vanished. A different encounter was related by Mr. Colin Eckley, who was riding home one afternoon on his bicycle past Tressech Farm. At a point where the road is narrow and bordered by steep banks he saw walking in front a woman in a long grey dress. He braked hard but unnecessarily for she had disappeared where even a young, athletic woman could not have escaped.

Still further sightings include 'the top half of a woman sticking out of the hedge'; a figure taken by a cyclist to be the schoolmistress on an evening stroll, but 'however hard he pedalled she was always the same distance away from him till at last she disappeared'; and a hooded figure 'like a nun, and deathly still at that standing under the trees by the roadside where the old Roman track from the ford joins the highway, greeted by a passer-by with a cheery "Goodnight" but making never a reply or a movement'. Yet another lady is unseen by the occupants of Upper Orchard House (formerly the Harp and Anchor Inn) but perceived by visitors. One more appears from time to time on the Wye in a boat travelling far faster than wind or current could propel it. Finally, 'Tom Reece's Ghost', a story noted by Rev. William Poole, vicar of Hentland and Hoarwithy from 1840 until 1901, is given in full in chapter 10.

Exorcism

A belief which lingered until the twentieth century was that money and also iron misplaced or hidden in life would prevent due repose in death. Ghosts haunt the sites of hidden treasure until it is found and their responsibility discharged. At Castle Farm, Madley, though, a ghost seems to have appeared only after a crock of gold was discovered in the cellar.

Since Biblical times the illegal moving of landmarks has been considered a great wrong. This, too, can cause a ghost to walk. Many years ago—the story was remembered in the 1870's by a nonagenarian—the White Cross, then just outside Hereford on the Brecon road, was haunted by 'Old Taylor' as a punishment for moving a landmark. One evening a local man called Dennis encountered the ghost, which persuaded him to return at midnight. Dennis related this in the Nag's Head to considerable disbelief, since he was known as an inveterate liar. He felt obliged to keep the appointment. Old Taylor led him to a huge pair of stones and asked him to move them. At first Dennis demurred at their size but discovered that after all he had the strength to shift them, as Taylor asked. Then he was told to lie down until he heard music, at which signal he was to get

Captain Bound's Stone

137

away as quickly as possible. After this he was a changed man, but he did not live long. His drinking companions perhaps posthumously conceded his veracity, for Old Taylor ceased to walk.

A mover of marks who went on to even worse things was Captain Thomas Bound of Upton-on-Severn, 'a desperately wicked man, very cruel and covetous and hard on the poor'. Bound moved the marker stones which are still to be seen on a meadow known as the Ham by the river so as to obtain more ground for himself. He married three wives in succession, and there were suspicions that he had done away with the first two. He lived at Soley's Orchard but moved to Southend Farm, which he secured by guiding the hand of a dying woman so that she bequeathed it to him. In retribution she haunted him. He in turn drowned himself in a pool by the Causeway, a raised path connecting Rectory Lane with Southend.

Bound undoubtedly existed. He was born in the time of James I, a member of an old Upton family. His handwriting as churchwarden can be seen in the church registers for 1640 and 1641. He was indeed married three times—to two Marys and a Margaret—with the first two both dying within twelve months of marriage. He owned Soley's Orchard, and leased Southend Farm from a Mrs. Bromley. He served as a soldier for Parliament during the Civil War, which may explain the opprobium in which local people clearly held him. On the day he died in late July 1667 a phantom cortège—black-draped coffin and black-cloaked men—was seen leaving the church.

Soon after Bound's death his ghost was seen at Soley's Orchard, Southend, the Causeway and Rectory Lane. An attempt to lay the unquiet spirit was made by a clergyman who dropped an inch of lighted candle into the fatal pool with the injunction to Bound to keep quiet until it was re-lit. This proved ineffective, and Bound grew so bold that he appeared in broad daylight on his grey horse. Three parsons next tried a ceremony in the cellar at Soley's Orchard, which was afterwards bricked up. They held hands in a ring, and tried to consign Bound to the Red Sea. One of them carelessly allowed his leg to move out of the circle. There was a 'whizz' and something hit him on the cheek; no hair ever again grew on that spot. Not surprisingly, Bound was soon seen again, sitting on a stone by the Causeway or riding up Rectory Lane with a land-measuring chain clanking behind him. To the terror of fishermen he would appear in early morning on the banks of the Severn, and as a further horror the spectral forms of his three wives were seen at Soley's Orchard.

Eventually the railway cut through what had been Bound's garden at Southend and the farm was demolished. The house at Soley's Orchard still exists, though it has been greatly modernised. Bound's grave and bones came to light in the mid-nineteenth century in the chancel of the old church at Upton. His skull was taken and turned into a macabre drinking cup. Bound's grim presence was long felt by timid people on dark nights in Rectory Lane, and it may be still.

Another unsuccessful exorcism was carried out in the 1870's at Childswickham House, where a blue lady was often seen at one of the bedroom windows. Twelve parsons gathered with bell, book and candle, and for some reason agreed that if one of them were to die within the year their attempt at exorcising the ghost would fail. One of them did die, and the blue lady resumed her appearances.

Other exorcisms were effective, perhaps because they were carried out in due form. The ghost of a grey lady on a grey horse was succesfully imprisoned in a goose quill at Haugh Pool, near Yarpole.

'And Peaceful ever after slept old Colles' shade'—once a well known saying—referred to Edmund Colles, who lived at Leigh Court in the early seventeenth century. He was very short of money, so much so that he was obliged to sell his house and estate to Walter Devereux, MP for Worcester. In a further attempt to raise money, according to tradition, Colles waylaid a friend from Cradley who was riding home from Worcester with a large sum. Colles seized the horse's bridle but the man lashed out with his sword, and spurred on. When he arrived home he found a bloody hand still grasping the reigns, and on one of the fingers he recognised Colles' signet ring. (The theme, by the way, is well known. It was first printed in 1579 and still turns up in the form of stories about attempted thefts from motorists in contemporary Britain and America.)

Next day the Cradley man went to Leigh Court to confront Colles. He found him in bed nursing his wound, and forgave him. Even so, after his death Colles' spectre drove a coach pulled by four fire-breathing horses down the road at Leigh, up over the great tithe barn at the Court, and into the River Teme. Eventually twelve parsons assembled to conjure the apparition by a ritual Bible reading. Colles' ghost was conducted to a pool, which was then filled in. His monument can be seen in the church of St. Edburga at Leigh.

A ceremony of exorcism is related in greater detail in the case of Black Vaughan of Kington. Thomas Vaughan, born in 1400 and nicknamed after his dark hair or possibly his nature, married Ellen Gethin from Llanbister, just over the Welsh border. Ellen was fiercely protective of her younger brother, David, and after her marriage brought him to live at Hergest Court, the Vaughans' seat. In 1430 David went to visit his cousin, John Hir, in Llanbister. For reasons now unknown there was a violent quarrel during which Hir killed David Gethin. Ellen watched for a chance to take revenge, which came with an archery tournament in which John Hir was competing. Ellen went there, dressed as a man, and put an arrow through his heart. Whether this was a blatant attack or an apparently accidental shot is not clear, but Ellen seems to have escaped retribution.

Black Vaughan died many years later during the Wars of the Roses. A supporter of the Yorkist king, Edward IV, Vaughan was marching in 1469 towards Banbury to join the battle when a Lancastrian party captured him. He was taken to Pontefract and summarily beheaded. His body must have been brought back to Kington, for it lies with that of Ellen in St. Mary's Church in a tomb surmounted by their striking alabaster effigies. Ellen seems to have slept peacefully but the spirit of Thomas was soon alarming the neighbourhood. Even in the daytime it would upset farmers' wagons, frighten their wives by jumping up behind them as they rode to Kington Market, and assume the shape of a monstrous fly to torment the horses. In the guise of a roaring bull it even charged into the church during a service. People began to avoid the town, and its prosperity suffered.

At last twelve priests—thirteen according to one account—were summoned. They stood in a circle, each holding a lighted candle and reading from scripture. The ghost would be compelled to present itself, then to shrink until it could be shut in a silver snuffbox, provided that at least one candle continued to burn and at least one parson continued to read.

One by one the candles sputtered and went out. One by one the clerics hesitated and fell silent. Yet one candle still burned and one parson still read; it perhaps helped that he was nearly blind and not very sober. At one stage he called out 'Vaughan, why art though so fierce?' The answer came 'I was fierce as a man. Now I am fiercer, for I am the devil'.

Undismayed, the parson read on. His candle flickered but stayed alight. Vaughan shrank and shrank until the lid of the snuffbox began to close on him. 'Vaughan, where wilt thou be laid?' asked the priest. 'Anywhere, except in the Red Sea'. When the lid was closed they buried the box at the bottom of Hergest Pool and put a great stone on top. There it was to remain for a thousand years. (Ghosts always seem to have been ritually threatened with the distant Red Sea before being confined to a pond or stream; it was thought that they found it difficult to cross water, especially running water).

Even so Hergest Court was haunted by a black dog which made an appearance every time a member of the Vaughan family was to die. Conan Doyle visited Hergest Court and, transposing the spectral beast to Dartmoor, created *The Hound of the Baskervilles*. (Both Doyle and the

Vaughans were connected by marriage to the Baskerville family). As recently as 1987 a Solihull woman, coincidentally called Miss Jenny Vaughan, saw the ghostly figure of a bull in the church, outlined against the blue curtain covering the north door. 'What struck me most', she said, 'was the incongruity of seeing a bull in a church'.

The Court still stands, and the pool to which Black Vaughan's spirit was committed remains. The wife of the present owner told me that he conceived a plan to fill in the pool. On the appointed day when JCBs arrived to do the work the water began to bubble ominously. The farmer changed his mind and dismissed the contractors.

Perhaps the last case of a full-blown exorcism dates from sometime between 1828 and 1854 when Rev. William Copeland was the rector of Acton Beauchamp. The ghost, that of the 'first wife of Hodges as used to have the blacksmithing at Acton Cross', was confined in Amstell Pool. Captain Andrew Haggard was told the story in 1920:

Mrs. Hodges dies and leaves two children, and the blacksmith marries again and very quick he did too—warn't that so, George?—and her was bad to children of first wife. And first wife's sperrit took to haunting her children, not tarrifying them as you might say but just standing at their beds. And the children they warn't frightened neither, 'cos you see her had her clothes on {that is, was not in her shroud}. But her come that strong that all the place was talking on it. And they tells parson and he lays un and says—parson say he don't never want no such job again—fair made him sweat it did. Copeland, yes, Copeland were parson then. And he got eleven other parsons so there was twelve on 'em each with a lit candle and they starts to read her small. Least they raised un first 'cos with sperrits you got to raise un afore you falls un. And her come that big and the lights went out and last there was only one candle left, and fortunate that candle kept burning else she'd a bested 'em. And they got reading her smaller and smaller and got her real small and pushed un in a matchbox and throwed un in Amstell Pond as I was telling you, and her aren't troubled no one since, ent that so, George? Ah.

The Anglican Church still nominates one clergyman in each diocese to carry out exorcisms as required, but there is no set form for the procedure.

Injustice, Accident, Murder
The first wife of Old Hodges returned after death to protest at the hasty re-marriage of her husband and the ill-treatment of her children by their step mother. Multitudes of injustices pass by without ghostly repercussions

while a few with no discernible principle of selection give rise to strange phenomena.

The village of Pembridge was once haunted by the spectre of a Mrs. Breton, the wife of a minister, who vainly attempted to return in death some land she had stolen in life from the poor of the parish. At Salwarpe the cutting of the Droitwich Canal was carried through at the expense of a big old house which had to be demolished. Its occupier of that time is sometimes seen gliding down the embankment into the water in protesting but ghostly form.

Barton Court at Colwall was either bought or leased from the bishop of Hereford late in the eighteenth century by Henry Lambert of Hope End (also in Colwall). Lambert had obtained Hope End by marrying Jane Pritchard, who had inherited it. Jane died at the age of 36, leaving only one child, a daughter, Sarah Pritchard Lambert.

In 1790 a penniless Yorkshire baronet, Sir Henry Tempest, heard that Sarah—by then aged 24—was a rich heiress, and travelled to Colwall to seek her out. Dressed as an old gypsy woman he contrived to meet her on Colwall Green and told her that next day at a certain time in Colwall Church she would meet the man she was to marry. Sarah was foolish or romantic enough to go to the church at the appointed time, and there met Sir Henry (now undisguised). A relationship flowered and the couple decided to elope.

One night when a ball was being given at Hope End Sarah quietly left, losing in the drive as she did so a satin slipper which was discovered the next morning. Sir Henry had arranged for a carriage to meet her at the bottom of Chance's Pitch (on the present A449) but the driver mistakenly went to Blackmore Pitch, some miles away to the east of the Malvern Hills towards Hanley Swan. She wandered for three hours in pouring rain before the driver found her, in Barton Holloway.

Having married Sarah, on 24 January 1791, Sir Henry promptly claimed Hope End—which she may have inherited from her mother—and turned out his father-in-law, who went to live at Barton Court. Tempest soon quarrelled with his wife, and turned her out, too. Sarah tried to go back to her father but he refused to see her; indeed, he probably never saw her again. She spent the rest of her life with an old relative.

After her death Sarah's ghost prowled round Barton Court and in Barton Holloway, a narrow, sunken road which passes close by. It was so persistent that the sons of the Peyton family who lived in the Court during the nineteenth century regularly shot at it. Twelve clergymen in time-honoured fashion eventually carried out a ceremony of exorcism but even today Barton Holloway has the reputation of being haunted, though few now know the story of the unfortunate Sarah Lambert. Barton Court still stands. Hope End was bought in 1809 (perhaps from Sir Henry Tempest) by the father of Elizabeth Barrett, who wrote some of her poems there— the Leigh Hall of *Aurora Leigh* may be Barton Court—before leaving to marry Robert Browning. Hope End was burned down in 1910; the present house has been developed from the old stables.

The misadventures of star-crossed lovers have undoubtedly produced their share of ghosts. The Red House at Barnt Green is haunted by the spirit of a love-sick woman who was cruelly jilted by a young man who lived a short distance away across the fields. Love led to the deaths of two young people at Goodrich. During the Civil War the castle was besieged by a parliamentary force commanded by Colonel John Birch (whose stormy career ended peacefully at Weobley in 1691). Birch's niece, Alice, had fallen in love with Charles Clifford, a member of the royalist garrison, and she contrived to join him in the castle. In attempting to escape together they plunged on horseback into the turbulent waters of the Wye, and were both drowned. In stormy weather they can be seen struggling in the water, and their desperate cries are heard above the noise of wind and wave.

Another tragic love story which resulted in a Wye ghost dates from the fourteenth century. During the reign of Edward II, Despenser, one of the king's favourites met and fell in love with Isobel Chandos, daughter of the governor of Hereford Castle. Despenser did not reveal his identity to Isobel, but one evening he warned her that there was to be a surprise attack on the castle, and implored her to leave with him. It seems that she preferred to warn her father. The attack failed. Despenser was captured and hanged in High Town. So runs the story, but the only Despenser who fits into the period in question was executed in 1326 at Bristol. Isobel, who had unwittingly betrayed him, was unhinged by grief. She took to rowing alone on the Wye, and on one of her outings she drowned. Her ghost now rows down the same stretch of river, coming ashore where she used to meet Despenser. It weeps and wails, then returns the way it came, disappearing before it reaches the city. Ill fortune comes to any who see it.

Hellens House at Much Marcle was the home in the sixteenth century of the Walwyn family (whose name still adorns one of the local public houses). Young Hetty Walwyn ran away with a lover and returned years later with nothing but a diamond ring he had given her. She was allowed back only on condition that she accept a form of solitary confinement for the rest of her life. Her room with its barred windows can still be seen, together with the bell she used to ring for attention. It is not clear whether her ghost is among the many which walk at Hellens. Servants once refused to stay in the house because of the hauntings. Early in the twentieth century a young naval lieutenant was disturbed several times one night by what he took to be a poor old lunatic clad in a long, dark dressing gown with a hood, who kept running backwards and forwards.

During the Second World War a chiropodist, Miss Sidebottom, who is described as a 'no-nonsense person', attended two ladies at Hellens. One day she found the front door open, and went in. On the stairs she met a nun coming down, and asked where the ladies were. The nun swept past, making no reply. On reaching Lady Eleanor Miss Sidebottom enquired after the guest, and received the reply 'That's no guest. It's our ghost'.

Still at Hellens is the case of a monk allegedly killed there by parliamentary soldiers during the Civil War. The room where this happened has a chilly atmosphere and indelible bloodstains. A dog belonging to a lady personally known to me would never enter it.

In 1405 during the Hundred Years' War a French expeditionary force supported by the Welshmen of Owain Glyndwr was forced to retreat after laying siege to Worcester. Sir John Washbourne of Wichenford in an attack on the stragglers captured a high-ranking Frenchman and detained him at Wichenford Court, for ransom. Sir John was then called away in the king's service. During his absence Lady Washbourne grew fond of the prisoner and tried to seduce him, but the Frenchman spurned her advances. She was so incensed that she gave him a sleeping draught, and as soon as he grew drowsy, stabbed him in the back. He fell to the floor, bleeding, and died. The bloodstain is said to have been indelible over five centuries.

Lady Washbourne was overcome by remorse. She could neither rest by day nor sleep by night, and when she died her spirit could still not find repose. Her ghost wandered, a cup in one hand and a blood-stained dagger in the other. Nor is hers the only ghost at Wichenford, for the Franco-Welsh retreat was cut off by a flood, and many men were drowned. When the brook floods their ghosts re-appear. Attempts were made to exorcise them but failed, perhaps because the French and Welsh spirits were unable to understand English.

Accidental deaths abound but only certain particularly striking or poignant cases seem to have produced ghosts. John Masefield heard tell of the ghosts of a coachman and guard who were killed when their stagecoach crashed on Chance's Pitch. It is strange that the thousands of road accidents which have since happened in the two counties seem to have produced no further ghosts.

Aylton Court in a tiny village near Ledbury was the home in the 1850's of a farming family called Foulgar. In 1855 little Emma Foulgar, aged fourteen, was going down the main stairs just as her older brother was coming in the front door on his way home from a shooting expedition. He stumbled, and his still-loaded gun went off. Emma was killed on the stairs, and her ghost subsequently returned to the spot. A macabre sequel to the story is that her body was stolen from its grave in the churchyard at Aylton by resurrectionists.

Hunting has its accidents, too. At Broadway the ghost of a lady killed while hunting rides along White Ladies Lane at the top end of the village. Broadway also has the ghost of a kennelman torn to pieces by his own hounds. Apparently he rushed out in the night when he heard them baying; they failed to recognise him in his night-shirt, and attacked him. His ghost appears in the same night-shirt.

A very similar story comes from Church Farm, Besford, where an eighteenth century kennelman went out at night after hearing a disturbance. He was not missed until the next morning. A search revealed only his jackboots with his lower legs and feet inside. It was never determined whether the dogs were responsible or whether he had been killed by a stranger and fed to the animals. In later years, though, the boots with their jingling spurs were heard walking in what is still called Dog Kennel Place. A strange tail-piece to the story is that a skeleton was found in the field in 1930, intact save for the lower legs and feet. Later more skeletons found at the same place were thought to be those of men killed in the battle of Worcester.

Violent death seems to leave a kind of supernatural legacy, at least in a few cases. The execution of Thomas Winter for his part in the Gunpowder Plot caused his headless spectre to pace up and down by Crowle brook and in an avenue of trees at Huddington called Lady Winter's Walk, where he had been in the habit of meeting his wife. Later in the same century—1681, to be precise—continuing religious tension led to the murder of a protestant magistrate, Robert Pye of the Mynde, by a catholic neighbour, Charles Bodenham, on whom he was trying to serve a summons. The deed took place at Bryngwyn House, Much Dewchurch, near a big walnut tree, and thereafter two figures were seen in ghostly struggle at the spot.

A farm at Weobley was haunted by 'Old Griggs' ghost' until it was shut in a silver snuffbox and dropped in a pond in Garnstone Park. Because of his tyrannical meanness Griggs was poisoned by his own grown-up children by means of cooked toads which they said were chicken livers. He took revenge by returning in the form of a calf which incessantly bleated round the house at nights, and vanished when approached. The murderers eventually abandoned the house, and it fell into ruin.

Murderers at Longtown in the far west of Herefordshire were brought to justice by suprahuman means. Two brothers killed a shepherd on the

Black Mountain but before he died he prophesied that the crows would speak out and reveal the crime. Undeterred, the brothers went ahead, and then buried the body on the mountain. When the corpse was discovered there was no evidence to link them with it, but whenever the brothers went out crows came croaking round their heads. Exasperated beyond measure, one finally said to the other 'Do you remember what the poor shepherd said before we killed him on the mountain?' The remark was overheard, and led to their both being hanged. The story seems, alas, no longer to be known in the locality.

In the early nineteenth century Callow Farm which stands near the church at Callow Hill, not far from Hereford, was a coaching inn. Over a period of time travellers staying overnight at the inn disappeared. Eventually there was an enquiry; it was discovered that they had been murdered, and presumably robbed. The bodies had been carried across two fields to a house where they were buried.

The house, subsequently demolished, re-appeared in ghostly fashion. In addition phantom figures carrying a heavy burden were seen crossing the fields towards it.

As recently as 1988 a stockman at Prior's Court, Staplow, saw the ghost of a woman by the brook, a tributary of the River Leadon. Mr. Jack Parry, who farmed for many years at Prior's Court, put into verse the story of how an insanely possessive miller murdered his daughter's lover:

> So nightly now she searches still
> In the murky waters round the mill
> To find her lover as of yore
> And woo him as she did before.
> She rakes the waters to and fro
> And searches for him high and low,
> Not knowing that her father lied,
> Or how her lover really died.
> The lovesick swain she never found
> For in the mill his bones were ground.
> Her father fed him to the swine
> And drank his blood instead of wine.
> So now when dark and bats take flight
> She searches in the dead of night.
> Now should you see her ghostly form,
> Face deathly white and quite forlorn,
> Remember her, this lovesick maid.
> Pass on your way—be not afraid.

Musical Ghosts

Not all hauntings have such a melancholy origin. Prior's Manse at Broadway is thought to have been built as a country retreat for Randulph, Prior of Pershore, in the reign of King John. People claim that it has an underground passage leading to another house in the village, Abbots Grange. Its ghost, that of a monk, is unseen but can be heard playing a violin.

A ghostly pianist plays at the sixteenth century Boot Inn, Orleton. A new landlord, Mr. Roger Broad, took over in 1991. On the first night after opening for business he and his family were awakened by the sound of doors slamming and the piano playing in the lounge. Mr. Broad got up and checked the premises. He found nothing untoward, save for an old, musty smell about the place. He said 'The ghost seems to be friendly. We don't know who it is but we have a theory it may be a former barman here who was painted out of a picture in the bar after an argument with a previous owner'.

Avenbury Church, near Bromyard, is now derelict but it is famous for ghostly organ music which was first heard by a number of people on 8 September 1896. A few years later the vicar himself, Rev. E.H. Archer-Shepherd, heard and described it:

The Boot Inn, Orleton

I was on my lawn and the sound of the music came up from the church quite clearly. It continued all the time I was walking down the meadow to ascertain the cause. When I got within ten yards of the churchyard it ceased. The church door was locked and there was no one within. It was like someone improvising a voluntary on a church organ.

The vicar pointed out that the instrument in the church would have been physically incapable of producing such music, and denied that he had tried to lay the spirit responsible by exorcism. Nevertheless local people tell (or used to tell) this story, which was transcribed by Andrew Haggard:

Avenbury Church? Ah, that's haunted all right. I heered un, I heered the organ a playing and nobody there. Ahd bin to Bromyard to buy a pair of shoes, one Thursday it were, and it were dropping night when I comes to Avenbury. I crossed the stile for the footpath and comes anunt the church and damn me, I hears the organ playing beautiful, and I tell yer, that frit me terrible and I runs all the way to the gate for The Hyde I was that startled.

Well, it come about this way I suppose, There was two brothers lived at Brookhouse, tells me, the one, he were a good chap and a used to play the organ in the church reg'lar. Everybody liked un. T'other he were a sclem {good-for-nothing}, never did no work, and was allus a-pothering his brother for money and such. Nobody couldn't suffer un. How it come to happen I don't rightly know, but one evening part they comes to blows on the water bridge over the prill {brook} just off the Bromyard road, and the one he kills his brother for dead. And that weren't the end of it, not by no manner of means for arter that the organ used to play nights and no lights nor nobody there. A could hear un on the road and all quiet—there's scores heered un one time or another.

That come to be the talk of the place, and presently that come on so powerful the passon he say he must fall the ghost, so one day at the same time as the murdering he comes to the bridge all in his clothes and he lights three candles and he starts to pray and presently the one candle that flickered and went out. The passon he prays harder but it warn't no good for the second candle that went out too. Then the passon he prays that hard till the sweat fair run off his nose, and the third candle that started to go down but the passon kep on a praying and just when it burned blue it come up bright again, and just so well it did as if it had a gone out the ghost would ha' bested un.

That didn't stop the music altogether but the pain had gone out of it and them as lived about there didn't take a lot of notice, but strangers as knowed about it wouldn't go near or nighst the place arter dark, and them as didn't know, well, they got tarrified.

Ah, I knowed the church well daytimes, my wife's brother was married there and it were there I stood {became godfather} for the daughter of Milly Preece as were cousin of my mother's, but after that Thursday I never went nigh the place again, nights, nor I wouldn't now, neither.

Perhaps the ceremony of exorcism denied by Rev. Archer-Shepherd was an ancestral memory of the one carried out for an earlier ghost at Avenbury, that of Nicholas Vaughan who in the Middle Ages burnt down a palace belonging to the bishop of Hereford. Twelve priests with twelve candles successively read the unquiet spirit into a silver casket which was buried beneath a stone in the River Frome, close by the church. Sceptics suggested that the story was put about to conceal the hiding of plate on the suppression of the monastery which once stood on the site of Avenbury's vicarage meadow.

Churches, churchyards and parsonages certainly seem to have their share of ghosts. The old church of St. Michael at Abberley and the nearby rectory are visited by a grey lady. At Astley what is simply described as 'a presence' manifests itself at the former rectory and in the vicinity of the church. The churchyard at Salwarpe has its whispering monks, passing to and fro, together with a carriage which crosses the river from High Park to the church. Workmen at Hanbury Church regularly refuse to be inside alone by day and will not go there at all after dark. One young man a few years ago was playing the church piano—alone, but in broad daylight— when he was seized by an overwhelming feeling of terror, and his hair stood on end. St. Helen's Church at Worcester had a little girl haunting the nave, crying, and searching for something lost. One wonders whether she still appears to startle the readers now that the church has been turned into a record office; perhaps not, for she may only come out at dead of night.

Hereford was once 'in a great flutter' about the ghost of a mysterious Mr. Hoskins which was haunting the cathedral at about the time (1786) when the west wall collapsed. Twelve parsons went in, each with Bible, prayer book and candle, and stood in a circle. As midnight struck one of them summoned Mr. Hoskins, who first said he was in Ireland, then appeared. He asked to be laid in the Red Sea, but the parsons decided that he should be under running water, and chose the Bye Street Gate bridge (near the present Kerry Arms). When the ceremony was over only one candle remained alight. Canon Underwood's servant girl later said that his shirt was wringing with sweat when he got home. Years later when the

Bye Street Gate was being pulled down an eye-witness heard one of the workmen say 'they hoped they would not disturb Hoskins' ghost'.

St. Peter's Church at Hereford had a cowled figure which two policemen saw one Christmas—in 1926—walking through stout iron gates and an oaken door. News of the incident prompted the son of a former organist at the church to tell how his father had always found 'something uncanny' about the place during the month of December, and avoided being there alone. On several occasions he had seen a robed figure which vanished through doors or into thin air. One explanation for the apparition connected it with the murder of a monk at the altar by marauding Welshmen; another with the death of Walter de Lacy who fell from the tower of the church he built for the monks in the thirteenth century.

The same cowled figure—or another like it—started to appear eight years later in the cathedral close, and was again initially encountered by policemen. Further sightings followed, and something of a vogue for ghost spotting arose, with up to 200 people congregating on the green— 'like going to a football match', said one—by the cathedral in the early hours of the morning. Local residents complained. The cathedral authorities alleged that a practical joker was responsible for the apparitions. The watchers gradually thinned out but the cowled and cassocked monk continued to be sighted from time to time. The story is perhaps not ended, for he may be seen again.

VII
WITCHCRAFT

The witch with her cat, broomstick and spells might now seem to belong only to the fantasy of Disney films or the horror of cult videos, yet she has a long and perhaps unfinished history. The twelfth century font at Shrawley Church still has staples used originally to insert a padlock to secure the consecrated water from witches. There are written records of Amisia Daniel, 'the Cradley witch', who lived on Wild Goose Hill, Storridge, between 1397 until 1400, but she remains a shadowy figure. Almost six hundred years later the planned re-enactment of a witch burning as part of the commemoration of a Civil War battle at Ledbury in 1991 was called off after a protest. The organiser commented: 'We were contacted by a witch who said it was very distasteful to hold a burning ceremony so we cancelled it rather than offend anyone'. Such mildness would have seemed very strange a few hundred years ago when witches faced the death penalty for their activities, and more recently still, when they were hated and feared by their neighbours.

Witchhunts
Witches were pursued by both church and state because they were thought to worship the devil.

The last trial for witchcraft in Hereford took place in 1712, but the heyday for prosecutions was the previous century. Patchy court records mean that some cases went unrecorded, while in others the sentences are not known. Four women were certainly executed for witchcraft at Worcester in 1649. Of these, Rebecca West and Rose Holybred protested their innocence to the last; Margaret Lundis and Susan Cook confessed. (Witches' confessions—often extracted under torture or the threat of it—were remarkably similar. No doubt reflecting what interrogators wished to hear, they included impossible feats like flying through the air and improbable deeds such as having sexual intercourse with the devil). A further case at Worcester in 1652 involved Mary Ellins, the daughter of an Evesham gardener. Apparently she had thrown stones at Catherine Huxley who then 'began to void stones and continued doing so' until Ellins was executed. Such were the things which could lead to a woman's death.

One test applied to a suspected witch was to bind the woman's limbs and throw her into water. The innocent sank; the guilty 'swam', or floated.

Either way the experience was unpleasant, and could even be fatal. In 1660 four suspects were taken from Kidderminster for a diagnostic ducking in the Severn. In the same year Joan Bibb of Rushock was 'tyed and thrown ynto a poole as a witch, to see whether she could swim'. She must have been a woman of rare spirit, for 'she did bringe her Act'n ag'st Mr, Shaw the Parson'—who presumably insitigated the proceedings—'and Recov'rd 10 lb Damadges and 10 lb for costes'. Perhaps the last instance in the area of such an ordeal by water was at Redmarley (now in Gloucestershire) in the 1820's. William Lygon, first Earl Beauchamp, happened on the scene, and stopped the ducking.

An incident at Upton Bishop in 1849 involved a punitive ducking rather than a water test. Hannah Goode, who lived at Hill Top, had the reputation of being a witch. A crowd one day surrounded her house with the intention of making her ride the stang—an ash pole decorated with stinging nettles and a ram's skull—to the nearest pond. When she came to the door she was stoned. A number of arrests were made, which led to fines of 2s 6d per person, with costs of 6s 6d.

Malicious accusations against women—to gratify spite, to avoid a debt, or simply to make mischief—were by no means unknown. In 1601 John Genifer laid charges of witchcraft against a midwife at Worcester—he said she 'had deserved burning seven years sithence'—when she asked for the return of money lent him by her husband, Edward Buckland. Almost at the end of the same century an Oldswinford nailer called Jospeh Orford was indicated as 'a common disturber' for boasting that 'he could have Barnes and his wife duckt for witches, and would procure one John Johnson, a drummer, to be present at the doing of it, to make the more sport'.

It is unusual for both a man and his wife to have been attacked as witches. The more typical victim was an old woman living alone, as in the case of Ann Bellett, a widow of Stacy Morton, who was accused in 1633 by three Inkberrow men of 'evil art' in the form of 'the jugling trick of the sire and sheves {scythe and shears} to find out goods lost and using the names of Peter and Paule therein in profane manner being saide to be founded on that sleight and cunning trick'. Finding lost or stolen goods was one of the standard functions of a village wise man or woman. A fine line divided it from witchcraft. Charming away disease or misfortune was usually acceptable, but not bringing them on by spells or curses.

As early as 1397 the bishop of Hereford was informed that whenever Alison Brown of Bromyard uttered a curse God always put it into effect. There is a record that in about 1598 John Smyth cursed William Walton of Yarpole, 'kneeling on his knees in the churchyard there, and upon him and

Burning witches, a sixteenth century woodcut

all his cattle'. A similar ritual was followed by Joanna Nurden when she cursed John Sergeant and his wife at Much Marcle in 1616; and in 1655 Rachel Dewsall of Hereford 'pulled up her clothes and kneeled down upon her bare knees and cursed her son and daughter and wished they might never prosper'.

Five years later Elinor Burt was accused at Worcester of healing the sick by the laying on of hands. She claimed 'a gifte from God' which indeed enabled her to cure 'by good prayers and laying her hands upon ... heads or faces'. The outcome of this case is not recorded. In 1662 Joan Willis of Great Comberton was charged not with healing people but killing them—namely, 'one Thomas Right's wife, and one Robert Price's child, both of Comberton'—by bewitchment. In addition, she 'behegged' another child, and gave Elizabeth Ranford 'several blows with a staffe, and ripped her quaife {coif} of her head, and profanely did swear, blood and wounds she would kill her'.

In the same year a citizen of Hereford, Philip Benny, alleged that he knew Mary Hodges was plotting against someone because at bedtime:

she is observed to take the andirons out of the chimney, and put them cross one another and then she falls down on her knees and useth some prayers of witchcraft. ... She then makes water in a dish and throws it upon the said andirons and then takes her journey into her garden. This is her usual custom night after night.

153

One smiles at reading such things until one remembers that they could have led to a horrible death for an alleged witch. Witchcraft ceased to be a legal offence in 1736 but its shadow lay over people for perhaps another two hundred years.

Strange powers

A wizard at Arley called Master Fidkin could put people under a spell which would make them wander the village all night. A sculptured pillar dial in the churchyard is said to have belonged to him.

Near Mansell Lacy a witch stopped a team of horses and agreed to lift the spell only when the carter threatened her with his whip. This might have been made of elder or mountain ash, both of which are feared by witches. The same woman put a spell on an old farmer so that he was powerless to go beyond a certain house on the edge of the village, nor could his horse pass the spot. The man used to wait there while his children posted letters in the village or collected what he wanted. Eventually there was such an outcry that the vicar went to the witch's house and burnt all her books, thus sapping her power. All this occurred in the 1840's.

A more recent incident was remembered by an inmate of Ross workhouse and told to Mrs. Leather:

He was coming over Whitney Bridge, many years ago, when behind the cart he was driving came a waggoner with three horses, and no money to pay toll. He defied the old woman at the toll house, and would have driven past her, but she witched the horses so that they would not move. 'I sin it meself, them 'orses 'ouldn't muv nor stir, and when I lent the mon the toll money they went right on through. There was funny tales about that old 'ooman: folks took care they didna give her offence: 'er'd make their pigs dance in their cots till they fetched her to stop 'em.

At Worcester two old women could halt carts in the mud of Salt Lane (now Castle Street) or free them from it. Waggoners learned to offer sixpence, so that their carts could go on their way. On one occasion a horseman happened to see straw lying across his horse's back, and cut it with a knife. Immediately one of the women fell dead. The other survived, to turn a troop of tax-gathering soldiers into the stones of the Tything. The full story is told in chapter 10.

At Leigh Sinton hounds kept by a Mr. Spooner would always start unseen game in a particular field called the Oak and Crab Tree Ground. The dogs would pursue the quarry but invariably lose it on Crampton Hill at Cradley by a cottage belonging to an old woman called Cofield. A similar tale, often told in Herefordshire, relates how as hounds scent a hare a little boy's voice is heard shouting 'Run, granny, run. The dogs be arter ee'. As the hare bounds through a hedge to safety one of the hounds manages to bite its hind leg. A few minutes later a huntsman knocks at a cottage door to ask whether the hare has been seen, and he finds an old woman bathing a fresh wound in her leg.

There is an animal connection, too, with Becky Swan, the last Worcestershire witch to be widely known. She was a healer and recoverer of stolen property who lived in Worcester Street, Kidderminster. One day in the 1850's a huge black cat came walking down the street, and dogs took to their heels before it. The cat scratched at Becky's door; she opened it, and turned pale. The cat went in. For three days it roamed the locality, then no more. Becky, too, failed to appear, so the neighbours broke down the door. The cat, which they found sitting on the hearthrug, dashed up the chimney and was not seen again. Becky's body lay on the floor, reduced to ashes, though nothing else in the room was even singed, and there was no smell of smoke. This was perhaps an early case of the spontaneous combustion which has been investigated in several television documentaries in recent years.

The doll with its curse, Hereford City Museum

Nancy Weaver lived at Bull Hill, Astley, in the early nineteenth century. She was in great demand when butter would not come or dough refused to rise. Liza Lloyd of Commonbach, Dorstone, is still remembered as a witch because she was born with only three fingers on each hand. Mary of Eldersfield, a herbalist who lived on Berth Hill, was also reputed to be a witch. Perhaps because she gathered witches' broom on Gadbury Bank.

Even women such as these could inspire fear. It was believed that the Scudamores of Holme Lacy had been punished by a curse that direct heirs to the estate would always die before their fathers. This happened twice. At Dorstone a farmer seduced his servant girl but refused to marry her when she became pregnant. She went to America with her baby, leaving behind a solemn curse. A rector's wife commented: 'Certainly, ill luck has in that case followed this man; his children without exception have died or behaved ill, his crops fail and his cattle die, though he is sober and fastidious'.

In Hereford Museum is a curse doll of the late nineteenth century found in 1960 at 21 East Street in the city. A paper with it bears these words:

Mary Ann Ward
I act this spell upon you from my holl heart wishing you to never rest nor eat nor sleep the rest part of your life I hope your flesh will waste away and I hope you will never spend another penny I ought to have Wishing this from my whole heart

The identity of the person issuing the curse is not known.

Another item in the museum, also from the nineteenth century, is a little wooden coffin with a human effigy, the body firmly pinned down by a nail. This was found only in 1987 at a house in the village of Woolhope. Soon after it came to light the lady of the house was visiting friends when an entire window fell on her from three stories up. Fortunately she was dealt only a glancing blow but she could easily have been killed. Then her daughter fell mysteriously ill, and the lady decided to rid herself of the object by taking it to Hereford Museum. The curator kept it in her office for a short time and almost immediately her husband was involved in a serious car accident. She hastily moved it to the more impersonal surroundings of a display case, where it can currently be seen.

Some Precautions

Walter Map in his *De Nugis Curialium* (Of Courtiers' Trifles), written in about 1190, tells of a sorcerer in a Welsh border town who would not rest in the grave after his death. Each night he came back and called on one or

Wooden coffin with effigy, Hereford City Museum

two of his former neighbours, who then fell ill and died within three days. When this had gone on for some time an English knight, Sir Walter Laudun, approached Gilbert Foliot, Bishop of Hereford, for advice. He was told to dig up the body, behead it, douse it with holy water, and then re-bury it. The instructions were carried out but they had no effect. One night Sir Walter heard his own name called by the sorcerer. He jumped up, snatched his sword and ran after the living corpse. Before it could return to the grave he cut off its head. Only then did the reign of terror end.

A less dramatic way of controlling witches was to find someone with superior powers. Such a person lived betwen Hereford and Bromyard during the second half of the nineteenth century. Mrs. Leather, who was told many tales of his exploits, is deliberately vague as to where he lived, and calls him Jenkins only to conceal his real name. Perhaps she wished to avoid giving offence to relatives still alive when she was writing.

Jenkins, known as 'maister o' the witches', became so well known that he was brought before the magistrates for imposture. He claimed that he indeed had power over witches. The magistrates said they did not exist. Jenkins, offering to convince them, asked whether they would prefer him to produce them in a high wind or a low wind. They declined either alternative.

One of Jenkin's exploits is attributed in a different account to a farmer from Preston Wynne. Perhaps he and the farmer were the same person. The man was renowned for his ability to remove spells. He also had second sight, and people travelled long distances to see him. Once he visited the Buck Inn (now closed) at Woonton. After the meal he called for the reckoning, and the landlady replied 'Fourpence for eat, fourpence for drink, eight pence on the whole'. Thinking the charge exorbitant, the farmer put the money on the table and drew a circle round it in chalk. When the landlady came to pick up the money she began to go round and round the table, repeating her request for payment. The servant came and tried to reach the money but the same thing happened to her. The ostler came in and tried: then there were three people circling the table. Another servant went out into the yard where the farmer was preparing to depart, and quietly asked him what was to be done. 'You take the money with a pair of tongs', he said. 'That will stop them'.

A similar situation occurs in a printed ballad entitled *The Enchanted Piss-pot* which came to light at Rhayader only in 1991 but was sold (and probably printed) in Hereford some two hundred years earlier. Here a wise man is enlisted by a farmer 'to know whether he was cuckold or no'. He sets up a spell which causes the farmer's wife and the parish clerk who is indeed cuckolding him to stick to a chamber pot and dance with it in their night attire through the town. They are released only when the clerk agrees to pay the farmer ten pounds in compensation.

Some people carried charms to counteract spells. A court at Stourbridge in the nineteenth century was shown a small bag of black silk containing pieces cut from a prayer book and Bible, together with some hairs from a cat's back. Its purpose was to cancel a spell of paralysis laid on one woman by another, and its use had been advised by a local wise woman.

Other objects were often kept in the home or farm to repel witches. A horseshoe was fastened over doors or bedsteads. The coloured glass walking sticks made at Stourbridge—now kept purely as a pleasing nick-nack—were once thought to protect a house against witchcraft. Another possibility was to draw a neat border of white chalk round a doorstep after it had been scrubbed, then to mark nine Xs in a row inside. The ancient Fleece Inn at Bretforton has an elaborate pattern of white lines painted on the floor of one room for the same reason.

Various plants were also deemed to be effective. A house leek (*sempervivum tectorum*) growing on a roof or wall was considered particularly good against witches—and also lightning. Twigs of wych elm or wych hazel—the latter ideally in bundles of nine—were also used, though their names are not in fact connected with witches since wych means pliant.

The fruits of the famous Whitty Pear (see chapter 5) in the Wyre Forest were carefully kept as another form of protection. The mountain ash or rowan was known as 'wittan', 'wittern' or 'witty' in Herefordshire, where a saying still current in the early twentieth century ran 'the witty is the tree on which the devil hanged his mother'. 'Witty-tree and birch, say the bells of Peterchurch' is another saying associating two anti-witch trees. The red berries of the rowan were thought a good protection in themselves against evil. Goads of the wood prevented horses from being 'overlooked', and cattle were given collars of it. Yoke-pins were made of yew or rowan. At least until the 1950's some farmers nailed a sprig of rowan or birch to barn doors to keep witches away.

Elder was unlucky to cut or burn, but a branch might be nailed over a door to keep witches out. A piece of the wood was often let into churns to prevent witches from spoiling the butter.

Persistence

The widespread use of such devices is an indication of the extent to which belief in the malevolent powers of witches continued until within living memory. Mrs. Leather was told by a Weobley man that he had gone to assist a policeman trying to arrest the drunken son of a local witch: 'I helped him and didn't think. My missis said when I came home I'd be sorry for it. Sure enough, my pig died next week'.

Malvern was feared for its witches. So were certain villages. 'There'll always be nine witches from the bottom of Orcop to the end of Garway Hill as long as water runs' was the firm belief in a remote area of Herefordshire. Near Little Shelsley in Worcestershire on the hillside above the River Teme is a hollow called Witchery Hole. According to local tradition witches were burned there in mediaeval times, and it is said that nothing of value will grow at the spot. When a cold wind blows strongly from the north villagers say that it comes from Witchery Hole.

A well known witch lived at Cockyard, near Abbey Dore. One account of her was written in 1928:

You could hear her a long way before you saw her. Her stick went thump, thump. No schoolmaster would stay long in Abbey Dore schoolhouse. Everyone gave the same reason, until a man who had failed in farming came there with two sons and two daughters. On dark nights they would hear 'thump, thump', and steps round the house; often the windows would shake as though every pane would fall out. They would go to bed, and then they would hear such a noise, as if a dozen people were moving the chairs, and plates and dishes rattling. When they came down in the morning, everything would be as they left it. This continued for years. The old Cockyard witch died; they never heard anything after. ...

These witches had the credit of going into stables and riding the horses; these would sometimes be found in such a state that they could not be worked. The last night in April was much feared. The waggoners always put boughs of two trees—one was birch {and the other was rowan}—each side and over the stable door; wherever you went, you would see these boughs on stables. If people were killed, it was laid to the witches. We often heard of horses being found dead at different houses, three and four the same night. Now, the witches are dead.

Yet at least one witch is still feared at Cockyard, and she may be the same one which terrorised the people of Abbey Dore schoolhouse. Her name is Nanny Gunter, and she is supposed to have killed some of her children and buried them in a wood. Her name is applied in Cockyard to a stretch of road, Nanny Gunter's Pitch. To this day some people find it eerie and avoid travelling along it, even by car.

Many miles away the story of another witch is remembered. Mrs. S. Rickhuss of Ronkswood, Worcester, has given me this version of it:

I'll tell you about a tale my mother told me, she herself a country-born lass from Herefordshire. It is the legend of Jumper's Hole. There was a gamekeeper's cottage near Bromyard as you travel towards Bishops Frome, on Dovehills Farm. On the outskirts of a wood at the bottom of a bank {between Stanford Bishop and Acton Beauchamp} runs a brook and above it {is} a gate. One time a witch came down from the woods on a horse and went to the cottage to ask for a loaf of bread. It being a poor farm the owner refused her request, so she cursed the homestead and stole the bread. It is said on her way back as she jumped the brook she dropped the loaf of bread, and its remains can be seen in the stone where she landed, along with two hoofprints. Also the gate above is said to be cursed, as nothing will grow around it. The cottage, believed to harbour ill luck, fell into disrepair and was eventually demolished. The address was Dove Hills Cottage, Jumpers Hole, near Bromyard.

VIII
WORK

It is not surprising that adjacent counties have great similarities in their main industry, agriculture. Common to both are arable, beef and dairy cattle, cider apples, perry pears and hops. Both have inevitably been affected by the enormous changes in patterns of work and life on the land since the Second World War. Along with farming practices, sayings, beliefs and customs have fallen into disuse—though many people remember them. The manufacturing industries more characteristic of Worcestershire than Herefordshire have been subject to changes of their own.

Needles, Nails, Carpets

The colliers of Dudley are long gone, their folkore with them; their town in any case ceased in 1974 to be part of Worcestershire. Elsewhere, some industries now flourish more in museums than in real life. Until the First World War the women and girls of Alvechurch and Redditch were noted for their delicate hands: they were employed in the needle and fish-hook trade, where very fine work was called for. Itinerant sellers tramped country and town with their wares:

> All sorts o' needles. O,
> The best o' Redditch needles, O.
> All sorts o' needles. O,
> And long, strong pins.
>
> A needle for to sew your gown,
> One to sew the flounces round.
>
> When your Sunday coat is torn,
> One will mend it in a rap.
>
> This will all your stockings darn,
> This will hem your cambric cap.
> All sorts o' needles, O,
> And long, strong pins.

At neighbouring Bromsgrove—as in many other centres, including rural Weobley—nails were made. Like the needlemakers, nailers had a turbulent history. They are credited with the invention of the 'tiswas', a four-spiked nail which always landed with one spike pointing up when it was thrown under the hooves of cavalrymen's horses when they mustered against striking nailers.

Robert Sherard, the biographer of Emile Zola, visited Bromsgrove in 1896 when he was writing a series of articles entitled *The White Slaves of England*. He found the town 'bright and sweet and clean, with many picturesque old houses and a fine, old church, and all round it, within two minutes' walk from the long, principal street, some of the of the prettiest country in the Midlands'. However, he described the nail trade as 'one of the cruellest industrial tragedies in England'. Pay was very low. Sherard met one man of 85 who had given up work after 77 years in the trade because he could earn only one shilling a week for six or seven hours a day.

The problem was compounded by what Sherard with heavy irony called 'a pleasant little custom of the trade': 'a thousand nails, between master and man, are twelve hundred nails, but only eight hundred (especially in the matter of hobnails), as between master and customer. Result, four hundred nails gratis to the warehouse'. No wonder that until living memory there was a saying in North Herefordshire and Worcestershire 'As busy as a nailer'.

Nevertheless Sherard noted:

The last sound I heard as I left Bromsgrove was the voice of a poor old woman, bowed and almost blind, who was working at her forge. She was singing in an enthusiasm of hope and fervour, 'The Lord will provide'.

Both nailers and chainmakers used an 'Oliver', 'a heavy hammer worked by a treadle, and restored to its upright position by a simple system of leverage'. The name comes from:

Cromwell, the heavy hammer-man; ... Oliver the Democrat, whose name, by the exquisite irony of things, is now attached to an implement used by slaves most degraded, by starved mothers fighting in sweat and anguish and rags, for the sop of the weazened bairns, who in the fiery sparks grovel in the mire of these shameful workshops.

Such shops are now a thing of the past, though they can be seen complete with demonstrations at the Black Country Museum, Dudley, and

Chainmaking, Oak Street, Old Hill, Dudley c.1910

the Avoncroft Museum of Buildings, near Bromsgrove. Hand chain-making ceased in the Black Country less than twenty years ago. One of its last practitioners was Lucy Woodall of Old Hill, who died in 1979. She started work in 1912 at the age of 13. 'I left school on the Friday and I started on the Monday. Four shillin' a week. Seven o'clock till seven o'clock. Two o'clock on a Saturday'. Sixty years later she still remem-bered the practical jokes played on her. Workmates would send her to fetch a left-hand spanner, or pass her a pair of tongs of which the handles had been heated enough to give an unpleasant surprise. Yet her recollec-tions were pleasurable. 'Them days were happier—tougher, but happier'. When the boss was safely out of the way Lucy and her workmates would sing in the chainshop. *Rosemary Lane* was one of her favourites; another, *My Chainmaker Lad*:

> My chainmaker lad he's a masher, he's allus a-smokin' his pipe.
> He's allus a' whistlin' the wenches, especially on Saturday night.
> Saturday night is my delight, Sunday morning too;
> Monday morning, off to school, he's allus after me.
> Collier boys, collier boys, come in;
> Down the road as black as coal but they're the chaps for me.

Other chainmakers felt rather more bitter about their trade. Caleb Southall of Cradley Heath wrote *The Donkeys* in the 1930's:

163

Like donkeys we stand in the chain-stall all day,
Thumping and banging and thrashing away.
If we work like hell there's little more pay,
So like donkeys we stand in the chain-stall all day.

Like donkeys we stand in the chain-stall all day,
Till our faces are scarlet, crimson and grey,
For we've homes to keep on, and we must pay our way.
So, donkeys we stand in the chain-stall all day,

And the donkey will stand in the chain-stall all day
When beer is his object and beer is his stay;
For this thing alone, I'm sorry to say,
The donkey will stand in the chain-stall all day,

And the donkey will stand in the chain-stall all day,
If a quid in the bank he can put away;
He'll work and save till he's under the clay,
The donkey who stands in the chain-stall all day,

Now some that won't stand in the chain-stall all day,
They sign on at the labour and pick up their pay;
They look all the better and feel it, they say,
Than the donkeys who stand in the chain-stall all day,

Now the Gaffer who sits in his office all day
Knows that our numbers are dwindling away,
That we are the last lot, I'm happy to say,
Of the donkeys who stand in the chain-stall all day.

Carpet weavers at Kidderminster were equally fond of a song. Their pro-
tracted and bitter strike of 1828 was fought with the aid of printed ballads
which promoted their cause. Titles include *The Carpet Weaver's True Tale*,
The Carpet Weaver's Lamentation, *Weavers Never Will be Slaves* and *The
Funny Rigs of Good and Tender Hearted Masters in the Happy Town of
Kidderminster*. Phraseology varies from the Biblical to the patriotic:

Therefore in union we will join,
Our rights and prices to maintain;
And never to oppression yield,
While yet Britannia rules the main.

The handloom carpet weavers of the nineteenth century were much given to drink and rough sports like dog and cock-fighting. They delighted in fairs, and kept up local customs such as Heaving and the Lawless Hour (see chapter 12). They also kept St. Monday, the practice of taking Mondays off—and sometimes Tuesdays too. Thus their independence was asserted but the price involved working longer and harder for the rest of the week:

> Dingle, dangle.
> Play all day,
> Work by candle.

Carpets are still made in Kidderminster though the trade was badly hit by the recession of 1992. Now it is probably true to say, though, that the attitudes and practices of carpet weavers differ little from those of other workers.

Farm Work
In spring and summer the working day for farm labourers once ran from six till six, and in winter from first light to dusk. The waggoner (horseman) would start earlier and finish later than the rest since he had his team to look after. He was the top man on the farm, and would deputise for the farmer in his absence. The waggoner was expected to work in all weathers save the absolutely impossible; a drenching downpour was wryly called 'waggoner's rain'. An acre's ploughing was considered a fair day's work, and in accomplishing it with their single-furrow plough the waggoner and his team would walk thirteen miles. Some still do, but only in popular ploughing matches such as the one at Trumpet, near Ledbury.

Such work was a source of immense pride. Bert Morgan of Dorstone looks back to when horses were still the standard motive power on the land:

> There's nothing better than going out ploughing with a team at seven o'clock in the morning with the horses all done up—tail done up, mane done up, brasses shining. It was a wonderful feeling walking behind them, their old ears going backwards and forwards as if they were really enjoying themselves.

Similar sentiments are expressed in *We're All Jolly Fellows*, which was amongst the best known of country songs. This version was sung to me in 1966 by Joe Gardiner, a farm worker from Hinton-on-the-Green:

The cocks was a-crowin', 'twas break of day;
Our master came to us and thus he did say:
'Come, rise my good laddies, come rise with goodwill,
For your horses want something their bellies to fill'.

The clock strikes four and so up we then rise
And into the stable so merrily flies;
With rubbin' and scrubbin' our horses I'll vow
You're all jolly fellows that follows the plough.

Then seven o'clock comes and away we then go,
And over the plains, boys, as nimble as does;
For when we get there so jolly and bold
To see which of us a straight furrow can hold.

Our master came to us and thus he did say:
'What have you been doing, boys, all this long day?
For you've not ploughed an acre, I'll swear and I'll vow,
And you're not jolly fellows that follows the plough'.

Then I steps up to him and I made this reply:
'We've all ploughed an acre. Why tell such a lie?
We've all ploughed an acre, I'll swear and I'll vow,
And we're all jolly fellows that follows the plough'.

Then he turns himself round and he laughs at the joke:
'It's past three o'clock, boys. It's time to unyoke.
Unharness your horses and rub them down well,
And I'll give you a jug of my bonny brown ale'.

So now all you fellows whoever you be,
Come take this advice and be ruled by me,
And never fear your master, I'll swear and I'll vow,
For you're all jolly fellows that follows the plough.

In caring for the horses waggoners employed many traditional cures
and recipes. Cobwebs were used to staunch bleeding, and for this reason
the chaff-house roof was never swept. The dosages and ingredients for
some potions were closely kept secrets. A horse tonic was supplied by
dried and powdered oxberry root, otherwise known as black bryony
(*bronica diocia*). Human urine was used to moisten the animal's bait if the

appetite needed stimulating. Tobacco rubbed each day on his bit kept him free of worms, and a pinch of blue vitriol (copper sulphate) made him lively enough to 'jump through his collar'.

Horses' names were chosen from a select, traditional list. The most popular were common to both counties: Bert, Blackbird, Bonny, Bounce, Bowler, Boxer, Brandy, Captain, Charlie, Darby, Diamond (always pronounced Diament), Dobbin, Dragon, Duke, Flower, Gilbert, Jerry, Jolly, Lion, Lively, Short, Smiler, Snip, Spanker, Surly and Tommy.

Other farm workers also had their role: the scythemen, for example, who at one time cut all the corn and hay. The scythe had a whole vocabulary of its own, including (in Herefordshire) sned (haft), nibs or tuts (hand-grips), rubber (round sharpening stone) and cayther (hazel or willow wand lashed to the scythe to lay all the stalks parallel). In Worcestershire the scythe was called an Isaac, after Isaac Nash, the Belbroughton maker.

A team of three or four men would contract to mow for so much an acre. They would work in echelon, the leader—known as the lord—setting the pace. The saying went 'You whet when the lord whets'. A rhyme on scythe sharpening ran:

Sowing, from a misericord at Ripple

167

Wet it to whet, wet it to whet. The mower be too lazy.
Give 'im a pint to make'im work. A quart will make 'im 'azy.

Until the First World War, when wages on the land were 12 shillings a week, labourers had an allowance of cider, usually two quarts a day. The drink was decanted from barrels in the farm cellar each morning and lunchtime into small wooden kegs called costrels by a boy who had to whistle at his task to show that he was not drinking. The men drank from their own cow-horn mugs. In the fields they would always take care to pour a small quantity on the ground as an offering to the gods or, as one Worcestershireman put it, 'a drap to the owd mon'. A mug would always be passed round in a clockwise direction, 'with the sun', and never against it. Casual labour sometimes received no wages, and was rewarded simply in bread, cheese and cider.

The labourer's meals were dawn-bit (breakfast), 'levenses (lunch), fourses (tea) and moon-bit (supper). Most of these were taken afield. Characteristic badges of the labourer were his bait-frail (lunch basket), yorks (thongs tied round the trousers below the knee) and white smock.

Apples and Hops

Many farms made their own cider. Apples were gathered from August to December, depending on variety, of which there are several hundred. Herefordshire favoured Dymock Red, Foxwhelp, Golden Pippin, Hagloe, Leather Coat, Oaken Pin, Styre Apple and Ten Commandments. Worcestershire preferred Badger Whelp, Bittersweet, Cherry Norman, Italies, Norman White (or White Norman), Roughthorn and Wilding. Kingston Black and Redstreak were popular in both counties.

Those apples which had not fallen to the ground were shaken or knocked down—the local word was pothered or panked—with long ash poles. Women picked up the fruit and put it into sacks to be taken to the press. There are still some 2,000 stone mills in Herefordshire alone, but their use was superseded by the scratter or scratcher mill driven by a small but noisy engine. The pomace (pulp) so produced was put between hairs (coconut matting; originally horsehair) and pressed.

The juice—at first muddy brown, then golden—was put into hogsheads to ferment. Some preferred if possible to add blood, beef, bacon or rabbit skins—all useful for adding nitrogen to feed the yeasts in the fermenting juice—but, contrary to popular belief, not rats. There is a story of a prize pig which disappeared during cider making one year. Twelve months later when a four-hundred gallon vat was cleaned out its complete skeleton was found. 'Best drop of cider we ever tasted', said the farmer.

Apples being tumped in a Herefordshire orchard in 1908

Many believed that cider-making should be done only when the moon was on the wane, otherwise the cider would turn sour. When it did become too acid it was known as 'belly vengeance'. Perry at the best of times was said to 'go round like thunder and out like lightning'.

Daniel Defoe was agreeably surprised to find in Herefordshire 'that several times for 20 miles together, we could get no beer or ale in their public houses, only cider; and that so very good, so fine, and so cheap, that we never found fault with the exchange'. Others deplored what they thought to be excessive consumption of cider. Two centuries after Defoe the bishop of Hereford asserted in evidence to the Licensing Commission of 1921 that there was much 'secret cider-drinking' in his diocese, a claim which inspired in *Punch* a poem entitled *Hell in Herefordshire*:

> The wild white rose is cankered
> Along the Vale of Lugg,
> There is poison in the tankard,
> There's murder in the mug;
> Through all the pleasant valleys
> Where stand the palefaced kine
> Men raise the devil's chalice
> And drink his bitter wine.

Unpseakable carouses
That shame the summer sky
Take place in little house
That look towards the Wye;
And near the Radnor border
And the dark hill of Wales
Beelzebub is warder
And sorcery prevails.

For spite of church or chapel
Ungodly folk there be
Who pluck the cider apple
From the cider apple tree,
And squeeze it in their presses
Until the juice runs out,
At various addresses
That no one knows about.

And, maddened by the orgies
Of that unholy brew
They slit each other's gorges
From one a.m. till two,
Till Ledbury is a shambles
And in the dirt and mud
Where Leominster sits and gambles
The dice are stained with blood.

But still, if strength suffices
Befre my day is done,
I'll go and share the vices
Of Clungunford and Clun,
But watch the red sun sinking
Across the March again
And join the secret drinking
Of outlaws at Presteign.

In fact there was a great decline in farm cider making. The extension of the Truck Acts to agriculture meant that cider could no longer legally be offered as part of the wages. One farmer told Michael Quinion why he had stopped making cider in the early 1920's: 'Well, I paid 'em to make it, and I paid 'em to drink it, and still the buggers weren't satisfied'.

In recent years there has been a tremendous revival in cider making and drinking. Old-established firms like Bulmer's and Weston's have been joined by Dunkertons (founded in 1981) and many small enterprises in both counties, some of whom have been featured in the Big Apple festivals organised since 1989 in the villages of Aylton, Preston, Putley, Much Marcle and Yatton.

Unfortunately the revival was not able to save the Plough at Elmley Castle, the only public house in England where cider had been made on the premises for generations. The same family ran the place for 135 years until the last landlord and his wife retired in 1991. Previously 150 tons of Vale of Evesham apples had been pulped and processed each year in a shed behind the pub. The resulting cider had an alcohol content of 8%. Traditionally, anyone falling into the village ditch on the way home would be dubbed Mayor of Elmley until the next person made the same mistake. The turnover was rapid.

The importance of cider means that apple trees are (or were) regarded with special affection, even reverence. People once thought it tantamount to sacrilege to cut them down. The feeling did not survive in those who grubbed up thousands of trees in the past twenty years, but this trend has now been reversed. We are unlikely to start throwing the afterbirths of cows into the branches of apple trees to bring them fertility, as people did up to the 1930's, but Weston's of Much Marcle have revived the ancient ceremony of wassailing the orchards on the nearest Saturday to Twelfth Night (see chapter 12).

'A certain care but an uncertain profit' was one Herefordshire saying about hop growing. Another observed that 'if it were not for the hops the farmers would have to hop themselves'. 'A hop picking morning' meant fine weather in late August or early September, with mists and dews followed by sunshine and sharp air. Hops are still an important part of agriculture in both counties, though the picking is now mechanised. The last picked by hand in Herefordshire were at Withington Court Farm. John Phillips (1676-1709) who lived at the Court wrote the poem *Cyder* which gained him a place in Poets' Corner at Westminster Abbey.

For many generations—until the 1960's—picking was done almost entirely by hand. The workers—mainly women, accompanied by their children—were brought in from Birmingham, the Black Country and South Wales. Kathleen Dayus (born in 1930) remembers being brought all the way from Birmingham by horse and wagon but most travelled on special trains arranged by the farmers. George Dunn (1887-1975) recalled:

When th' 'op pickin' season come, about the beginn' o' September or the latter end of August we'd sometimes be away for six weeks. The train was 'ired an' if you were 'ired you 'ad a ticket of th' agent. That was goin' from Cradley {Heath} to Worcester, an' went on to Leigh Court an' Tenbury an' Knightwick, Suckley, Leigh Sinton, Bromyard, Pershore. There's not many I 'aven't bin to. I used to love the 'op fields. We stayed in the barns, all the stables an' cowsheds an' that, just accordin' to the amount o' pickers they wanted. The animals were taken out and the stables white-washed and plenty o' new straw put in.

The work was exacting, pay (by the bushel) modest and conditions spartan, but there was a tremendous camaraderie among the pickers, and plenty of singing:

Lovely in th' 'opyard. Everybody was a-singin'. You sung while you were pullin' the 'ops off. We 'ad sing-songs round the fire. I've 'ad some good times down the' 'opyards. I 'ardly missed a year. It was the best o' my days.

The sentiments were echoed by thousands of other pickers.

Hops were picked into a crib, a piece of sacking supported on a wooden frame nine feet long by four wide and four deep. By ancient tradition any

Hop picking (Alfred Watkins)

172

stranger wandering into a hopyard would be 'cribbed', which a censorious commentator described as 'a custom (happily falling into disuse) by which female pickers seized upon, lifted into a crib, and half smothered with hops and kisses, any strange man who entered the hop-yard'. The victim was also expected to give money for drink.

At the end of the season as the last bines were pulled down for picking the pole-pullers took hold of any unmarried woman and dropped her into a crib. Photographs give a fairly sedate impression of what in fact was vigorous horseplay with clear sexual overtones. The women would sometimes band together to retaliate by up-ending the binman or busheller into a crib and covering him with bines. In earlier times a woman would be thrown in with him too, thus enacting a kind of fertility rite meant to ensure a good harvest the following year.

Another custom was described in the *Worcester Journal* in 1956:

On some farms, the last day of picking had its age-old ceremony of hoisting the last and best pole of hops, saved specially for the occasion. The pullers' caps and hats were decorated with rosettes, dahlias and asters and sprays of hops. Then a procession was formed, making its way to the farmhouse, headed by the busheller beating his metal measure to a drum, and followed by the pole-pullers, sack-holders and the pickers. At the farmhouse a feast was prepared and the farmer and his wife were toasted.

Mrs. Leather reports a similar but more elaborate ceremony:

At the conclusion of the hop picking ... it was formerly the custom to choose a King and Queen of the Hop-pickers. The head pole-puller, gaily bedecked with ribbons and sprays of hops, walked in front of the last load of hops from the hop-yard. Behind this came the two hop-pickers, who were chosen to be King and Queen; the woman wore male clothing, and the man a woman's dress. They, like the pole-puller, were adorned with hops and streams of coloured paper; all three carried poles of hops decorated in a similar fashion, the finest poles being reserved for the purpose. This procession went from the hopyard to the homestead, followed by all the other hop-pickers and labourers, singing and making merry. The King, Queen, and pole-puller removed their decorations at the barn door, while the poles they carried adorned the barn or granary until after the ball, which usually took place the same evening. Afterwards the hops would be carefully dried and hung in the farmhouse kitchen.

A pale echo of such vivid ceremonies is the practice still followed of displaying hop bines at harvest festivals or using them to decorate rooms in public houses. The Boot Inn at Orleton holds a barbecue and blessing each October to mark the successful completion of the hop harvest and to look forward to the next.

Farm Wisdom and Custom

'Live as though you were going to die tomorrow; farm as though you were going to live forever', so runs a wise Herefordshire saying. A great deal of lore was transmitted in the form of memorable axioms and rhymes. Of the poplar it was claimed:

> Cut me green and keep me dry,
> And I will oak or elm defy.

The birch had similar properties:

> Heart of oak is still and stout;
> Birch says, If you keep me dry I'll see it out.

On the subject of oaks, people believed that 'the man who plants oaks, like the man who plants pears, plants for his heirs'. Alternatively:

> Who sets an apple tree may live to see its end.
> Who sets a pear may set it for a friend.

For planting acorns, nuts, cherry or other fruit stones to grow into trees the best time is from the fall of the leaf until Christmas. For crops of grain the conventional advice used to be four seeds in each hole:

> One for the rook, one for the crow,
> One to rot and one to grow,

Wheat should be sown in the dirt (moist soil), and rye in the dust. Farmers expected to complete sowing wheat by Allontide or Allhallows (1 November). If they had finished by the previous night a cake was divided between the dairymaid and the waggoner. However if the latter could succeed in getting into the kitchen by a certain hour at night, and cracking his whip three times, the cake belonged to him; but if the dairymaid, by any means in her power, could prevent this she could claim half the cake. She would be on the lookout well before the appointed time, and the duel of wits between the two parties afforded much amusement to the spectators.

In earlier times, though, the aim was that 'At Michaelmas Fair {29 September} the wheat should hide a hare'. All seeds were set as the moon waxed, roots as it waned. Pigs were killed at the moon's waxing, otherwise—it was believed—the bacon would waste away with the moon. Every pig has four small holes in the skin inside the front ankle, and it was believed that this showed where Old Nick entered the Gadarene swine. Conversely, the black cross on the back of every donkey is a reminder of Christ's journey to Jerusalem.

A donkey was kept with cows in the belief that it would ensure that they never aborted. In the days when farmers took a lantern to visit their cowsheds at night it was considered that on no account should they put it on the table when returning to the house or a cow would lose her calf. At Ledbury a cow was not named until after having her first calf. That is perhaps why vague appelations such as Fillpail were once used. (Some of these figure in wassail songs). In Worcestershire the Christmas mistletoe bough was fed to the first cow to calve in the New Year, and was thought to bring good luck.

A horse found unaccountably sweating in the stable, first thing in the morning, had been ridden overnight by witches or fairies. This could be prevented by nailing over the door a cross made of mountain ash and birch. For a horse to have three white feet was very unlucky; hence the rhyme, 'One buy, two try, three don't go nigh'; and also:

> One white foot, buy him;
> Two white feet, try him.
> Three white feet, doubt him;
> Four white feet, do without him.

On the other hand, according to a Herefordshire maxim, 'a good horse is never a bad colour'. As to the animal's treatment:

> Up the hill press me not;
> Down the hill trot me not.
> On the level spare me not;
> In a stable forget me not.

In Herefordshire until late in the nineteenth century the custom was kept of bleeding horses on St. Stephen's Day. The occasion was sacred in Scandinavia to the goddess, Freya, and horse races were held in her honour.

It was thought unlucky to keep sheep in the same field for two Sundays running, so before they heard the church bells on the second Sunday they should be moved to fresh pasture. When any animal was sold a little of the purchase price was returned by the seller to the buyer as luck money, a custom still widely followed, and even extended to motor vehicles.

Corn was once measured by the bushel, the size of which varied from place to place. A bushel measure for hops has been preserved in the church in Bromyard. The tod (28 pounds) was employed for wool. In hedging and ditching until relatively recently the rod, pole or perch (five and a half yards) and the chain (22 yards) were used. The latter still applies to cricket pitches.

Farm tenancies ran from Candlemas (2 February) or Lady Day (25 March), and the latter is still the date on which many farm rents fall due. A tenant destined to move into a farm at Candlemas had the right of access to plough land from the previous 1 November, together with stabling for two horses and a room for a ploughman. Similarly, a tenant leaving at Candlemas could keep his cattle on the pasture and retain the use of the house and some of the buildings until 1 May. It was customary when a young couple took possession of their first tenancy for neighbouring farmers to help them establish themselves during the first season.

A number of calendar customs were kept on farms. On Easter Sunday there was a ceremony called corn showing, when the bailiff, the men and their families went into a wheat field with supplies of plum cake and cider. They ate and drank in the field, then marched across it with joined hands, saying:

> Every step a reap, every reap a sheaf,
> And God send the master a good harvest.

A small piece of cake was buried in a corner, with a drop of cider poured on top. A similar procedure was followed in orchards. In the wheat fields, according to Fosbroke, the ceremony originated as a mass weeding of the crop to ensure that no corn cockle (*agrostemma githago*) were present, since if its seeds were ground with the corn and got into the bread, anyone eating it would suffer from dizziness. The best weeder was allowed to claim a kiss from the prettiest maid, together with the biggest piece of cake at the feast.

Every year on Ascension Day the master gardeners of Evesham gave their workpeople a treat of baked peas, both white and grey, with pork.

Farm workers, both male and female, indoor and out, were hired on an annual basis at 'mop' fairs held in May or October. In Worcestershire—for

176

example at Alvechurch, Bewdley, Evesham and Worcester—October was preferred; in Herefordshire, May. Even so, there were variations. Bromyard held to May but Ledbury only ten miles distant kept October. Both events still exist though they are now purely pleasure fairs.

Mops were bitterly attacked by clergymen and police. A rare defence, urging reform rather than abolition, was an anonymous pamphlet—possibly written by Rev. William Poole of Hoarwithy—entitled *Old Mops Mended*. By contrast Rev. E. Jackson, the Herefordshire Inspector of Schools, wrote this in 1860:

When the *business* of day has drawn to a close, the *pleasures* of the evening commence. The inexperienced lad and lass, with the fruits of their last year's labour in their pockets, are naturally led for refreshment to the neighbouring public-house. ... To the stupefying effects of tobacco are added the intoxicating consequences of deleterious beer and spirits, and the maddening results of dancing and music. Each female selects her male companion for the evening, whose duty it is to see her to her distant home at the close of the amusements in the darkness of the night. Decency forbids me from entering into further details, and I cannot picture to you the proceedings of the night to its close. The very devils in hell would delight and be satisfied with the orgies and revels that follow.

Mr. Chipp, Superintendent of Police at Worcester, echoed these views—albeit in slightly apocalyptic terms—with reference to St. John's Mop:

After the Mop is over drinking, cursing and swearing, and fighting are carried on to a fearful extent, and I have many times been called out to quell the disturbances. When night comes on, there is scarcely a place in the parish in which couples are not seen elated with drink. In many cases the females are easily taken advantage of. I have known young women entrapped by procuresses, and have often been employed by their distracted friends to find and restore them. But when they have once been tainted they often break out again. Mops are calculated to bring trouble and misery, without producing the least benefit to society.

An agency called the Worcester Servants' Registration Society was set up, and by the 1870's hiring had ceased at St. John's Mop, though a pleasure fair continued.

Bromsgrove's mop ended in 1914; Bewdley's lasted until the 1920's, for hiring, that is. At Hay-on-Wye, just over the Welsh border, hirings continued until the Second World War. Both farmers and farm workers from West Herefordshire attended, and many still have recollections. One Dorstone farmer remembers hiring a young Welsh lad who lasted only a few days before home-sickness proved too strong for him.

At the hirings workers wore an emblem of their calling: some wool in the hat for a shepherd, a piece of plaited straw or even a miniature corn dolly for a waggoner, a few strands from a mop for a housemaid (and hence one explanation for the name of the event). At one time 'each man had to carry his clean Sunday smock on his arm, to show he possessed one, or no good master would engage him'. When a bargain was struck the farmer would give a shilling, known as earnest money, to seal it. Normally, both sides would respect it. A waggoner at Ross-on-Wye was told 'If your character is satisfactory you can start work on Monday morning'. Next day the farmer received a postcard with the laconic message 'I a yeard on yer, and I bent a-coming'.

Another story, unconnected with hiring, comes from Tenbury Wells. A very rich farmer there was excessively mean. Any animals—cows, sheep, poultry—which started to ail were quickly killed and dressed, either to be sold for meat or cooked for the workman's dinner. One morning the postman called at the farm and found the workman packing up ready to leave. On asking the reason why he was told: 'Everything that is about to die is dressed and put out for dinner. Well, this morning the gaffer died, so I'm off'. Such a tale goes against the conventional wisdom that 'Herefordshire farmers live rich. Monmouthshire—or Radnorshire—farmers die rich'.

Generosity was certainly evidenced in Worcestershire where at Hanbury until the 1930's at least it was the custom for all farmers to give milk to any who asked for it on Whitsun Eve. No milk was sold on that day since it was considered that ill luck would befall anyone doing so. As a result of the farmer's largesse everyone ate baked custard on Whit Sunday.

Harvest was—as it still is—the climax of the farming year. The last few stalks of the last field were called the mare. The reapers tried to cut it by throwing their hooks or sickles at it. The one who succeeded had the mare, and either plaited it himself or gave it to the mistress of the farm to do so. The plait would be hung with the bush burned in the early hours of New Year's Day (see chapter 12) in the farm kitchen to bring luck. Other plaited corn dollies were fastened to the thatch of ricks or used to adorn harvest suppers or harvest festivals in church. The art of making them dates back to mediaeval times, and is still widely practised. The dollies, which symbolised the harvest spirit, were carefully kept through the winter and ploughed in during the following spring.

Harvest Home from Chamber's Book of Days *(1864)*

The arrival in the stackyard of the last load of sheaves was greeted with due ceremony. Until the 1890's in Worcestershire men and boys shouted:

> Up, up, up, up, harvest home.
> We have sowed and we have mowed,
> And we have carried the last load home.
> Up, up, up, up, harvest home.

Then followed a harvest supper given by the farmer to his workers and their families in the great kitchen or even a barn spruced up for the occasion. A liberal meal would be followed by a bout of drinking, dancing and singing until anything up to six o'clock the next morning. In Herefordshire the custom was for the main dish at the meal to be goose. A farm feast at Leigh for hop-pickers was described in 1930 in the *Worcester Journal*:

The long hop-room, gaily decorated with brilliant streamers, its walls and windows draped with softer hues, is the scene of the annual feast. The fare is all prepared in the Great House kitchen, or in the cookhouse whose furnace boils the Christmas pudding and whose 'stick-oven' roasts the great joint of beef. The master, his light-grey suit protected by a blue-striped apron, carves, and the wide plates circle to receive from busy helpers potatoes, creamed swedes, brussels sprouts and gravy (such gravy, founded on boiled goose and stuffed fowls).

Each guest, and there are at least seventy, is supposed to bring hs own eating tools, but a pile is available for novices and the forgetful. Plum pudding and rum sauce are the second course, and mammoth jugs of beer and cider pass freely round the long trestle tables. When no-one can eat any more, the tables vanish and the fun waxes warm.

The guests are of both sexes and all ages and sizes; there are grandfathers and babies in arms, great strapping lads and bonny well-built lasses, and a host of small fry who scramble for the nuts, sweets and biscuits thrown to them. A professional entertainer with song and speech and dance performs on the dais, but the company furnish their own contributions too. The same songs, the same pieces are clamoured for each year.

Harvest suppers continue in many villages but they now tend to be a kind of community celebration organised by volunteers, with participants paying their own way.

After the corn had been carried from the fields gleaners were normally allowed into the stubble to pick up any loose ears for their poultry. 'Though the new binders swept the cornfields clean', wrote John Masefield in 1943, 'the farmers still gave gleaners leave to glean'. Some farmers moved their own poultry houses into the fields so that their hens could glean for themselves. Some fields might be left with their covering of loose ears to attract game and sticks might be scattered to snag the nets of poachers before the local estate agent could organise shooting parties. 'The full moon used to see many people out into mischief', says Mr. Stanley Yapp.

Taking corn for malting, from a misericord at Ripple

There was also once a kind of gleaning from orchards, called griggling. An anonymous Herefordshire contributor to Hone's *Every-day Book* wrote in 1826:

Leasing in the corn-fields after the sheaves are borne to the garner, is performed by villagers of all ages, that are justly entitled to glean, like ants, the little store against a rainy day. But after the orchard is cleared, ... the village ... climbing boys collect in a posse, and with poles and bags, go into the orchard, and commence *griggling*.

The small apples are called *griggles*. These, the farmers leave pretty abundantly on the trees, with an understanding that the urchins will have mercy on the boughs, which, if left entirely bare, would suffer. Suspended like monkeys, the best climbers are the ring-leaders; and less boys pick up and point out where an apple still remains. After the trees are cleared, a loud huzza crowns the exertion ... Then the hostess, or her daughter, brings a large jug of cider and a slice of bread and cheese, or twopence, to the great pleasure of the laughing recipients of such bounty.

Another climactic moment was New Year's Day. Some farms roasted their finest ox to be eaten by their workers on 1 January. In parts of

181

Herefordshire it was customary for farm workers to go on strike. Anyone failing to join in was forcibly carried on a ladder to the nearest public house, and released only on putting sixpence into the drink kitty. Few people in any case can have been fit for work on New Year's Day after the bush-burning celebrations of the early morning.

Nor did they work on Plough Monday—the first Monday after Twelfth Night—which traditionally marked the resumption of farm work after Christmas. In Worcestershire thirty of forty men would turn out to drag a plough by long ropes round local houses and farms. Their hats and white shirts would be bedecked with ribbons and emblems. A boy or young man dressed in women's clothes—and known as the Bessy—carried a collecting box. In return for a contribution the ploughboys brought luck; in default of it they would wreak some mischief by way of reprisal. On the same day if by rising very early indeed a ploughman could place his whip, plough staff or hatchet by the fireside before the maid could get her kettle on the fire she would in due course have to surrender her Shrovetide cockerel to him.

IX
SONGS

Traditional songs have a rich and lengthy history in Herefordshire and Worcestershire. They were part of the pattern of life for ordinary people, both on special occasions such as harvest suppers or family gatherings, and during the daily round of work in field or factory. Their subject matter covered the whole breadth of life: love and marriage, crime and punishment, sport and entertainment, politics and religion. It is sad that their place seems now to be more in schools and folk clubs than in everyday life, but at least many people continue to take delight in them.

Street Music

The waits were originally civic musical watchmen who patrolled the streets by night and sang out the hours. Later they played at official functions, in the streets, and on festive occasions. In Hereford they existed from about 1300 until the late sixteenth century. The Worcester waits performed as far afield as Coventry in 1613, 1623, and 1631. Their livery consisted of cocked hats and blue cloaks or coats, and by the end of the the eighteenth century they had become a drum and fife band. They continued to play, though only at Christmas, until the middle of the nineteenth century.

Unofficial street music was provided by wandering players such as the man encountered in about 1789 by Martha Sherwood's father, who was rector of Kidderminster at the time:

One day ... there was a poor blind fiddler passing through the town, and by some accident he was knocked down, and his violin broken to atoms. My father, not having any cash about him, could not bear to see this scene of distress unrelieved; he went into his field and caused a tree to be cut down, which he sold, for the benefit and consolation of the poor itinerant musician.

Such players continued to perform in the Shambles at Worcester until the 1930's. In the 1980's they re-appeared in the pedestrianised High Street, as they did in the High Town at Hereford.

Street songs were supplied by ballad singers who sometimes faced persecution, or prosecution by the authorities. At Hereford before the Civil

War a man was sent to the palace prison by the bishop's bailiff for singing and attempting to sell his ballads without leave during St. Ethelbert's Fair. At least three times during the same war action was taken at Worcester:

We do order and ordain that all ballet singers shall be put out by the heels. (1649)

It is ordered that to suppress all ballat singers, their ballats shall be burnt and themselves imprisoned by the space of three days. (1653)

That ballad singers be put in the stocks. (1659)

Three hundred years later one writer, J. Kyrle Fletcher, was asking whether any ballad singers remained in country towns, or whether they had all gone 'in this age of jazz to join the old men who wore smocks and billycock hats, and spoke with the slow, rich speech of the border country'. From his boyhood in Worcester during the 1880's he remembered the singers who came round on market and fair days. He mentions others who 'went to the markets of the three L's. Ledbury, Leominster and Ludlow'.

Some of the very same people might well have been encountered by John Masefield, who writes of Ledbury at much the same period:

I never crossed the town without the sight
Of withered children suffering from blight,
Of women's heads, like skull-bones, under shawls,
Of drunkards staggering with caterwauls,
And starving groups in rags, with boots unsoled,
Blear-eyed, and singing ballads in the cold.

Over twenty years later, in 1908, the composer, Ralph Vaughan Williams, had this experience:

One evening in Ledbury he heard a girl singing a ballad to two men. The pubs were just closing and these three, standing in the road outside in the light of the still open door, looked like a group in a story.

It is not clear from these accounts whether the ballads at Ledbury were merely sung, or were also for sale in printed form. Fletcher leaves no room for doubt in writing about Worcester:

The best remembered of these {performers} was an elderly blind man with a concertina who had a regular stand on the Cornmarket. He was a big stout man with a large white face fringed with grey whiskers. His sightless eyes were closed and he had a perpetual smile, a most unpleasant grin I should better describe it. He was led about by a small boy who carried a number of printed ballads still wet from the printing press, and as the old man sang he moved through the crowd selling the ballads at one penny each. We called this blind ballad singer The Welshman, but anyone who came from west of Malvern Hills was usually called Welsh, even those who spoke with the broad Hereford accent.

From where came these ballads?

Printed Ballads

Most early street ballads seem to have been printed in London. Some of them make reference to provincial places but have no real connection apart from the mention of a name. *Love Overthrown* from Samuel Pepys' collection looks interesting, but almost any county would do in the compendious sub-title:

The Young Man's Misery; and the Maid's Ruine: Being a True Relation, How a Beautiful Hereford-shire Damsel (who coming to Live in London, and being greatly Beloved by her Master's Son) was, by her Mistress, Sold to Virginia: and of the Great Lamentation her Disconsolate Lover makes for her.

The same would hold true for Martin Parker's ballad of 1663, *A Fayre Portion for a Fayre Mayd: Or, The Thriftie Mayd of Worstersheere*, and for *The Valiant Virgin: Or, Philip and Mary* of about 1671 which tells how a 'young Gentlewoman of Worcestershire (a Rich Gentleman's Daughter), being in love with a Farmer's Son, which her Father despising, because he was poore, caus'd him to be Prest to Sea; And how she disguised herself in Man's apparel and followed him'.

Other sheets issued in London genuinely dealt with provincial events but are now lost. The titles survive to tantalise, such as *The Miraculous Judgement of God showen in Herefordshire, where a mightie barne filled with Corne was consumed with fure begynninge last Christmas Eeve, and During ffyftene Dayes after* (1595) and *A new Ballad of the late Commotion in Herefordshire occasioned by the Death of Alice Wellington A Recusant*. We do know that the latter refers to an event in 1605 when the vicar of Allensmore refused burial to a catholic woman, and a party of fifty of her co-religionists carried out the interment despite him.

The background remains obscure to three more lost ballads of 1564-5 which appear to concern the Malvern Hills. Their titles are *An Answere to the Dystruction yat Men agaynste thayre Willes beynge answered by thayr Wyves muste Digge downe Malbroue hilles*; *An newe Instruction to Men of such Willes that are so Redy to Dygge up Malbron hilles*; and *A Seconde Destruction agaynste Malborne y hylles sett fourth by us Wyves consente of our Wylles.*

The killing of a man by his brother was the subject in 1577 of *A lamentable Songe of a cruell Murder Donne in Worcester* but we have only the title of the ballad. Details are also lacking on *A Doleful Ballad of a Cruel Murther in Worcestershire* (1605) but a sheet issued the following year must refer to some of those involved in the Gunpowder Plot: *A Ballett Declaring the Arraignment and Execucon of the Traytors late executed at Worcester.*

Murder ballads were very much part of the stock-in-trade of the printers concerned, and at least one issued in London but dealing with a local crime has survived. It was printed by the ballad printers, F. Coles, T. Vere, J. Wright and J. Clarke between 1674 and 1679, some twenty-five years after the events it narrates (and may be a re-issue of an earlier sheet which is now lost). Under the title of *The Downfal of William Grismond; Or, A Lamentable Murther by him committed at Lainterdine {Leintwardine}, in the County of Hereford, the 12 March, 1650* the ballad is in gothic or black-letter type, adorned with crude woodcuts. Its 22 verses begin:

> O Come you wilful young-men,
>   and hear what I shall tell,
> My name is William Grismond,
>   at Lainterdine did dwell:
> O there I did a murder,
>   as it is known full well,
> And for mine offence I must dye.
>
> There was a neighbours daughter
>   that lived there hard by,
> Whom I had promis'd marriage,
>   and with her I did lye,
> I did dissemble with her,
>   my lust to satisfie,
> And for mine offence I must dye.

The unnamed woman becomes pregnant but Grismond knows that because she is poor his well-to-do parents will not agree to their marrying. He murders her and, when the body is found three days later, runs away .

The title illustration from The Downfal of William Grismond

He attempts to flee to Ireland but the ship he sails in is 'troubled'—the superstition is as old as Jonah:

> There is some wicked person
> the shipman they did say,
> Within this Ship we know it,
> that cannot pass away:
> We must return to Land here,
> and make no more delay.

Grismond is arrested, imprisoned at Chester, then taken to Hereford to stand trial. The ballad ends as he faces the gallows, warning other young men to take a lesson from his fate. Under various titles it was to live on in Britain and America for over 250 years.

Heavy-handed moralising is also a feature of *Newes from Hereford*, which tells of 'A wonderful and terrible Earthquake' of 1661:

> On *Tuesday* last *October* the first day,
> In *Herefordshire* there happened such a fray,
> By a most terrible Earthquake that did hap,
> And violent storms too by a Thunder-clap.

The conclusion is pointed by a woodcut in which huge forearms issue from stormclouds over the city, one with a sword and the other with a three-thonged whip; between them a trumpet points down, and from it comes a balloon with the single word, 'Repent'. The message recurs in *The Worlds Wonder. Being strange and true news from Leompster in Hereford-shire of one Alice Griffiths, that had four men children at a birth, upon the 25 th. of April last past, 1677*. All four babies died after 25 days of life.

Almost a century passed before such ballads were printed in Herefordshire and Worcestershire. The earliest local printer of such material seems to have been S. Gamidge who was in business at Worcester from 1758, issuing both single sheets and eight-page booklets of ballads known as garlands. At Hereford Thomas Davies set up either in 1788 or 1795 (the records are contradictory) but he is represented by a single ballad, *The Enchanted Piss-pot* (see chapter 7), which came to light only in 1991.

Such printers were usually in a small way of business, producing jobbing work as well as ballads, and supplementing their incomes by such activities as selling stationery and medicines, binding books and running circulating libraries. Some traded only for short periods, others for twenty or thirty years. Their output of ballads—so far as one can tell from what survives, which is probably a mere fraction of the whole—varied from a single example through a handful to several dozen. The most prolific were Thomas Ward of Ledbury, with 53 sheets extant, and Richard Houghton of Worcester, with 33. The total number for the whole of Herefordshire is no more than 175 sheets; for Worcestershire, perhaps 100 sheets and garlands—but it should be remembered that many of these carried more than one ballad.

Distribution was in the hands of the hawkers mentioned earlier. H.F. Sefton advertised his wholesale and retail warehouse at 41 Broad Street, Worcester, 'where travellers may be supplied'. As well as his own ballads he sold those produced by Edward Taylor of Birmingham. John Butler operated from premises in the High Street, Worcester, 'where Country Dealers may be furnished with Histories, Old and New Songs, Ballads, Carols'. His stock was also on sale in Gloucester. S. Gamidge had outlets at Alcester, Bromyard, Evesham, Kidderminster, Stourport and Tewkesbury. Matthew Child of Eign Street, Hereford supplied shops at Gloucester, Hay-on-Wye, Kington, Leominster and Worcester.

The most plentiful source of material for printers was the stock of their colleagues which they shamelessly appropriated. In this way popular and sentimental songs were reprinted all over the country—*Auld Lang Syne*,

The Country Carol Seller, by Cuthbert Bede

Cherry Ripe, Highland Mary, Home, Sweet Home, Lash'd to the Helm, Maid of Llangollen, Robin Adair, and many more. Printers also happily re-issued traditional songs such as *The Baffled Knight, The Blind Beggar's Daughter, The Cuckoo's Nest, The Golden Glove, Lord Marlborough* and *The Sheffield Apprentice.*

Printers sometimes achieved apparent local reference by a simple change of name. *Bartholomew Fair* (the first word pronounced Bartlemy) was originally printed in London by Johnny Pitts of Seven Dials. It became *Hereford Fair* when reprinted—without acknowledgement, of course—by T.B. Watkins of Hereford. On other occasions far more adaptation or re-writing was done to provide local interest. *Jump Jim Crow* was a song and dance act devised in 1828 by an American showman, Thomas D. Rice. The song soon reached England, where it gave rise to a series of adaptations including *Jim Crow's Visit to Worcester*:

> I leave the gay metropolis,
> To Worcester then I go,
> To see the country people
> And to jump Jim Crow.

(Chorus)
Wheel about, turn about,
Do just so:
Every time you turn about,
Jump Jim Crow.

Then followed a number of verses specifically about Worcester, including these:

In Foregate-street they're building
The new County Court:
But they spent all their money
And that spoilt their sport.

Down in Copenhagen-street
I saw Saint Andrew's spire.
I think there's one at Coventry
Stands a great deal higher.

The Severn navigation
Is a very useful thing:
But the cunning knaves at Gloucester
Will stop it if they can.

Still other ballads seem to have been genuinely local productions from the outset. *The Herefordshire Fox Chase* chronicles an epic pursuit:

All you that love hunting attend to my song,
I'll beg some indulgence that will be rather long,
I{t}'s concerning the huntsman, the horse, and the dogs,
That never fear'd mountains, hedges, ditches, or bogs.

The year 97, Twelfth Eve was the day,
Bright Phoebus shone clear, and the morning was gay,
Resolv'd on a chase to which Reynard gave birth,
I'm sure such a chase was ne'er equal'd on earth.

Squire Percy well mounted, away he did ride,
James Careless with hounds coupled close by his side,
Then off to St Margaret's Park did repair,
For Reynard long time had been harbouring there.

No sooner arriv'd, as I've since understood,
But the drag of the Fox they cross'd near the wood,
Cries James, Hark to Rounder! for that was the hound,
Which led the whole Pack, and old Reynard first found.

Twenty-two verses and 98 miles later the hunt reaches its conclusion:

Now Reynard is dead, and my song ends at last.
Excuse me, I'm thirsty, then push round the glass,
So I drink with a wish that all great men in place,
To their king stick as true as these hounds to their chase.

The ballad was printed by T.B. Watkins of Hereford, some time
between 1810 and 1836. The author is unknown, but there is evidence that
the piece entered oral tradition, though it is not clear whether this
preceded or followed its publication by Watkins. A manuscript version of
the early nineteenth century—which names the tune used as *Six Bottles
More*—has many minor differences of phraseology, and spells some
places phonetically: dorson (Dorstone), brainton (Breinton) and comb
(Cwm), for example. Many years later Noah Richards, a Moorhampton
blacksmith, was able to write out the words (albeit reduced to 21 verses)
and sing the tune for Mrs. Leather.

A rather more sedate form of recreation features in the Worcester bell-
ringing ballad quoted in chapter 3. The powerful exploits of Tom Spring
seem to have been left to printers in Birmingham, Bristol, London and
even Gateshead (chapter 2). Even a celebration of high jinks under the
title of *Evesham Race Ball* was printed in Birmingham.

Crime

Locally produced ballads, following in the footsteps of *William Grismond*,
did chronicle various crimes. *Elegy on Mary Perry* (1781) laments the
murder of a woman by her jealous lover as she was returning from a
dance at Leominster to her home at Cholstrey, a short distance away. *The
Leominster Tragedy* relates at inordinate length the murder of Mary
Cadwallader by her blacksmith husband who was hanged at Hereford in
1816. The sheet, one of the few to acknowledge an author (W.
Cartwright), first appeared in Leominster but was evidently thought of
enough interest to warrant reprinting in London (by J. Evans and sons).

Gritton of Garway, or The Murdered Man's Lament, issued by B. Powle
of Ross some time between 1821 and 1839, tells in the first person how an
unnamed wrestler goes unwillingly to a contest and meets his death:

191

To Garway's cruel Feast I went, it was a hapless night,
I bring my God to witness I did not wish to fight,
But Orcop's men are ignorant and savage to degree,
And nothing else would so but they must have the life from me.

Two seconds they were false and pretended friendship there,
Oh of such hollow friendship I bid you all beware,
For long I was a fighting 'till I was out of breath,
When they held my hands behind me, and I was beat to death.

The dead man is made to argue that such events should be suppressed:

Oh cruel are these feats indeed, they should be done away,
And thus to pass in drinking the holy Sabbath day,
Good gentlemen I pray you, and magistrates be brave,
And you'll prevent the poor man from sinking to his grave.

A further sheet published in Cheltenham, *The Death at the Feast. A True Tale*, seems to be another commentary on the same incident, but the full background awaits exploration.

Better documented is a ballad dealing with the robbery of a farmer called Jones as he was on the way home from Kidderminster Market to the village of Rock, by way of several public houses in Bewdley. At 10 p.m. when he left the last of these, the Union, he was followed by James Carter (aged 22) and his brother, Jospeh (30). Outside the town Jones was knocked into a ditch and robbed of his remaining money, just a few shillings. He was not seriously hurt but the Carters' smock frocks—they were probably agricultural labourers, fallen on hard times—were spattered with blood, and this eventually led to their arrest and trial. They were found guilty of the robbery and also of stealing a Kidderminster £5 note—many different banks issued currency at the time—on the same day. They were sentenced to death.

The Lamentation of James & Joseph Carter was printed by R. Houghton of 5 Merry Vale, Worcester:

Come all you wild and wicked youths, wherever you may be,
An example take while you have time to shun bad company,
Refrain from all your former sins, reform & take good ways,
Then you'll be blest with sweet content, live and see happy days.

192

(Chorus)
Take advice young men all,
And think of our downfall.

We was brought up near Bewdley town, all in fair Worcestershire,
Where our parents now reside in sorrow, grief, & care,
When from them last we took our leave, the tears flow'd from their
eyes,
Desiring to take good ways, we heeded not their cries.

Soon after we left our parents dear, employment we did gain,
But being prone to wretched vice, not long we did remain,
For in lewd harlots company, we spent each night and day,
And to maintain this wretched set we robbed on the highway.

In eighteen hundred & thirty-three, Feb. the 7th day,
We did attack one Mr. Jones, all on the king's highway
We robbed him of his property, and also beat him sore,
Dispersed and left him on the ground weltering in his gore.

But soon we apprehended were & unto Worcester sent,
Within strong prison walls to dwell in grief & discontent,
And at the last assizes we were guilty found and cast,
And then the awful sentence of the law was on us past.

Now with strong bars we are confin'd in a dismal cell,
And soon upon the fatal drop must bid this world farewel,
Ah young men all we little thought of this any more than you,
That we should meet our fate so soon & bid this world adieu.

So all young men a warning take who hath sweet liberty
And for two dying sinners sake, shun harlots company,
For they will soon your pleasure blast, and prove your overthrow,
And then like us you will get launch'd into a gulph of woe.

It is probable that the Carters' sentences were commuted to terms of
transportation to Australia. Other ballad sheets featured executions. One
printed by H.F. Sefton of Worcester is comprehensively titled: *Life and
Career of Robert Pulley Who was Executed in front of Worcester County
Gaol, on Monday, March the 26th, 1849, for the Wilful Murder of Mary
Ann Staight, aged 15, in Windmill-Hill Lane, near the "Sister Elms"*

(which stand on each side of the London Road, about 6 miles from Worcester) at Broughton, Near Pershore, Wednesday, December the 5th, 1848. There is a large engraving of a prison, showing a hanged man. Lengthy prose passages report the trial and condemnation, sentence of death, confession and 'awful execution'. Finally, in a prominent position a song points the inevitable moral:

Now may this fate a warning be, to all both far and near,
And shun such deeds as he has done, when his sad fate you hear!
There's scarcely one will pity him, he better should have known,
He was not like a thoughtless youth, he was to manhood grown.

I will conclude this mournful song, may every mother take
This copy to their children, for Robert Pulley's sake;
To instruct them in their early days, to shun all murderous ways,
And he that reigns and dwells above, will bless their fleeting days.

This is the last execution ballad from Worcester which seems to have survived but the genre still had several decades to run at Hereford. *Double Execution of John Hill and John Williams (1885), convicted of murdering Ann Dickson,* records the first hanging at Hereford to be carried out in private. An engraving shows the gaol with a black flag waving over it. The verses were intended to be sung—incongruously—to the tune of *Ehren on the Rhine:*

The victim had been labouring,
In the hop gardens we're told,
When her work was over then,
Alas her life was sold,
She met with Williams & John Hill,
At a public in the town,
And before the dawn of early morn,
In death she was struck down.

(Chorus)
Side by side they had to die,
In Hereford goal {sic} they both condemned did lie,
For the cruel Weobley murder,
For mercy they did cry.

Excited by the drink they had,
They followed her thro' the field,
Twas only for a purpose bad,
To them she would not yield,
With a little baby in her harms {sic},
No resistance could she give,
And they gave her wounds while on the ground,
Till she had ceased to live.

The same format and the same engraving but a different tune—*Just before the Battle, Mother*—were employed three years later for a sheet headed *Execution of Scandreth & Jones At Hereford for the Brutal Murder of Mr. Ballard at Tupley* (Tupsley):

In the county goal {sic} at Hereford,
Two young men has met their doom,
No sorrowing friends they had around him,
There last days past in prison gloom,
For murder at Hereford they were convicted
And by the judge condemned to die,
That sentence now as been inflicted,
They both in the grave does lie.

(Chorus)
Scandreth and Jones has been executed,
There soul as {sic} gone beyond the skies,
They cruelly murdered poor Mr. Ballard,
And on the gallows had to die.

It is unlikely that such ballads were of more than ephemeral interest, but some of the carols printed in the two counties continued to be sung locally for generations afterwards.

Carols
As we have seen, John Butler of Worcester specifically advertised his printed carols in the 1780's. He issued at least five small collections, of which four have survived:

Part the first   1. God's dear Son without Beginning
                  2. God rest you merry Gentlemen
                  3. Oh! fair Jerusalem

Part the second	1. Now when Joseph and Mary
	2. Awake, awake sweet England
	3. Joseph was an old man
Part the third	1. Let all good Christian people here
	2. God bless the master of this house
	3. When Jesus Christ was twelve years old
Part the fifth	1. My master, your servants & neighbours, &c
	2. A virgin most purely, &c
	3. Remember, O thou Man
	4. Let Christians now with joyful mirth

In the 1820's and 30's titles such as *The Angel Gabriel*, *The Bosbury Carol*, *Christians Awake*, *A Hymn for Christmas Day*, *Righteous Joseph* and *The Virgin Unspotted* were printed at Hereford, Ledbury or Ross. Few carols seem to have been produced by the Worcester printers of that time, save for *The Virgin Unspotted* by Sefton, but in 1847 George Walters of Dudley published in book form—under the title of *A Good Christmas Box* and at the price of 1s 3d—58 carols.

The old carols continued to be reprinted. An engraving (see page 189) of 1869 by Cuthbert Bede—a pseudonym for Rev. Edward Bradley, a former pupil of Kidderminster Free Grammar School—shows an intinerant vendor at work in the countryside. Over forty years later Mrs. Leather noted that a sheet of carols which included *The Moon Shines Bright* was still being issued at Christmas by a member of the Elliott printing family of Hereford.

With such support from print, many carols entered oral tradition. Tunes were not included on the sheets, so they were passed on by ear, a practice which could lead to strange unions of words and music. In the 1850's some carollers at Marden were heard singing *A Virgin Unspotted* to a tune normally associated with a ballad about Admiral Benbow, *O we sailed to Virginia*. Conversely, a tune sung in Herefordshire to *The Truth sent from above* turns up elsewhere with the words of a drinking song, *Ye Mariners All*.

Mrs. Leather, Ralph Vaughan Williams and Cecil Sharp all took down carols from Herefordshire singers. Those sent to Lucy Broadwood from Worcestershire include *The Angel Gabriel* (from Leigh Sinton, 1902) and *Mary's Lamentation at the Sepulchre* (from Eckington, 1907), both of which had been issued forty years or more earlier by R.H. Elliott of Hereford. From Leigh Sinton, too, came *The Saviour's Love* (1899), which was earlier printed in *A Good Christmas Box* and on a sheet issued by E. Heath of Monmouth. The same carol was sung by Charlie Jones, a

Castle Frome farm worker, at Christmas 1978 in Bromyard hospital, where he was recorded by Daphne Davies:

Have you not heard of our dear saviour's love,
And how he suffered like a harmless dove?
And if we in our wickedness remain
Christ will not shed his blood for us again.

If we were going to be put to death
It would be hard to find a friend on earth
Who would lay down his life to set you free,
Yet Christ with patience shed his blood for thee.

The sin of drunkenness leave off in time,
For that's another, a notorious crime.
Lead sober lives and lay that sin aside,
Nay, likewise too that odious sin of pride.

Some do by gaining lose their whole estate,
And then are sorry when it is too late.
Therefore in time leave off such foolish things
Which heavy sorrow and destruction bring.

Attend thy church, the sabbath don't neglect;
The holy scriptures will thy path direct,
And do no more abuse the name of God,
Lest he should smite you with his heavy rod.

Some carols were never printed, others weren't popular enough to be learnt and passed on by word of mouth. A manuscript copy of *The Bosbury*

THE CELEBRATED CAROL, CALLED
HAVE YOU NOT HEARD OF
Our Saviour's Love.

And another composed by an eminent Writer.

HAVE you not heard of our Saviour's love,
 And how he suffer'd like a harmless dove?
But still we in our wickedness remain,
And crucify our blessed Lord again.

If you were going to be put to death
You wou'd find it hard to meet a friend on earth,
That would lay down his life to set you free,
But Christ did shed his precious blood for thee.

Consider what our Lord did undergo,
To prevent them from the gulph of woe:
Repent in time, from wickedness refrain,
Christ will not shed his blood for us again.

Let's love each other as we ought to do,
'Tis God's command, tho' it be kept by few,
For little love does in the world abound,
Nothing but spite and malice to be found.

Yet if we one another do not love,
How shall we think that our great God above,
Will ever take us to his throne on high,
If we each other scorn and vilify.

Here is a thing the Scripture shows
To pray for them that are our greatest foes,
If you think ever for to meet in heaven,
You must forgive, as you expect to be forgiv'n.

'Tis very apt for some to curse and swear,
But let me now persuade you to forbear,
And do not more abuse the name of God,
Lest he should scourge you with his heavy rod.

The sin of drukenness leave off in time,
For that's another sad notorious crime,
Live sober lives, and lay that sin aside,
Nay, likewise the horrid sin of Pride.

Some men make wealth their God, as we do
 know
And to their neighbour no charity will show,
'Tis good to help the widow in distress,
Relieve the needy and the fatherless.

Give to the Poor, you lend it to the Lord,
The cheerful giver God doth oft reward,
In that sweet place, where saints and angels
 dwell,
How soon your death may come, no tongue can
 tell.

Our latter end now let us well consider,
For when our life is gone we know not whither,
Our precious souls may be condemn'd to go,
Lord keep us from the burning lake below.

Some men by gaming spend their whole estate,
And they are sorry when it is too late,
Therefore in time ward off these foolish things,
Which surely will destruction to you bring.

Keep to the Church, your Sabbath don't
 neglect,
The holy Scripture will your soul direct,
Then let it always be your chiefest care,
To spend the Lord's Day in most fervent prayer.

CAROL II.

Away dark Thoughts.

AWAY, dark thoughts, awake my joy,
 Awake my glory, sing,
Sing songs, to celebrate the birth,
 Of Jacob's God and King
Oh, happy night, that brought forth light,
 Which makes the blind to see,
The day-spring from on high came down
 To cheer and visit thee.

To wakeful shepherds, near their flocks,
 Were watchful for the morn,
But better news from heaven is brought,
 Our Saviour Christ is born:
In Bethlehem town the infant lies,
 Within a place obscure,
Oh, little Bethlehem, poor in walls,
 But rich in furniture.

Since heaven is now come down on earth,
 Hither the angels fly,
Hark how the heavenly choir doth sing,
 Glory to God on High.
The news is spread, the Church is glad,
 Simeon o'ercome with joy,
Sings with the infant in his arms,
 Now let thy servant die.

Wise men, from far, beheld the star,
 Which was their faithful guide,
Until he pointed out the babe,
 Whom then they glorify'd.
Do heaven and earth rejoice and sing?
 Shall we our Christ deny?
He is for us, and we for him,
 Glory to God on high!

Monmouth; Printed and Sold by E. Heath.

198

Carol dates from 1791 or perhaps earlier. It was printed in the 1830's by T. Ward of Ledbury, in eighteen verses which retell the Christmas story:

> When we were all through Adam's fall,
> Once judged for to die,
> And from all mirth brought to the earth,
> To dwell in misery;
> God pitted then his creature man,
> In Scripture as you may see,
> And promised that a woman's seed
> Should come for to make us free.
> (Chorus)
> Oh! praise the Lord with one accord,
> All you that present be,
> For Christ, God's Son, has brought pardon,
> All for to make us free.

This was undoubtedly sung, but there appears to be no record of the tune, nor does anyone remember it.

On the other hand, a considerable number of carols seem to have circulated orally, perhaps with some help from handwritten copies. Again at Bromyard in 1978, Charlie Jones sang a seven-verse carol beginning:

> How grand and how bright was that wonderful night
> When the angels to Bethlehem came;
> They burst forth like fires and struck their gold lyres
> And they made not a sound with their playing.

I have been unable to trace this in print, but a manuscript version taken down in 1907 from Alfred White of Eckington has this interesting comment:

This carol my father says has been sung as far back as he can remember. (He is nearly eighty). It is sung by children, usually only by those who do not know any other, and is rather despised by them. It is sung rapidly and generally gabbled through and its singing has been for that reason discouraged.

It is possible that a printed text for *How grand and how bright* may turn up—it has an eighteenth century literary flavour—but *The Bitter Withy*, apart from a single verse in 1868, was certainly not printed at all until

1905, and then only in the periodical, *Notes and Queries*, which was far from being the preferred reading of farm workers and their families. Yet at least a dozen versions were noted in the two counties between 1908 (remembered from over forty years earlier) and 1952. These words were sent to Vaughan Williams in December 1907, with an accompanying letter:

Sir,

Being 62 years of age, at the age of 10 years I learnt this carol from my mother, in the parish of Yarkhill, Herefordshire.

W. Holder

Duke St, Withington, Nr Hereford

I can sing the Carol in the old Tune but have never saw the Music.

Our Saviour asked leave of his Mother Mary
    If he should go to play at Ball
To play at Ball my own dear son,
    It is time you was gone and coming home
But pray do not let me hear of your ill doings
    At night when you do come home.

It is up Leencorn and down Leencorn {Lincoln}
    Our Saviour did he run
Untill he met with three Jolly Jerdins {young lords}
    And asked them all three.
Now which of you all three Jolly Jerdins
    Will play at Ball with me.

Oh we are Lords and Ladys sons
    And born in power all in all {bower and hall}
And you are nothing but a poor maids child
    And born in an Oxen's stall.

You are safe you are safe you are safe said he
    You are safe you are safe I plainly do see
For it is at the latter end I will make it appear
    That I am above you all.

So our saviour made a Bridge of the beams of the sun
    And our {o'er} it went he went he
And the three Jolly Jerdins followed after he
    And drowned they were all three.

So it is up to Leencorn and down Leencorn
    Their mothers they did hoot & hollow
O Mary Mary mild call home your Child
    For ours are drowned all.

So Mary Mary mild called home her child
    And laid him across her knee her knee
And she with her hand full of these cold cold bitter withies
    She gave him the lashes three.

Oh you cold you cold O you cold bitter Withy
    That has made me so bitterley to smart
You shall be the first and the very first tree
    That shall perish and die at the heart.

Vaughan Williams' notation of Mr. Holder's tune was included in Mrs. Leather's book, *The Folklore of Herefordshire*.

Other Themes

Although carols had a favoured place in local repertoires they were not the only traditional songs circulating orally. People sang on all manner of subjects at work, in public houses, at family gatherings. Sometimes they wrote down words to help their own memories or to oblige friends. What was obviously a treasured little collection of songs in careful handwriting has been preserved at the Hereford Record Office. It includes *The Herefordshire Fox Chase*, *Gritton of Garway* (which must have been copied from the ballad sheet since it even reproduces the epigraph from *Proverbs*, 'Envy thou not the oppressor, and choose none of his ways'), *Plato's Advice* and *Jenny Jones* (both probably from ballad sheets), and what seems to be a home-made composition called *The Farmer's New Mill*:

I'll tell you of a welthy farmer of late
And how he was diddled oute of his Estate
It was for himself and his neighbours good will
He sent for a millwright to build him a mill

(Chorus)
I de deredoun O deredoundee I &c

The millwright, notorious for seducing old women so as to obtain their money, conquers the farmer's wife, who announces she will be leaving:

> Hur husband went to hur and fell on his knees
> Saying nancy dear nancy come back if you please
> Be a wife unto me as you used to be
> And all that I have I will settle on the

> O no she replied while life do remain
> I never intend to come with you again
> The ring of her finger she instantly drew
> Saying here take your ring for I am no wife unto you
> With this his heart full of sorrow then straight home he went
> To his seven children his case to lament
> Your hard hearted mother do grieve me full sore
> She says she will come to you no more

Later, despite producing twins for the millwright ('If his foot had not slipt she shewerly had three'), Nancy has second thoughts:

> Then she did repent but it was in vain
> She sent for her husband to take her again
> On no he replied while life do remain
> In the same house as me she shall not come again

> Then she returned the millwright to tell
> O then says the millwright I will mach him wright well
> I will send him to goal {sic} if you will keep it still
> For he has not paid me for building his mill

The farmer goes to gaol, as a result of which his 'counsellors and lawyers ... diddled him out of the farm and mill'. Nancy has a second bout of regret:

> When she did live with the farmer at home
> She had plenty of white bread and strong beer and rum
> Now as I tell you if I am not mistaken
> She is the greatest part of her time on potatoes and bacon

She and the millwright decide to go to America but have a change of heart before sailing. The despairing conclusion is lightened by the man's remark that 'He never will forget the cutting of firs' {furze}—the expression means sexual intercourse. A final stanza deals with the authorship of the piece:

If you wish to hear who made this fine song
It was the poor quarre man a riseing of stone
The stone being wet and his fingers did smart
He made these few lines just to cheer up his hart.

It is impossible to say to what extent the poor quarryman's song circulated but a few years later another lyric, *The Red Herring*, was noted
which would become known throughout England. A hatter, Mr. Alderman
Slayney, sang it at the Bewdley Bailiff's Feast in 1831:

As I was Walking Down by the Sea Side
I saw a Red Herring was forty foor Wide
he was forty foot wide & fiftey foot Square
if that beant a Lie I wil Come no more thear.

(Chorus)
Hark how thou liest Why Marry thou Liest
Why Marry thou mights have told Mee so
Yes Marry So I do—Sing I O lantre lo Larl lal Larriel I O

And wat Do you think I maid of my Joley Red herrings
Head as good an Oven as Ever Baked Bread
Oven & Baker and every thing
Don't you think I maid wel of my Joley Red Herring
And wat Do you think I maid of my Red Herrings hears
forty pair of Taylors & fiftey Pare of Sheers
Needles & Thimbles & every thing
Don't you think I mad wel of my Joley Red Herring

And wat Do you think I maid of my Red hearrings Eys
forty pare of fesants & fifty pare of flies
fesants & flies & Everey thing
Dont you think I maid wel of my Joley Red Hering
And wat Do you {think} I maid of my Red Hearrings Nose
forty pair of Stockins & fiftey pare of Showse
Stockings & Shows, Buckles & garters & Everey thing
Dont you think I maid wel of my Joley Red herring

And wat Do you think I maid of my Red Hearrings Skin
As good a Ship as Ever did swim
Ship Men Mast Pole and Everey thing

Dont you think I maid wel of my Joley Red hearring
And wat Do you think I maid of my Red herrings Ribs
Saint Pauls Church Steeple & London Bridge
Steeple & People & Everey thing
Don't you think I maid wel of my Joley Red herring

And wat Do you think I maid of my Red Hearrings Guts
forty pair of Morkins {scarecrows}, and fifty Pare of Sluts
Morkins & Sluts and Evereything
Dont you think I maid wel of my Joley Red herring.
And wat Do you think I maid of my Red Herrings Tail
As good a Windmill as ever had Sale
Windmill & Miller, Toal {?} Dish & Everey thing
Dont you think I made wel of My Joley Red hearring

This is the earliest known record of the song in question. *The Jovial Hunter of Bromsgrove* has a much longer pedigree, but the version given in chapter 10 was noted from Benjamin Brown at Upper Wick, near Worcester, in 1845. Just six years later Mary Hayes learned from a dairymaid at Upton Warren the narrative ballad, *Spare me the Life of Georgie*, which in turn was noted from her at Hartlebury in 1908. She also sang *Three Gypsies betrayed her* and *Cold Blows the Wind*.

Song collecting in the Twentieth Century
Cecil Sharp seems to have made his first visit to Worcestershire in 1909, when he took down *The Holly Twig* at Hunnington and *Rosetta*, *Mary of the Silvery Tide*, *The Outlandish Knight*, *The Battle of Waterloo* and *Young Henry the Poacher* at Evesham from a Mr. Gibbs who may have been the person of the same name who supplied versions of *The Bitter Withy* and *General Wolfe* to the local newspaper in 1908.

Another song-hunter, H.E.D. Hammond, found that his landlady at Bath in 1906—a Mrs. Webb—was a Worcestershire woman who had lived at King's Norton and Malvern. She knew seventeen songs, all of which she had learned from old singers in her native county.

There was a long period from before the First World War until well after the second when interest waned in seeking out the traditional songs of Worcestershire, but a revival started in the 1960's. By then, many singers had died but there was nevertheless a modest harvest of songs, which may well turn out to be the last.

A similar pattern can be traced in Herefordshire. Mrs. Leather was initially the key figure. She lived in Weobley from her marriage in 1893 till her death in 1928, and during that time she scoured the villages round about in search of singers. Her niece, Nona Swire, recalled:

Ella used to take me round in the dog-cart to visit the old folk where she had heard folk songs could be sung. My part was to note them down with the aid of a tuning fork and my own ear. Later a phonograph was produced and we sallied forth with that. Pembridge was about the greatest distance we covered.

Others also helped. John Griffiths, the miller's son; R. Hughes Rowlands, the village schoolmaster; and Annie Webb, governess to the Leathers' sons, all noted tunes. The singers were labourers, a blacksmith, a molecatcher's widow, servants and gypsies. Mrs. Leather even learned how to pick hops—an extraordinary step for a middle-class lady of the time—so as to work alongside gypsy women and gain first their confidence, then hear their songs. She also regularly visited the work-house at Weobley where to the suppressed fury of the matron she would sweep into her sitting room, take over the piano and gather the old people round it. Among the singers she found there was William Colcombe, who was born in 1827 and learned many of his thirty or so traditional songs from an old nailmaker with whom he had lodged in the village as a youth.

At Pembridge Fair in 1908 Mrs. Leather heard two gypsy fiddlers, John Lock and his brother, possibly Polin. They were two of the nine children of Ezekiel, and were known as the Gentlemen Locks. 'Polin Lock often visited me afterwards', wrote Mrs. Leather in 1926, 'introducing himself by playing away under our windows until we came to listen; but lately I have not seen him, and his wife tells me he is now crippled with rheumatism, and unable to play'. One of the Locks, again possibly Polin, was found dead in the snow near Church Stoke, Montgomeryshire, with his fiddle by his side, and was buried with it.

Mrs. Leather was anxious to share her discoveries and she arranged for Cecil Sharp to meet the Locks at Leominster in 1909. He took down from them several tunes. Sharp returned to Herefordshire in 1921 and during the course of several days spent mainly in the workhouse (later Dean Hill Hospital) at Ross-on-Wye noted some 40 songs from eight men and women whose ages ranged from 64 to 82.

In 1908 Mrs. Leather met the composer, Ralph Vaughan Williams, at the Three Choirs Festival in Hereford and took him on to meet some of her singers. Vaughan Williams returned in the late summer or autumn— usually hop-picking time—every year from 1909 to 1913 and then again in 1922. During the course of visits to Ashperton, Aylton, Dilwyn,

Hardwick, King's Pyon, Madley, Monkland, Monnington, Pembridge, Weobley and Withington he took down some 80 songs, many of them in several different versions. Unfortunately he often neglected the words, but always noted the tunes. One of his excursions—to a hopyard at Monkland—was described by Vaughan Williams as his 'most memorable musical impression for the year 1912' because of the singing of a gypsy. Mrs. Leather's description of the occasion sheds light on her attitude to singers and their songs, and to Vaughan Williams' manner of working:

> After some trouble Dr and Mrs Vaughan Williams and I found their camp in a little round field at dusk, on a fine September evening. There were several caravans, each with its wood fire burning, the Stephens and other families being there, besides Alfred Price Jones, whom we were seeking.
>
> His wife was very ill, and we found him with her under an awning near one of the fires. He agreed to sing, so we all sat down on upturned buckets, kindly provided for us by the gypsies, and while Dr Vaughan Williams noted the tune his wife and I took down alternate lines of the words.
>
> It is difficult to convey to those who have never known it the joy of hearing folk-songs as we heard that pathetic ballad {*Cold Blows the Wind*}; the difference between hearing it there and in a drawing room or concert hall is just that between discovering a wild flower growing in its native habitat and admiring it when transplanted to a botanic garden.

Such was Vaughan Williams' fascination with Alfred Price Jones that he again made a special visit to hear him at Monkland, ten years later. Jones and his wife, Harriet, ended their days in Clun Workhouse.

Cold blows the wind on my true love,
And a few small drops of rain.
I never had but one true love
In a greenwood he was slain.

I'd do as much for my true love
As any young girl may.
I'd sit and weep all on his grave
For a twelvemonth and a day.

When twelve months and a day were gone
This young man he arose:
'Why do you weep down by my grave,
That I can take no repose?

'O fetch me a nut from a dungeon deep
Or water out of a stone,
Or white, white milk from a fair maid's breast,
Or from me begone'.

'How can I fetch a nut from a dungeon deep
Or water out of a stone,
Or white, white milk from a fair maid's breast
When fair maid she is none?

One kiss, one kiss from your lily-white lips
You days will not be long;
My lips are as cold as any clay,
My breath is earthly and strong'.

Unfortunately, the words so carefully taken down have not been preserved, so with Alfred Jones' tune a text obtained by Mrs. Leather from Mrs. Powell of Westhope, Canon Pyon, has been given here.

There was a lengthy period in Herefordshire when traditional singers and their songs received very little attention. Then in 1952 Peter Kennedy made several recordings in the county for the BBC Sound Archive, some of which were later issued on disc or cassette. Later, during the 1960's and 70's Dave Jones discovered more singers at Ledbury and Kington whose repertoires included *Branston's Ale* (better known as *Jones's Ale*), *The Farmer's Boy*, *John Andrew*, *Mary Ann*, *Rainbow Hill* and *Young Sailor*. In 1968 Henry Clayton of Ledbury sang *I loves My Sarah*:

Oh I loves my Sarah, she works at the farm,
And as long as she's true to me I'll do her no harm.
For she's fat and she's beautiful, she's proud and she's fair
As the buttercups and daisies that grows everywhere.

207

(Chorus)
For I follow her all day, I follow her all day.
I follow her, I follow her, I follow her away.

When we two goes courting she's like the vicar's wife,
She never says nothing and neither do I;
But she gives me a squeege and I squeeges she,
The more Sarah squeege I the more I squeege she.

When we both get married there's sure to be fun,
For they tell me the parson makes two into one.
For thinks me I'll puzzle him, between you and me,
There's enough meat on Sarah to make two or three.

It is unfortunate that no anthology or cassette of traditional songs from Worcestershire or Herefordshire is available, for even if the old singers have gone there are many who still take an interest in their art.

X
STORIES

Much of this book consists of stories passed on originally by word of mouth in the local vernacular, sometimes over long periods of time. They range from anecdotes to lengthy tales which have been condensed or summarised. In this chapter some examples are given in complete form.

In our day listening to stories is thought to be a pastime for children, yet adults spend a great deal of time in listening to narratives ranging from anecdotes told in the pub to 90-minute or two-hour television programmes. In the past traditional stories of different kinds were enjoyed by both children and adults. Their role was not only to give pleasure but to provide information and to convey attitudes.

Martha Sherwood—famous in Victorian times for her series of novels, *The History of the Fairchild Family* (published 1814-47)—was born at Stanford-on-Teme in 1775. She looked back with great affection to the stories she heard there as a child from her father's curate, Robert Nash, who was also a relative:

Oh! it was a happy day when he was seen coming across the park, in his great bushy wig, his shovel hat, his cravat tied like a King William's bib, his great drab coat, and his worsted splatter-dashes {leggings}. ... As soon as it was dark, in a winter evening, I took my place on his knee, and calling him Uncle Robert, begged for a story. Again and again I heard the same, but the old tale never tired. He told of dogs which were supposed to have been spirits, and which were always seen in certain rooms when any of the family were about to die, and other marvels of like description.

Mrs. Sherwood mentions the title of two tales told by Uncle Robert— *Robert and the Owl* and *Henry Milner*—but I have not been able to trace them.

John Masefield, a writer who considered himself to be mainly a story-teller in prose and verse, was born at Ledbury in 1878. 'From the first', he remarked, 'I delighted in stories, that I contrived to wheedle out of my nurses. ... I liked best the chain-stories:

The fire began to burn the stick,
The stick began to beat the dog,

The dog began to bite the pig,
The little pig got over the stile, etc'.

Other tales inspired a terror which Masefield remembered for the rest of his life: accounts of boys gored by bulls or stolen by gypsies; ghosts; the Severn Bore.

Adults, too, relished stories told round the hop-pickers' fire, under the hedge when farm workers took their bait, or round the inglenook as the family gathered on a winter's night. Some of the tales could have come from printed sources. Little booklets of eight or sixteen pages were issued by printers such as S. Gamidge, who set up at Worcester in 1758. Gamidge published ballads and 'histories'—potted versions of novels such as *Gulliver's Travels*, *Moll Flanders*, *Pamela* and *Robinson Crusoe*, together with traditional stories like *Children in the Wood*, *Patient Grissel*, *Robin Hood*, *Sleeping Beauty*, *Tom Thumb* and *Valentine and Orson*.

These were from the national repertoire. Many local tales were also told, and some of these did not find their way into print until the twentieth century. Indeed, others did not emerge at all until the twentieth century, which shows that a need to make and tell stories is still with us.

All those which follow were noted from oral tradition during the past 150 years. Originally they would have varied in the telling, with different narrators adding, omitting, embellishing. In print they become fixed, but can still serve as points of departure for oral narration.

The Long Ladder

My brother's boy Tom went to Hereford to learn to be a carpenter. Well, once Tom and the carpenter were mending a church spire, and they had a long ladder. The carpenter forgot a tool and had to go all the way back down and into the village. When he comes back he calls up to Tom from the churchyard. 'Hey, Tom. Don't go to climb down the ladder'. 'Oh', says Tom, 'I be halfways down 'im already'. 'Oh', says the carpenter, 'I've took 'im away'.

A Horse called Dragon

Many years ago, when I was a little boy, a relation left me to mind his horse outside an inn—the Chequers at Cutnall Green, to be particular—while he did business near by. Outside the inn, a-drinking of his ale, sat an aged person in a smock-frock, who began to talk to me. A carter was also there, and his horse was black—he called it Dragon. I said I wondered why black horses were so often called Dragon, and my gossip replied that he did not know, but they always had been so named. 'I've heard', he said, 'that as long ago as when the French came—we was farmers by Martley then—my grandfather's grandfather rode into Worcester from there on a black horse called Dragon. He had his little lad afore him and his missis behind him; and they shot her when he started and killed her; and he rode with her all the way to Worcester and never knowed her was dead till she fell off when he pulled up on Worcester Bridge'.

Now this was a picturesque tale and laid hold on my fancy; but I didn't believe it since I knew that the French had never invaded Worcestershire. It may have been twenty years afterwards before, reading Monstrelet's *Chronicles*, I learned that when Owain Glyndwr invaded the county he was indeed accompanied by a French force, that they actually came by Martley, and made their headquarters on Woodbury Hill. There is another curious little twang of truth in the tale—'he pulled up on Worcester Bridge'. Why should he? Because there was a gate-tower on the middle of the bridge, where of course in wartime everybody would be stopped and examined.

I never knew who the old man was, but I shall never forget the tale. It seems strange that those details should have been remembered for nearly five hundred years, but on the other hand would it not be stranger still that they should be forgotten?

Tokens of Death at Droitwich

Well, sir, I do believe in tokens afore death. I do, for I sin 'em, sir. The folks in this row says as a crow flyin' over the roof is a sign o' death. An' a dog howlin'.

When I was a lad, me an' me two brothers was down by the hedge when 'Hullo', says I, 'thar's a white rabbit'. An' we chased un as fur as the hedge, an' then a was clear gone—not a track of him nowhur. An' up we went to the house, an' first thing we saw was mother at the gate a-cryin' an' sayin' as how father had been taken that very hinstant. Me an' my brother, we seed it an' thot we'd got a prize; an' 'twas but a token o' death, sir. An thar was some lads in a archard—a happle-orchard—an' says they, 'Let's have a bit o' them apples'. So up tha climbs, an' thar tha was, a-settin' in the tree on the branches like, sir, when 'Lord bless us', says one, 'thar's a tame rabbit, a white 'n'—an' the rabbit run right under the tree. An' 'twas a token of thur master's death, an' die a did.

I have a heerd tell by men as I knows, an' they sin it themselves, that a Christmas eve, at a certain hour, all the cattle an' beasts, be they what you will, 'll kneel down whar they be. No, sir, I haven't sin 'em meself, but I knows them as have.

O yes I saw something

After the late French war, when the army was disbanded, a soldier who was making his way home through an out of the way part of the country near Bewdley knocked at the door of a farm house to ask for food. The farmer's wife who had never seen a soldier was so dazzled at the splendour of his appearance that she took him for an angel. She welcomed him with much awe and hastened to get dinner ready for him. Presently she ventured to ask where he had come from. 'From Paris', he answered. 'From Paradise! Then you will have seen my first husband, John Jones', said she, adding some particulars of John Jones' appearance. The soldier recollected everything that was expected of him. He said that John Jones was very comfortable in heaven, only rather tired of having nothing to do, and that he wanted a little money to set up a peppermill. 'Ah', said the old woman, 'that is so like my poor dear John Jones! He would always be making a bit of money'. Then she gave the soldier twenty guineas out of an old stocking hanging in the chimney corner, and an old grey mare to turn the peppermill.

Soon after the soldier had gone the farmer came in, and was very angry when he heard of his wife's visitor. He set out in pursuit forthwith, and soon met a shepherd, of whom he asked tidings of the soldier and the grey mare. But the shepherd who had been bribed by the soldier replied:

Oh yes, I saw something just now
That very much startled my wit,
For a man and a mare rode together through the air
And methinks I see them yet, yet, yet.

Oh, yes I saw some - thing just now Which ve - ry much sur - prised my wit, For a man and a mare rode to - ge - ther through the air And me-thinks I see them yet, yet, yet. (Chorus) Fol de rid - dle di - do, fol de rid - dle di - do, Fol de rid - dle did - dly di - do.

212

(Chorus)
Fol de riddle dido, fol de riddle dido,
Fol de riddle diddly dido.

Then the old man lay down on his back
And into the elements he did stare,
To try whether he could discern or not
The young man on his bob-tailed mare.

The Jovial Hunter of Bromsgrove
Sir Robert Bolton had three sons—
Wind well thy horn, good hunter;
And one of them was called Sir Ryalas,
For he was a jovial hunter.

He rang'd all round, down by the wood side,
Till up in the top of a tree a grey lady he spy'd.

'Oh! what does thou mean, fair lady?' said he.
'Oh! the wild boar has killed my lord and his men thirty,
As thou be'est a jovial hunter'.

'Oh! what shall I do this wild boar to see?'
'Oh! thee blow a blast and he'll come to thee,
As thou be'est a jovial hunter'.

Then he blow'd a blast full north, east, west and south,
For he was a jovial hunter;
And the wild boar heard him full into his den,
As he was a jovial hunter.

Then he made the best of his speed unto him,
Wind went his horn as a hunter;
And he whetted his tusks as he came along
To Sir Ryalas the jovial hunter.

Then the wild boar being so stout and strong
He thrash'd down the trees as he came along
To Sir Ryalas the jovial hunter.

'Oh! what dost thou want of me?' the wild boar, said he.
'Oh! I think in my heart I can do enough for thee,
For I am the jovial hunter'.

Then they fought four hours in a long summer's day,
Till the wild boar fain would have gotten away
From Sir Ryalas the jovial hunter.

Then Sir Ryalas draw'd his broad sword with might,
And he fairly cut his head off quite.

Then out of the wood the wild woman flew:
'Oh! thou hast killed my pretty spotted pig,
As thou be'est a jovial hunter'.

'There are three things I do demand of thee,
It's thy horn and thy hound and thy gay lady,
As thou be'est a jovial hunter'.

'If these three things thou dost demand of me,
It's just as me sword and thy neck can agree'.

Then into his locks the wild woman flew
Till she thought in her heart she had torn him through,
As he was a jovial hunter.

Then Sir Ryalas draw'd his broad sword again,
And he fairly split her head in twain.

In Bromsgrove Church they both do lie;
There the wild boar's head is pictur'd by
Sir Ryalas the jovial hunter.

Sir Ryalas has been identified with Sir Humphrey Stafford who, in about 1430, killed a wild boar which was terrorising the neighbourhood of Bromsgrove. He died in 1450 at Sevenoaks while fighting against Jack Cade and the Kentish rebels and is buried in Bromsgrove Church, where there is an alabaster effigy of him and his wife, Eleanor. The family crest, a boar's head, is shown on the tomb.

Bromsgrove Church in the nineteenth century

The Tything Witches

Once upon a time—and it were a very long time ago—there was a little house in the Tything at Worcester, and in it lived two old women. They was witches, and what they didn't know the devil had kept to himself. They sold charms and spellings, and sent things, and they'd cure warts and toothaches and find anything as was lost; but they would have made a poor living of it if it wasn't for the carts. Because every now and again a cart as it was passing by their house would stick in the mud, and all for whatever the horses and men could do that cart couldn't go on.

Then one of these here old women would come out of the house, and the men would give her sixpence, and she'd say 'God bless the cart', and then the horses would start away with it as easy as if it weren't loaded. Folks didn't like it but nobody never said anything to the old women about it. For one thing they never meddled with carts that belonged to the town—it was mostly the salt carts as was stopped—and for another thing it wasn't reckoned gain to cross them.

Well, this here went on a long time, and at last a salt cart came along and stuck afore the house, and out comes the old woman. The man as the cart belonged to had been stuck a good many times before and he was going to pay the money; but he had a new man with him, one as knew something himself, and he says: 'Wait a minute, master. Don't you give her nothing yet. Just you talk to her while I has a look'.

So he goes round the team and sees a long straw lying across the wheel-horse's back. He outs with his knife and cuts it in two, and the horses screamed and started on, and away went the cart; and there in the road lay the other old woman cut clean in two, and the blood running round about.

After that the old woman as was left didn't stop no more carts, and she got very poor. One day she was coming out of the town with a loaf as she had been to buy, and in the road she meets a big regiment of soldiers on horses that had come to see about the taxes. In front of them a very brave gentleman was riding, and he pulls up to talk to her.

'Good day, old woman', he says. 'Where did you get that loaf?'

'In Worcester', she says, a-bobbing.

'How much did you give for it?', he says, and she says, 'A penny, captain'.

'Ho', says he, 'by the time I've done with the town you won't be able to get a loaf there for a penny, nor for sixpence neither'. And all his men laughed.

Then the old woman was very angry. 'Worcester?' says she. 'You'll never get to the town, and you'll never be done with it'.

They all laughed again, and the captain says, 'Never get to town, old woman? Why, we'm nigh there already. There's the gate'. And they all laughs again.

'Yes', says she, 'you'll get to the gate and no furder. Stone you are, all the lot of you, and stones you'll be to Judgement Day', she says. And she pointed her finger at them and away she goes.

So they rode on and came to the gate, and as soon as ever the captain's horse came to it, it fell down and turned to a stone, and so did the captain and all his men and horses; and there they lay by the roadside, a long heap of grey stones. And the old woman laid a word on them that they should stay stones till someone would come by the light of a new moon and put a loaf on each of them and say the Lord's Prayer over it. Nobody did it, and after a while she died.

The stones lay a long time by the side of the road and nobody durst cross the old woman's word, but at last there was a brave man—but he were a gallus random lad—as said he would do it for the sake of the poor soldiers like. So he went in the new moon and he put a loaf on every stone and said his prayer over it. But when he came to the last stone but one, as soon as he had said the prayer it started up into a live horse in the light of the moon. And he were that afeard that he dropped the last loaf and ran

216

away and never finished it; and nobody else ever darst do it. So the stones lay there by the roadside for ever and ever, and it is because of them that the Tything is called Whitestones.

The Old Woman of Oddingley

Long and long ago there was a wise old woman lived at Oddingley. She was a witch but I never heard tell that she did any harm to man nor beast: only she couldn't always wish them well. One day she was going along the road carrying plants in a basket when she met four handsome young gentlemen. The first two were very strong and big, but they touched their hats to her very gallant and polite and said, 'Good morning, mother', Of the next two one was slim and pretty like a maid, and the other was short and had a gammy back. The pretty one says, 'Well, old woman, how long is it since you was kissed for your beauty?' and the gammy one takes off his hat and makes a low bow, mocking like. 'Tell us our fortunes, old woman', he says, 'if you be a witch'.

'Young gentlemen', she says. 'fortunes are things best left alone: they're most in general bad enough when they comes, without troubling one aforehand'.

'Then don't tell us the bad part', says one of them. 'Just wish us well like'.

'My lad', she says, 'I'll wish you all as well as I can but my wishes won't mend what's got to be'. But they werrits her till she gives way, and she says to the eldest one, 'What fortune would you like to have?'

'I'm a prince', says he, 'and I'd like to be a great king and a great conqueror and have the master-hand over all my enemies'.

'And how would you die?' says she.

'I'd like to die in my castle like a great king, with all my people looking up to me and loving me, and leave my kingdom to my heirs for ever'.

'Well wished it is', she says; 'and what do you want, young sir?'

'I don't reckon on being a king', says the second one, 'but I'd like to be a brave soldier and die in battle in the hour of victory'.

'Well wished it is', she says; 'and what do you want, my pretty gentleman?'

'No king nor battles for me', he says. 'Fine clothes and fine houses and wine and dancing and the love of ladies and soft living is what I want'.

'And how would you die?'

'I don't want to die at all', he says, 'but if I must you can drown me with wine at a feast'.

'Well wished it is', she says. 'And what do you want, young lad with a smile?'

'I'm not tall and straight like my brothers but I'd like to be a famous knight and ride over my enemies so that the best soldiers in the world will be glad to follow me. Fame's what I want', says he, 'and to die in battle victorious and leave a name in honour for ever and ever'.

'Well wished it is', says she. 'Well, my lads, I can promise you all the best part of your wishes. You shall have what you've asked for but not quite as you've asked for it'.

'How's that?' they says.

'I reckon it's the way of the world, my dears', she says. 'We all wants a lot and we mostly gets the best part of what we wants; but there's always somewhat a-missing, and if we do get it all it's never quite the same as we reckoned it would be. Howsoever I wish you all as well as I can, and God bless you all.' So they thanked her and went their ways.

The young men of the tale were four of eight brothers of the house of Mortimer. They included the future Edward IV; George, Duke of Clarence, who was allowed to choose the manner of his death—ordered by the king for treachery in 1478—and who selected to be drowned in a butt of Malmsey wine; and the Duke of Gloucester, who reigned for two years as King Richard III before being killed in 1485 at the battle of Bosworth. Why their encounter with a witch was set at Oddingley remains a mystery.

The White Cap

Once there was a boy who wandered off the path on his way home in Herefordshire and found himself in a big wood. Darkness fell, and as he was tired out he lay down and fell fast asleep. Two or three hours later he woke to see a bear lying beside him with its head on his little bundle of clothes. It got up and the boy was very frightened at first, but the bear seemed tame and gentle so he let it lead him out of the wood to a spot where he could see a light.

As he got nearer he saw that the light was coming from a little turf hut. He knocked at the door. A little woman opened it, and invited him in. He saw another little woman sitting by the fire. He was given a good supper and was then told he would have to share the only bed with the two women.

He lay down and fell fast asleep but was wakened when the clock struck twelve. His bedfellows jumped up and put on little white caps which hung on the bed posts. 'Here's off', said one. 'Here's after', said the other. Then they disappeared, as if they were flying.

The boy was frightened to stay there alone, so he took another white cap from a bed post, put it on and said: 'Here's after'. He was straightway transported to the fairy ring outside the hut where the little women were dancing merrily.

'Here's off to a gentleman's house', said one. 'Here's after', said the other. 'Here's after', said the boy, and found himself on the top of a tall chimney. 'Down the chimney', said the first fairy. 'Down the chimney', said the second. 'Down the chimney', said the boy.

Down they went, first to the kitchen and then to the cellar. There they began collecting bottles of wine to take away. They opened one and gave it to the boy who drank so greedily that he soon dropped to sleep. When he woke up he was alone, and frightened. He crept up the stairs to the kitchen, where he was grabbed by the servants, and hustled in front of the master of the house. He told his story but the master would not believe him. He was tried for theft and sentenced to be hanged.

From the scaffold he saw a little woman pushing her way through the crowd. She was wearing a little white cap, and carrying another one. She asked the hangman if the prisoner might be hanged in the cap, and he agreed. So she walked up to the scaffold and put it on the boy's head. 'Here's off', she said. 'Here's after', he quickly added. And away they went like lightning to the turf hut.

The fairy explained that she had been angered by his taking the white cap. 'If ever you are befriended by fairies again', she said, 'you must never take liberties with their property'. 'I promise', he said. He was given a good meal and allowed to go home.

The Devil and the Farmer

The devil once called on a farmer at Little Comberton and asked if he could give him a job. 'What con'st do?' said the farmer.

'Oh, anything about a farm', said the devil.

'Well, I wants a mon to help me to thresh a mow o' whate', says the farmer.

'All right', says the devil, 'I'm yer mon'.

When they got to the barn the farmer said to the devil, 'Which 'ould thee do, thresh or throw down?'

'Thresh', said the devil. So the farmer got o' top o' the mow and begun to throw down the sheaves of whate on to the barn floor, but as fast as he could throw 'em down the devil with one stroke of his nile {flail} knocked all the corn out on 'em, and sent the sheaves flying out the barn door. The farmer thought he had got a queer sort of a threshermon, and as he couldn't throw down fast enough for 'im, he says to 'im, 'Thee come and throw down'.

'All right', says the devil. So the farmer gets down off the mow by the ladder but the devil he just gives a lep up from the barn floor to the top o' the mow, athout waiting to go up the ladder.

'Be you ready?' says the devil. 'Iss', says the farmer. With that the devil sticks his shuppick {pitchfork} into as many sheaves as 'ould cover the barn floor, and throws 'em down. 'That'll do for a bit', says the farmer, so the devil sat down and waited till the farmer'd threshed that lot, and when a was ready again, he throwed down another floor full; and afore night they'd finished the whole o' the mow o' whate.

The farmer couldn't help thinking a good deal about his new mon, for he'd never sin such a one before (He didn't know it was the devil, thee knowest, 'cause he took care not to let the farmer see his cloven foot). So in the morning he got up early and went and spoke to a cunning mon about it. The cunning mon said it must be the devil as had come to him, and as he had asked him in he couldn't get shut on him without he could give him as job as he couldn't do.

Soon after the farmer got wum {home} again his new mon wanted to know what he was to do that day, and the farmer thought he'd give him a teaser; so he says, 'Go into the barn, look, and count the number of corns there be in that heap o' whate as we threshed out yesterday'.

'All right', says Old Nick, an off he went. In a few minutes he comes back and says, 'Master, there be so many' (naming ever so many thousands or millions and odd, I don't know how many).

'Bist sure thee's counted 'em all?' says the farmer.

'Every corn', says Satan. Then the farmer ordered him to go and fill a hogshead barrel full of water with a sieve. So off he shoots again but soon comes back and tells the farmer he'd done it; and sure enough a had; and every job the farmer set him to do was the same. The poor farmer didn't know what to make on it, for though he was getting his work done up so quick, he didn't like his new mon's company.

However, the farmer thought he'd have another try to trick him, and told the devil he wanted him to go with him a-mowing next morning. 'All right', says the old un, 'I'll be there, master'. But as soon as it was night the farmer went to the field and in the part the devil was to mow he drove a lot of harrow tines into the ground amongst the grass. In the morning they got to the field in smartish time and began to mow. The farmer he took his side and told the devil to begin o' the t'other, where he'd stuck in the harrow tines, thee knowst.

Well, as it went the devil—who but he?—he soon got in amongst the stuck up harrow tines; but they made no odds, his scythe went through'em all, and the only notice on 'em he took was to say to the farmer every time he'd cut one through, 'A burdock, master'; and kept on just the same. The poor farmer he got so frightened at last he throwed down his scythe and left the devil to finish the field.

As luck would have it sooner after a got wum a gipsy woman called at the farm house, and seeing the farmer was in trouble asked him what was the matter. So he up and told her all about it. 'You a-got the devil in your house sure enough and you can only get shut on him by giving him summat to do as a can't manage'.

'Well, woman', says the farmer, 'what's the use o' telling me that? I a-tried everything I can think on but I darned if I can find him any job as a can't do'.

'I'll tell you what to do', says the gipsy woman. 'When a comes wum you get the missis to give him one of her curly hairs, and then send him to the blacksmith's shop to straighten him on the blacksmith's anvil. He'll find a can't do that and he'll get so wild over it he'll never come back to you again'.

The farmer was very thankful to the gipsy woman and said he'd try her plan. So bye and bye in comes the old fellow and says 'I a finished the mowing, master. What else a you got for me to do?'

'Well, I can't think of another job just now', says the farmer, 'but I thinks the missis got a little job for thee'. So he called the missis and her gave the devil a curly hair lapped up in a bit o' paper, and told him to go to the blacksmith's shop an 'ommer that hair straight, and when a was straight to bring him back to her. 'All right, missis', says the devil, and off a shot. When he got to the blacksmith's shop he 'ommered and 'ommered at that there hair on the anvil but the more he 'ommered the crookeder the hair got. So at last he throwed down the 'ommer and the hair and bolted, and never went back to the farmer again.

The Devil and the Hedgehog at Malvern

A hedgehog made a bet with the devil to run him a race. The hedgehog was to have choice of time and place. He picked night-time, up and down a ditch. When the time came the hedgehog rolled himself up at one end of the ditch and got a friend to do the same at the other. Then the first hedgehog started the devil off. At the other end his friend said: 'Now off we go again'. This went on at either end of the ditch until they ran the devil to death.

Silver John, the Bonesetter

John Lloyd, who was born in the late eighteenth century, lived on a farm in the Harley Valley on the Herefordshire-Radnorshire border. He knew the art of making poultices of herbs for sick sheep, and also that of manipulating and mending their bones. He was asked to help when, down the valley at Haines Mill, a young man—the miller's son—broke his leg.

A deeply reflective man, he pondered whether it was right to use his gifts to help a human being. The decision made, he set the limb— successfully. He would take no payment from the grateful miller, but agreed to take a small gift of silver, and accepted two little buttons.

Demand for his services quickly spread. More buttons followed, and also shoe buckles, a snuff box and an embossed cane. Lloyd became widely known as Silver John, the Bonesetter. Decked in his finery, and driving his own horse and trap, he travelled the border country to treat patients and to visit markets and fairs.

One autumn, though, he failed to return from the Michaelmas Fair at Builth Wells; the horse brought home an empty trap. A large-scale search found no trace of him. Early the following year at a time of severe frost {and possibly therefore in 1789} the Radnor Candlemas Fair was held on the frozen Llyn {Lake} Hylin. Fires were lit round the edge. People drank hot cider, ate cakes and skated on the ice.

In one corner of the lake a woman—the daughter of the Fforest Inn landlord—slipped, and fell face down. She was unhurt, but below her in the thick but clear ice she saw the face of Silver John. The people decided not to smash the ice to release the body, for they feared that if John's bones were broken his spirit would not rest, and they waited for a thaw. It was then discovered that Lloyd had been murdered for his silver. Those responsible were never brought to justice, but a local rhyme implied that they came from New Radnor:

> Silver John is dead and gone,
> So they came home a-singing.
> Radnor boys pulled out his eyes
> And set the bells a-ringing.

Despite the care of those who recovered his body, John's spirit is still said to haunt Llyn Hylin. His body was buried on the slopes of Great Graigau at a place where to this day the grass grows greener. Among those who have passed on his story is David Green Pryce, otherwise known as Dai the Rabbit Catcher.

Tom Reece's Ghost

Tom, like so many other of our young farm lads, was given to occasional excess in the matter of cider, and seldom, I suppose, visited Ross on a market day without bringing back a full allowance of drink. It takes a great deal, however, to make one of these practised cider-drinkers in any proper sense of the word drunk. And so Tom, though he had taken any number of pints, was still able to walk tolerably straight, and to see tolerably clear. In this state he plodded homewards one autumn evening from Ross, and without having experienced any very remarkable divergence of course found himself about 8 o'clock by the wood side on Sheppon Hill.

There he became conscious that a large Newfoundland dog—one which he had never seen before, and which he was certain was no regular dweller in the neighbourhood—was steadily keeping pace by his side. If he stopped, the dog stopped. If he hurried on the dog was still in a line with him. It turned its head neither to the right nor the left. It gave no heed to Tom's attempts at attracting it. His whistling, not the most brilliant certainly, had no effect.

'Blow the brute', said Tom. 'What the deuce is up?' And he pulled up just under a gnarled oak that hangs over the road. The dog pulled up also: and they stood for a moment, side by side, in calm contemplation. But patience was not one of Tom's most eminent qualities, nor was he very remarkable for a delicate choice of words. So with much superfluity of oaths he announced his intention of 'stopping this fuss', and he went to a hedge and drew out a stake, tried its strength on the ground, and then with courage and determination and a fresh volley of anathema he rushed at the animal telling it to go off to some unpopular region or other. But our friend had met his match. The dog had no intention of being dispatched at such short notice. When Tom began showering his blows perpendicularly, horizontally, diagonally, in every possible direction and with vehemence of all degrees, the dog quietly removed to the further side of the road, sat there in the easiest and most composed manner possible, and assumed the appearance of Tom's father, a worthy who had died a few weeks before, and whose death had given occasion to much village gossip.

The effect on Tom was immediate. The stake dropped form his hand, and he himself veering rapidly round from blasphemy to devotion, fell down on his knees in the road; and with a sort of nervous yell, which was heard, they say, in the evening breeze as far as Red Rail, poured out something between a sarcasm and a prayer.

How he got home that night Tom never told his most intimate acquaintance; only it is certain that he walked into the house about 10 o'clock 'dead sober', as his brother called it, and 'glum as a reaper when his bottle is empty'. He would give no account of himself; but day after day the change still continued to be observed. He was no longer seen at his usual haunts. He went about his work in a dull dogged temper, very different from the light-hearted vivacity which made him so popular in the village. No wonder, then, that the rumour spread through Hoarwithy that Tom had 'seen something'. What it was, when it was, why it was, was supplied at discretion according to the taste of each speaker. Everything from murder to love had its advocates. But nothing oozed out. Tom was not communicative, and his brother told no one, and little by little this nine days' wonder yielded to some other incidents. Tom's secret remained intact.

But one stormy night in February the whole family of Tom's brother, where he lodged, were cowering over the fire. Suddenly Tom got up from his seat and said 'Joe, I am going out for a bit'.

'Out tonight, Tom. Why, what ails you?'

'Oh, nought very particular. I just want to go a step or two, that's all'.

'Be easy, Tom, can't you? What's to be got going off such a night as this? Tomorrow'll do, surely'.

'Tomorrow won't do no ways, Joe'.

'Where be'est off to then?'

'Oh, not far'.

Joe's wife came to the charge. 'You know, Tom, you've been under the doctor this two weeks, and he said most particular that you wasn't to catch cold no how'.

'I tell you I must go', was his answer, 'and what's more I will go, and all the men and women in Hoarwithy shan't stop me, no nor couldn't, let 'em try ever so. Joe', he added in a low and very solemn voice, 'I'm bound to'.

And he took his hat and a stout ash stick, and just beckoned his brother to the door. 'Joe', he whispered as he set out, 'father's summoned me tonight, and I could never rest if I did not go. God knows whether I shall ever come back. No use your coming. I must go by myself. God bless you. Good night'.

He came back about 12 o'clock, and went to bed, saying very little. After a while he became more like his old self; and little by little his gloom and gravity passed away and Tom was much as he used to be. It was some days, however, before he told his brother what had happened to him.

He said that on the night in question he had received some way—he could hardly tell how—a notice to meet his father. When he went out of the house and shut the door, he did not know 'no more than a baby' where he was to go. But something put it in his mind to go to Sheppon Hill 'by that oak opposite Riggs Wood, you know, where the brute of a dog dashed me so'. And there accordingly he went. And there once again he saw his father who beckoned him to follow. And so he did, across the field to the little spinney on the bank above the river just as you go to Craddock. He took him into this wood, walking as easy as if it was clear daylight; though Tom ran his head and shoulders and his arms against boughs and stubbs at almost every step. Well, he brought him to the corner of the little wood, and told him to turn up the ground. Tom had no spade and did not relish the notion of scratching in the ground with his fingers but dared not refuse, and he had no sooner begun than the ground seemed to open of itself, and there lay a bag 'like a bag for grist, or such like'.

'Take it and throw it in the Wye', was the command. 'And which was the queerest of all', said Tom, 'though I knew quite well what the old fellow meant, as well as if he spoke it as loud as the parson, yet never a word did he really say'. There was no sound but the wind among the trees, and once or twice an old owl hooting in the air. 'Yet I knew what I must do and no mistake'.

'And what was in the bag, Tom?' said his brother.

'Heaven knows, Joe. I weren't to look, and I wouldn't have looked, not for a hundred pound. But I know that I took it and carried it straight to the river, and pitched it in as far as ever I could'.

'Was it heavy, Tom?'

'Ay, about as heavy as half a bushel of potatoes, only much smaller; and it went slick and smooth into the water making no noise at all, and then I looked to see where father was, and he was nowhere about. And then all at once a dathering came over me from my feet upwards, till it got upon my head, and then I fell down and knew nothing for I don't know how long. And when I came to again there was a half moon just got up, and the sky was all clear and dark, and the stars about here and there— and there was Walter's house standing quite plain in the moonshine. So I knew where I was, and I walked up the path in the road and came straight home. But I can tell you this, Joe, I didn't feel like myself for the deuce of a time and sometimes at my work I would feel that queer feel come over me just as if the old fellow was close to me still. I had much ado to keep from going off. But bit by bit it passed away, and I'm just, you see, pretty smart again. But I'm not a-going to hang about here any longer. I've got a mind to try some other parts'.

So Tom went to the 'works' and the last accounts state that he is getting on well, and is troubled by no further visits or comments from the 'old fellow', his father.

Beating the Rush

One summer, a friend of mine from Bromsgrove was going on holiday with his wife to the West Country. To beat the rush they decided to leave late on the Friday and travel through the night. They set off as planned, towing a little caravan.

After some hours the wife said she was feeling very tired so the husband said 'Well, go into the caravan, get undressed and put your head down, while I drive on'.

'But it's against the law to be in the caravan while it's on the move'.

'Who's to know about it?'

So he stopped the car, waited while his wife undressed and got into a bunk, and then drove on. Some hours later he felt the call of nature and stopped the car in the middle of nowhere to go over the hedge. A few moments later his wife woke up, realised what was happening, and decided to spend a penny herself. She was wearing only a short night-dress, but the night was warm and dark.

However, no sooner had she got out of the back door of the caravan and walked a few steps across the grass verge towards the hedge than she heard the car start to pull away. She called out but her husband, who'd been rather quicker than she thought in returning to the vehicle, didn't hear.

There she was in the middle of the night in the middle of nowhere, wearing only a short nightdress. What should she do? 'I'd better ring the police', she said to herself. 'I shall just have to walk along till I find a 'phone box'.

Off she went. A few cars passed but she didn't want to flag any stranger down, dressed as she was, so each time she had to hide in the hedge. It wasn't too long, fortunately, before she came on a 'phone box. The police told her to wait there.

She was relieved to see their car about ten minutes later, but also embarrassed because of her attire. One of the two policemen gave her his raincoat to put on, though. She explained what had happened. 'We'd better try and catch that husband of yours up, then'.

After a little time they saw him and pulled him over. They told the woman to wait in the car, and went over to speak to him. 'I see you're towing a caravan, sir. You wouldn't have anyone in the back, would you? You know that's against the law while the vehicle's in motion. Well, would you mind showing us in the caravan, then, sir?'

At this stage, the husband admitted that his wife was in the caravan. 'I still think we'd better check, sir', said the policeman. The husband was dumbfounded when his wife was nowhere to be seen, but then the policeman took him to their car and the story all came out. The couple, suitably embarrassed and chastened, were let off with a caution.

Did this really happen to a friend of yours from Bromsgrove? Well, the friend of a friend.

XI
DANCE & DRAMA

Traditional dance and drama flourished for centuries. The latter, in the form of mumming plays, persists in only a very few revivals but both country and morris dancing continue to thrive. Some claim that morris and mumming are relics of fertility rites whose origins lie in the distant past. This is just possible, but the point is never likely to be proved since the earliest records go back only a few hundred years. As it is, dancers and actors provide colour, music, movement and spectacle, which already amounts to a great deal. If they can bring good luck and even fertility to land and people in addition, so much the better.

Morris

The origin of morris—the word comes from *morisque* in French, though this knowledge does not advance us very far—remains obscure. Scholars cannot agree whether the dance is indigenous to the British Isles or an early import from Europe. There is no recorded trace in England before the time of Henry VII (1485-1509), but the morris dance was already well established in Herefordshire by 1609 when an anonymous pamphleteer wrote 'Lancashire for Horne-pipes: Worcestershire for Bag-pypes: but Herefordshire for a Morris-dance puts downe not onely Kent, but verie near (if one had a line enough to measure it) three quarters of Christendome'. The pamphlet was published for the occasion when twelve dancers whose ages amounted to 1,200 years performed after a horserace on Widemarsh Moor, just outside Hereford. A speech was made to introduce the event:

> Ye servants of our mightie king,
> That come from court one hundred mile
> To see our race and sport this spring,
> You are welcome—this is our country stile—
> And much good doe you, we are sorie
> That *Hereford* hath no better for yee.
>   A Horse, a Cocke, Trainsents {drag hound chases}, a Bull,
> Primero, Glecke {card games}, Hazard, Mumchance {dice games}:
> These sports through time are growne so dull,
> As good to see a Morris dance.

The twelve dancers are carefully listed, and their ages given:

James Tomkins, gentleman, of Lengerren {Llangarron}, the foreman 106 yeares
John Willis, bonesetter, of Dormington 97
Dick Phillips of Middleton 102
William Waiton, fisher and fowler, of Marden 102
William Mosse 106
Thomas Winney of Holmer 100
John Lace, tailor, of Madley 97
John Carlesse of Homlacie 96
William Maio, 'an old Souldier, and now a lusty labourer', of Egelton {?Elton} 97
John Hunt, the Hobby Horse 97
John Mando of Cradley 100
Meg Goodwin of Erdisland 120

In addition there were four 'whifflers' or crowd marshals:

Thomas Andros of Beggar Weston {Weston Beggard} 108
Thomas Price of Clodacke {Clodock} 105
William Edwards of Bodenham 108
John Sanders, ironworker, of Walford 102

Andros, Price and Winney were subsidy-men, people liable to a pay a subsidy—pecuniary aid granted by Parliament to the king for special needs—and therefore people of substance. Both Edwards and Tomkins had small children of six and eight respectively.

Music was provided by two Hereford men, Squire (aged 108), who 'tickled a trebble Violin', and Hall, a 'quack-salver' (healer) (97), than whom 'the Wayts of three Metropolitan Cities make not more Musicke than he can with his Pipe and Tabor'.

Of the oldest of the company, Meg Goodwin, we are told that she was Maid Marian to John Mando's Robin Hood, and that she was 'at Prince Arthur's death at Ludlow {in 1502} and had her part in the dole; she was threescore years (she saith) a Maide and twenty yeares otherwise'.

The costumes worn were described in this way:

The Musitians and the twelve dancers had long coates of the old fashion, hie sleeves gathered at the elbows, and hanging sleeves behind: the stuffe, red Buffin {coarse cloth}, stript with white, Girdles with white,

Morris men at the Ledbury Folk Fair, 1991

stockings white, and redde Roses to their shoes: the one sixe, a white Jews cap, with a Jewell, and a long red Feather: the other, a scarlet Jewes cap, with a Jewell and a white feather: so the Hobbi-horse, and so the Maide-Marrion was attired in colours; the Wiflers had long staves, white and red.

Sporadic references to the morris continue over the years. Edward Hall, a Ledbury innkeeper, was recorded in 1618 as being a keen amateur actor and also morris dancer. In Herefordshire women took part in the morris— as we have seen with Meg Goodwin—though the practice arouses the disapproval of some men even in the twentieth century. Villages particularly keen on morris dancing during the seventeenth century were Avenbury, Tedstone Delamere, Withington and Yazor.

'The morris dance {is} kept with great spirit', wrote Fosbroke in 1821, but less than a century later Mrs. Leather observed that 'the only morris dancers I can discover in the country {?county} ... are from Brimfield'. However, between 1800 and 1940 morris was recorded not only at Brimfield but at Bromsberrow Heath, Bromyard, Cradley, Dilwyn, Elton, Leominster, Orleton, Putley, Richard's Castle, Ross-on-Wye, St. Weonards and Weobley.

In Worcestershire during the same period the morris was regularly danced all over the county. There are records of sides appearing at Abberley (c. 1910), Drake's Broughton, Droitwich (1847), Evesham, Grafton Flyford, Hanbury (1851 and 1884), Inkberrow (before 1884), Kidderminster (1839 and 1884), Kinver (1884), Lowesmoor (c. 1917), Ombersley (1890-91), Peopleton (c.1890), Pershore (1884 and 1925), Shrawley (c.1880), Stourport, Upton Snodsbury, Upton-on-Severn (1910 and 1925), White Ladies Aston (1907) and Worcester. But this is doubtless not an exhaustive list.

Some sides danced on high days and holidays such as May Day, Midsummer, Whitsuntide or Christmas; others turned out when they were short of money, which was usually in winter. Writing in 1856, John Noake commented:

Morris dancing is still resorted to by boatmen on the Severn and the canals, whenever frost interrupts their ordinary occupations, on which occasion small parties of them, dressed up fantastically with ribbons, and carrying short sticks, which they strike together in time with parts of the dance, perform in the streets, soliciting alms.

In 1961 a Claines woman aged about 50 told Lavender Jones that she remembered exactly the same thing at Lowesmoor, a suburb of Worcester. Her mother took her as a small child to the Pheasant Inn to see the canal boatmen dancing outside when ice interrupted navigation.

In the border morris—that of Herefordshire, Worcestershire and Shropshire—the characteristic dance is done by multiples of four men, often totalling twelve in all. This is unlike the six a side of the Cotswolds, though the formation described at Hereford in 1609 mentions two groups of six. The dances were vigorous. Short sticks were clashed, except in the handkerchief dances of Evesham, Pershore and Upton, and the stepping dance of Bromsberrow Heath. The costumes worn ranged from perfunctory to elaborate. For example, the Upton dancers made do with a few ribbons attached to their shirts while those of Cradley preferred a dense garment made of matted rags. Finally, as one old dancer put it, 'You're not a morris man unless you black your face'.

Bill Scarrett of Pershore, who died in 1986, came from a fairground family which settled in the town after their equipment was destroyed by a flood in the Weir Meadow. He was a fiddler and dancer for thirty years, starting at the age of eight, two years before he left school. 'We went out before the First World War as youngsters; after the war as real dancers'.

The side would get down to practice each October so as to be ready for the Christmas season, of which the high point was Boxing Day. The men went on foot to places like Malvern or Ledbury. 'We used to walk ... As you came to a village, so you danced'. At night they put up if need be at a lodging house. One of Bill Scarrett's memories—told to Dave Jones—was dancing for two hours at Worcester in the old market opposite the cathedral. On another occasion the Pershore men went to Ross-on-Wye, pushing a handcart with their sticks and other equipment, and taking turns to ride on a tandem.

Members of the side included 'brickies, carpenters, plumbers, ordinary working fellows, fellows off the ground'. Competition for a place was lively because 'there wasn't the work about at that time of year'. Eight men usually danced. In addition there were two musicians—playing fiddle and concertina usually, but also at different times piccolo, tin whistle, triangle, tambourine and bones—together with the all-important collector, the person responsible for going round with the hat.

The favourite dance was *The Black Boy* which went to the tune of *Not for Joe*. This in turn gave the name to this style of dancing of Not for Joeing. It was not, of course, confined to Pershore—I have seen an account of something very similar from Oxfordshire—but it certainly occurred there. As well as having the tune played instrumentally the dancers from time to time would break into a snatch of the words:

Not for Joe, not for Joe,
Not for Joseph if he knows it;
Not for Joe, not for Joe,
Stick him in the garden, let him grow.

The original song was a composition—which sold 80,000 copies—by Albert Lloyd, a music hall singer of the 1860's and 70's, whose other works include *Married to a Mermaid, The Street Musician, The Organ Grinder* and *Policeman 92X*.

To the delight of Bill Scarrett, Dave Jones was able from his descriptions to reconstruct the costumes, steps and figures of the dances. In 1987 Jones founded the Old Wonder Not for Joes morris side, and it continues regularly to perform from its base at Putley, near Ledbury.

No morris side in the two counties has an unbroken history of any length but there are several flourishing revivals. Sides such as the Silurian (Malvern) and Old Wonder favour border dances. Others—Leominster and Faithful City (Worcester), for example—prefer the Cotswold Morris. Their personnel is made up no longer of hungry workmen but more often of professional people, akin to the subsidy-men of 1609. Nevertheless, old traditions are carried on, albeit with a different emphasis and function.

Mumming

As with morris there is a long history of popular drama in the two counties. Until the Reformation lavish and colourful street pageants were mounted by the city craft guilds in Hereford and Worcester. In 1503 there were twenty-five in Hereford alone; Worcester was more modest, with five a year. The Corpus Christi pageant continued in Hereford until the mid-sixteenth century—but was stopped after the accession of Edward VI—and a labourer rode into the city on an ass every year in Passion Week until 1706.

Favourite subjects for the pageants included Biblical themes such as Adam and Eve, Noah, the Annunciation and the Nativity. To some extent they were replaced by plays given by the travelling theatre companies which toured from the time of Henry VIII onwards.

Village drama in the form of Robin Hood plays staged as parish fund-raisers is recorded in Worcestershire as early as the 1470's. It is possible that Christmas mumming plays were also on the go at the time. Some claim that their central theme of death and resurrection is connected with the death of the old year and the birth of the new. Yet no example of such a play was recorded until 1738, at Exeter. The earliest text from Worcestershire was taken down by Cuthbert Bede (Rev. Edward Bradley) over the Christmas season of 1865-7. He saw 'several performances of a set of mummers who lived in the hamlets of Upper and Lower Howsell in the parish of Leigh ...; and went the round of the Malvern district with their masque'. Their version, he says, was 'handed down by oral tradition; and had been taught to the boys by their elder relatives, who had learnt it from the dictation of their seniors'. He continues:

The lads were well up in their parts, and were spirited performers. The Valiant Soldier wore a real soldier's coat; Old Father Christmas carried holly; the Turkish Knight had a turban; and all of them were decked out with ribbons and scarves, and had their faces painted. Little Devil-doubt had a black face, and carried a money-box, a besom, and a bladder; with the bladder he thwacked the performer whose turn it was to speak—a proceeding that reminds us of Mr Lemuel Gulliver and the philosophers of Laputa. Little Devil-doubt having brushed away the snow and cleared a space, the performers ranged themselves in a semicircle, and the play began.

A performance recorded by the BBC at Great Malvern in 1946 seems to have been a revival, using the Great and Little Howsell text of ninety years earlier. The Cradley play (see below) also had similarities, but then these places are only a few miles apart.

No text came to light in Herefordshire until 1908, when William Powell wrote out for Mrs. Leather the version previously performed at Ross-on-Wye. He said that 'the mumming had been discontinued of late years. He had taken all the parts at different times; the dresses worn were various and fantastic'.

The Ross-on-Wye text was the only one from Herefordshire until Dave Jones unearthed another at Cradley, some fifty years later. Even references to the play are sparse. In a poem of 1943 John Masefield mentions the youthful memory at Ledbury of the 'mummers {who} went at Christmas with their play, with Mrs Vinney who revived the dead' and he refers elsewhere to 'the figure of the St. George of a crew of mummers', this time placing the performance at an October Fair in his native town.

The relative absence, apparently, of the play from Herefordshire remains a mystery. Worcestershire is a little better off, with five places chronicled over a period ranging from 1856 to 1946: Broadway (c. 1874), Evesham (c. 1870), Great Malvern (1923 and 1946), Shrawley (c. 1880) and Upper and Lower Howsell (1856).

Performances were given in town streets and on village greens, in public houses, farms and (by invitation) mansions. The actors—always

Mummers at Much Marcle, 1987

male—stood in a line or semi-circle, stepping forward with the formulaic 'In comes I'. Speeches were delivered with due solemnity punctuated by comic relief and even horseplay, especially where the doctor's part was concerned. The series of stylised combats and deaths, followed by rapid restoration to life, was the essential point of the play. Its text—perhaps one should say texts, for there are many variations, all very similar— might not read very well on the page but both for actors and audience was (and still can be) very satisfying in performance. There are no instances in the two counties today where traditional performances survive, but revivals occur from time to time. For example, the Cradley play is now performed every Boxing Day by the Old Wonder morris side. The text concludes this chapter. It is preceded by another which dates from a century earlier.

Broadway

Taken down in 1909 by Helen Dorrill of St. Louis, Missouri, from her father who had been one of the performers in Broadway, Worcestershire, some thirty-five years previously. The players ranged in age from 14 to 21. They toured farmhouses, asking permission to perform: 'Would you like to hear the mummers tonight?' They were usually invited into the front kitchen. Old Father Christmas wore a fur cap and gloves, a long red coat and topboots. He had a wig and beard of long white hair, and the end of his nose was reddened. Beelzebub carried a club and wore a big black hat and long black coat. The doctor wore a top hat and swallow-tail coat. The soldier had a blue uniform and military cap. Little Dick Nip had a hat with a wide brim, a short coat, and carried a long stick, with a pig's bladder tied to the end. St. George wore a small hat with a feather, a dark red coat, knee-breches and low shoes. After the play the performers were usually given hot spiced ale or cider and bread and cheese, together with from two to five shillings.

Characters

Father Christmas, Beelzebub, St. George, Turkish Knight, King of Spain, Soldier, Italian Doctor, Sweet Moll, Little Dick Nip.

FATHER CHRISTMAS
In comes I, Old Christmas.
Christmas or Christmas not,
I hope Old Father Christmas will never be
  forgot.
Christmas comes but once a year,
And when it comes it brings good cheer.
Roast beef, plum pudding, and mince pie,
There's no Old Father Christmas loves better
  than I.

BEELZEBUB
A room, a room, brave gallant boys,
And give us room to reign,
For we have come to show our bold activity,
Here on a merry Christmas time.
Activity of youth, activity of age,
The like was never acted upon any stage.
If you don't believe what I say,
Enter in, St. George, and clear the way.

ST. GEORGE
St. George, that man of courage bold,
With sword and spear all by my side,
Hoping to gain the twelve crowns of gold.
'Twas I who slew the fiery dragon,
And brought him to the slaughter,
And by those fiery means I hope
To gain the Queen of Egypt's daughter.
Seven long years I was kept in a close cave
Where I made my sad and grievous mourn.
I have led the fair Sarepta from the snake,

	Which neither man nor mortal would undertake.
	I brought them all most couragely,
	And still I gain the victory.
	Show me the man who dare me.
TURKISH KNIGHT	I am the man who dare fight thee,
	The Turkish Knight,
	Come from my own Turkish land to fight.
	I will fight St. George, that man of courage bold.
	If his blood is hot I will quickly made it cold.
	(They fight)
(dropping on one knee)	Hold, hold, St. George. Another word
	From thee I have to crave.
	Spare me this time and I will arise
	To be thy Turkish slave.
ST. GEORGE	Arise, arise, thou Turkish Knight.
	Go over to thine own Turkish lands and fight.
	Tell them there the champions grow in England.
	Tell them the wonders I have done:
	I have slain ten thousand for thy one.
TURKISH KNIGHT	No, rather than tell them that,
	I cut thee, hew thee small as flies,
	And send thee to Jamaica to make mince pies.
ST. GEORGE	Mince pies I do not like;
	But another battle, then, and I will fight.
	(He kills the knight)
BEELZEBUB	A room a room, and let the prudent King of Spain come in.
KING OF SPAIN	In comes the prudent King of Spain.
	All with my glittering sword
	I have cut and slain St. George
ST. GEORGE	Thou prudent King of Spain,
	Hast thou come here to fight?
KING OF SPAIN	Yes, bold champion, and I think it is my right;
	And with thee I have come to fight.
ST. GEORGE	Firstly, thou hast challenged me, king.
	Secondly, thou hast challenged me.
	Stand forth, thou figure of a tree,
	And see who gains the victory.
	(He kills the king)
BEELZEBUB	A room a room,
	And let the valiant soldier in.

SOLDIER	In comes the valiant soldier.
	Cut and Slasher is my name,
	All from the fiery wars of Spain.
	'Twas I and seven more
	Who slew eleven score,
	And could have slain twelve thousand more,
	All brave marching men of war.
	Many a battle have I been in,
	And still fight St. George, that noble king.
	(Soldier kills St. George)
BEELZEBUB	A room, aroom, a gallant room,
	And let the little Italian Doctor walk in.
ITALIAN DOCTOR	In comes the little Italian Doctor
	Lately come from Rome, France, and Spain.
	I carry a little vial bottle
	In the waist of my break, with which I can cure.
BEELZEBUB	What canst thou cure?
ITALIAN DOCTOR	What thou canst not cure, old dad.
BEELZEBUB	Old dad, what's that?
ITALIAN DOCTOR	Rheumatic gout,
	Pains within and pains without.
	Bring me an old woman
	Of three score years and ten
	With the knuckle of her little toe broke,
	And I can set it again.
BEELZEBUB	Set it, then.
ITALIAN DOCTOR	Drop on thy brow,
(who goes round slain,	Drop on thy heart.
who lie on the floor,	Arise up, Jack,
and says over each)	And take thy part.
	(All arise. Sweet Moll enters)
ST. GEORGE *(sings)*	Sweet Moll, Sweet Moll, where art thou going
	So early and so soon?
	I have something to say to thee
	If yet that thou canst stay.

Sweet Moll, sweet Moll, where art thou go-ing, So ear-ly and so

soon?__ I've some__thing to say [to thee] If yet thou canst__ stay.__

SWEET MOLL *(sings)*   What hast thou got to say?
                        Pray tell it to me now,
                        For I am spending all my time
                        In what I can't tell how.
ST. GEORGE *(sings)*   Thy parents and mine had well agreed
                        That married we should be,
                        So pull down thy lofty looks
                        And fix thy love on me.
SWEET MOLL *(sings)*   But I must have a little boy
                        Who speaks a peevish tongue,
                        A pair of silver buckles
                        That ladies oft have on;
                        And I must have some butcher's meat
                        Of every sort and kind;
                        And in the morn a cup of tea,
                        At night a glass of wine.
ST. GEORGE *(sings)*   Won't bacon serve thy turn, Sweet Moll,
                        Some good fat powder puffs?
                        And in the morn a cup of tea,
                        And that's the farmer's cut.
                        Sweet Moll, thou hast no cause
                        To talk of silver things,
                        For thou wast not brought up in palaces
                        Amongst lords, dukes and kings.
                        And the little thou hast learnt
                        Thou hast almost forgot;
                        And if thou wilt not marry me,
                        Then thou canst go to rot.
LITTLE DICK NIP   In comes I, Little Dick Nip,
                        With my big head and my little wit.
                        My head is so big and my body so small,
                        Yet I am the biggest rogue of all.
                        My forehead is lined with brass,
                        My head is lined with steel;
                        My trousers touch my ankle bones,
                        Pray, doctor, come and feel.
DOCTOR   Yes, yes.
ST. GEORGE   A room, a room, a gallant room,
                        And let old Beelzebub in.

BEELZEBUB	In comes old Beelzebub.
	On my shoulder I carry a club,
	In my hand my dripping pan.
	Don't you think I'm a jolly old man?
	A mug of good ale will make us merry and sing,
	And a few of your half-crowns and five-shilling pieces
	In our pockets would be a very fine thing.
	(They collect, dance and sing a carol)
ALL	Here's health to her stock,
	Likewise to his flock.
	We'll take this small cup
	And we'll drink it all up;
	And then there's enough to fill it again.

(The tune for St. George and Moll's song comes from Mrs. Webb—for whom see chapter 9—an can be found in Roy Palmer (ed.), *Songs of the Midlands* (1972), page 15).

Cradley

Noted in the 1960's by Dave Jones from Albert Philpotts of Cradley, who knew it as the Cradley Morris Dance. The play was performed throughout Boxing Day at houses and pubs. All the characters were dressed in the same way, their trousers, jackets and hats being smothered in strips of rag of many colours, the effect being like that of an old pegged rug. Their faces were blacked. Some carried instruments—melodeon, tambourine, accordion, mouth organ or bones—with which to accompany the songs.

Characters

Belzebum, Noble King, Doctor, Raggety Jack, Little Billy Funny.

BELZEBUM	In comes I, Belzebum.
	On my shoulder I carry a gun,
	In my hand I carry a can.
	Don't you think I'm a jolly old man?
NOBLE KING	In comes I, the Noble King,
	Just arrived from France,
	And with my sword and lance
	I'll put old Belzebum to a dance.
	(He hits him with a sword and knocks him down)

DOCTOR	In comes I, the doctor.
NOBLE KING	How did you come to be a doctor?
DOCTOR	By my travels.
NOBLE KING	Where have you travelled?
OCTOR	I've travelled England, Scotland, Ireland and Wales; three times round the world and back again.
NOBLE KING	What can you cure?
DOCTOR	I can cure the its, the pits, the palsy and gout, Pains within and pains without. If there's nineteen devils in this man I can guarantee to knock twenty out.
NOBLE KING	Set about it, then.
DOCTOR	In my left-hand coat pocket I carry a box of pills called goosifer lucifer pills. Take one of these, old man. In my right-hand coat pocket I carry a bottle, and this is goosifer lucifer syrup. Take a drop of this, old man, and I guarantee to put you back on your feet again. *(Belzebum gets to his feet and they all sing)*
ALL *(sing)*	He'll be strolling round the town, Knocking the people down, Tasting every kind of wet, Having a fair you air you bet. Fair-o, fair-o, ricketty, racketty crew.
RAGETTY JACK	In comes I, Ragetty Jack, Wife and kids on my back. Two at the Union, two at home, Two in the corner chewing the bone. Out of ten I've got these five, And the rest have gone to the workhouse.
ALL	Fair enough, fair enough. He's only a local lad.
LITTLE BILLY FUNNY	In comes I, little Billy Funy. I'm the one that collects the money. All silver, no brass. Bad money won't pass.
ALL *(sing)*	Christmas comes but once a year And it's everyone's delight to keep it up, keep it up. We started going down the town and finished with a fight, When half a dozen of us got run in for the night.

Christ - mas comes but once a year And it's ev' - ry one's delight to keep it up,____ to keep it up.____ We start - ed go - ing
down the town and fin - ished with a fight____ When half a do - zen
of us____ got run in for the night. Just__ the same,____ boys____
yes - ter - day was we,____ For how the wind do blow____ and
all of the peo - ple know____ We all got drunk and full of dev - il -
ment,____ We left our dar - ling wives at home and arm in arm we
went____ Strol - ling round the town, Knock - ing the peo - ple
down, Tas - ting ev - er - y kind of wet, Ha - ving a fair you
air you bet. Fair - o, Fair - o, rick - et - ty, rack - et - ty crew.

241

Just the same, boys, yesterday was we,
For the wind do blow and all of the people know
We all got drunk and full of devilment,
We left our darling wives at home and arm in
    arm we went.

Strolling round the town,
Knocking the people down,
Tasting every kind of wet,
Having a fair you air you bet.
Fair-o, fair-o, ricketty, racketty crew.

XII
SEASONS

Calendar customs marking the passing of the year and its seasons have a tenacious hold on people's affections and emotions. Many of those relating to churches and farms have been considered in chapters 3 and 8 respectively; others feature here.

Although they may give the feeling of dating from time immemorial, few rituals have an unbroken history of any length, and some are of recent creation. The custom of decorating the Guildhall at Worcester on Oak Apple Day (29 May) has died and been brought back to life more than once. Several seasonal rituals listed as defunct in 1912 by Mrs. Leather—burning the bush and heaving, for example—were resurrected sixty or seventy years later. Indeed, there seems to be a current fashion, which must respond to a profound emotional need, for reviving calendar customs in particular and folk culture in general.

Commercial motives may play a part, and also civic pride or the desire to promote tourism. In other cases the joy and satisfaction generated are their own reward. For whatever reason, the celebration of turning points in the year is deeply ingrained, and one can safely predict that in one form or another it is destined to continue.

January

New Year's Day
The desire to greet the New Year now leads some people to assemble in the centre of Hereford and Worcester. Smaller places, too, have their crowds, whose enthusiasm sometimes crosses the borderline into rowdiness. Arrests were made and policemen injured at Ross-on-Wye in 1991. Undeterred the following year 1,500 people turned up outside the Market Hall. The same town has a New Year's Day walk and fun run from Court Farm, Hole-in-the-Wall, to the Hope and Anchor Inn at Ross, which in 1992 attracted 200 entrants.

In private houses many still prefer the first caller of the year to be a dark-haired male. Such a person is invited to enter by the front door and leave by the back, contrary to normal superstition which holds that a caller should enter and leave by the same door so as not to take the luck away from a house. The first footers used to greet the occupants with this rhyme:

Good master and good mistress and everybody here,
We wish you a merry Christmas and a happy New Year;
A pocket full of money and a cellar full of beer,
And a good fat bacon pig for to last all the year.

A male caller was also required both on Christmas Day and the first Monday of the New Year at Ross-on-Wye, or the household would have no luck for a year. Boys were often recruited at the price of a few coppers (pence) to act as first footers. In addition they would go round gifting—asking for a gift or a tip—on New Year's Day. At Castlemorton and also (until the 1950's) at Longdon boys and girls would go gifting round the farmhouses and say, all in one breath:

Bud well, bear well,
God send you fare well.
Every sprig and every spray,
A bushel of apples on New Year's Day.
Morning, master and mistress,
A happy New Year,
A pocket full of money,
A cellar full of beer.
Please to give me a New Year's gift.

It was considered unlucky for a house to be without mistletoe, so a small sprig was kept throughout the year, to be thrown out and replaced by another on 1 January. Until at least the 1930's Worcestershire people believed that clothes should not be washed on New Year's Day, or the person they belonged to would be dead before twelve months.

In parts of Herefordshire there was great competition to be the first to drink water from certain wells or springs after the midnight chimes had announced the New Year. For this practice at Aconbury Well, see chapter 1. At Dinedor the water of the holy well—now no longer in existence, but recorded in the name of Holywell Farm—was especially prized since a drink from the first pailful, 'the cream of the well', was thought to promote health and happiness throughout the year.

At Bredwardine Kilvert made this note in his diary for 31 December 1877 (though it refers in part to the following day):

I sat up till after midnight to watch the Old Year out and the New Year in. The bells rang at intervals all the evening, tolled just before the turn of the night and the year and then rang a joy peal, and rang on till one o'clock. After I had gone to bed I saw from where I lay a bright blaze sprung up in the fields beyond the river and I knew at once that they were keeping up the old custom of Burning the Bush on New Year's Day in the morning.

The bush was in fact a hollow globe made of twisted hawthorn shoots. In the early hours of New Year's Day it was removed from the farm kitchen where it had been kept for twelve months, filled with straw, fixed on a long pole, and set on fire. Sometimes the burning bush was used to light twelve small bonfires, after which it was consigned to a thirteenth and larger fire. A variant was that one of the men ran with some of the fire on a pitchfork across thirteen ridges of ploughland; if he could keep it alight for all thirteen it was a sign of good luck to come.

Cider was poured on a newly-prepared bush, which was then singed in the fire. The company would chant several times 'Auld ci-der', and then perhaps walk round the fire singing a carol. In liberal measure cider was drunk and cake eaten. The new bush was carefully put in the kitchen to await the following year's ceremony.

As early as the 1850's the custom was beginning to die, to the consternation of some people, one of whom (at Kington) told a farmer who was proposing not to burn the bush 'Well then, depend on it, sir, you will have no crop if you do not'. The prediction, sadly in some ways, proved unfounded.

Bush burning did continue in much of Herefordshire and parts of Worcestershire (and also Radnorshire) until late in the nineteenth century. It survived at Malvern until 1900 and at a few places near Kington and Leominster until the First World War, or perhaps even later. At Knighton-on-Teme a bush was burnt until the 1930's. Then the custom died, or at least went into limbo, but it was revived at Putley by Dave Jones in 1975 and has continued every year since.

Twelfth Night
Twelfth Night (5 January) and Twelfth Day (6 January) are otherwise known as the Vigil and Feast of the Epiphany. By act of Parliament the calendar was changed in 1752 from the Julian to the Gregorian. Eleven days were omitted in the first year, but from then on many country people insisted on sticking to the old dates, at least for certain important occasions. As well as being Twelfth Night, 5 January was therefore Old Christmas Eve. We are told that until the middle of the nineteenth century Old Christmas was observed in Worcestershire 'as much as Christmas Day itself'. In Herefordshire, and at Ross-on-Wye in particular, there was

a rooted belief that no one should borrow fire on Old Christmas Day or the following eleven days. In emergency, fire could be bought at the price of a pin.

To return to Twelfth Night, a ceremony was held then which partly resembled that of burning the bush—though without the bush. As early as 1791 this description appeared in the *Gentleman's Magazine*:

In Herefordshire, at the approach of the evening, the farmers and their friends and servants meet together, and about six o'clock walk out to a field where wheat is growing. In the highest part of the ground, twelve small fires, and one large one, are lighted up. The attendants, headed by the master of the family, pledge the company in old cider, which circulates freely on these occasions. A circle is formed round the large fire, when a general shout and hallooing takes place, which you hear answered from all the adjacent villages and fields. Sometimes fifty or sixty of these fires can be seen all at once. This being finished, the company return home, where the good housewife and her maids are preparing a good supper. A large cake is always provided, with a hole in the middle. After supper, the company all attend the bailiff (or head of oxen) to the wainhouse, where the following particulars are observed: The master, at the head of his friends, fills the cup (generally of strong ale), and stands opposite the first or finest of the oxen. He then pledges him in a curious toast: the company follow his example, with all the other oxen, and addressing each by his name. This being finished, the lage cake is produced, and, with much ceremony, put on the horn of the first ox, through the hole above mentioned. The ox is then tickled, to make him toss his head: if he throws the cake behind, then it is the mistress's perquisite; if before (in what is termed the boosy), the bailiff himself claims the prize. The company then return to the house, the doors of which they find locked, nor will they be opened till some joyous songs are sung. On their gaining admittance, a scene of mirth and jollity ensues, which lasts the greatest part of the night.

With variations, similar rituals continued for perhaps a century. One explanation of the thirteen fires is that they represented Christ and the apostles. The thirteenth, taken to represent Judas Iscariot, was quickly put out, and the materials kicked about. Near Ross-on-Wye twelve fires were lit on Twelfth Day, with one larger than the rest intended 'to burn the old witch'. At Ledbury the thirteenth fire was affectionately known as 'Old Meg'. The farm workers gathered round it to drink warm cider, eat plum cake and toast the master and crops.

At Eardisland more drinking went on in the oxen's—later the cows'—stalls, with toasts such as:

> Here's to the plough, the fleece and the pail.
> May the landlord ever flourish and the tenant never fail.

And:

> Here's to thee champion, to thy white horn,
> Here's God send the master a good crop of corn,
> Of wheat, rye, barley and all sorts of grain;
> If we live to this time twelvemonth we'll drink his health again.

Specific animals might be addressed:

> Here's to the heifer {by its name} and to the white teat,
> Wishing the mistress a house full of meat,
> With cruds {curds}, milk and butter fresh every day,
> And God grant the young men keep out of her way.

At Ledbury the song concluded:

> The leaves they are green and the nuts they are brown,
> They all hang so high they cannot come down.
> They cannot come down until the next year,
> So thee eat thy oats and we'll drink our beer {or cider}.

At Tretire the oxen were excused work throughout the twelve days of Christmas in commemoration of Christ's birth in an ox's stall. There, if the holed cake were thrown forward it belonged to the bailiff; back, and it went to the boys. Elsewhere the forward fall favoured the cowman; the backward, the dairymaid. Some places thought the former denoted good luck; the latter, bad.

Thomas Hardy's poem, *The Oxen*, begins:

> Christmas Eve, and twelve of the clock.
> 'Now they are all on their knees',
> An elder said as we sat in a flock
> By the embers in hearthside ease.

We pictured the meek mild creatures where
They dwelt in their strawy pen,
Nor did it occur to one of us there
To doubt they were kneeling then.

The notion that oxen knelt lingered in both Herefordshire and Worcestershire until the early twentieth century, but on Twelfth Night rather than on Christmas Eve. Mrs. Leather remarked that she had 'talked to many people who believed this'. She did not see Kilvert's diary—it was not published till after her death—but it has an entry (5 January 1878) which reports the experience at Staunton-on-Wye of 'old James Meredith'. 'I was watching then on old Christmas Eve and at 12 o'clock the oxen that were standing knelt down upon their knees and those that were lying rose up on their knees and there they stayed kneeling and moaning, the tears running down their faces'. A different account, published in 1924, relates how at Michaelchurch a man had witnesed 'the oxen falling on their knees, sighing and groaning piteously, with tears rolling from their eyes in torrents'.

Another renowned phenomenon, still on Twelfth Night, was the flowering of the holy thorn. The original thorn at Glastonbury in Somerset claims descent from the staff of Joseph of Arimathea, which rooted in the ground as he leaned on it. Cuttings from the Glastonbury tree or its scions were widely distributed to different parts of the country.

With his usual interest in such matters Kilvert went in January 1878 to Dolfach, near Rhayader, to see the holy thorn blooming there. He was given a sprig from it. A year later he noted 'Last night the slip of Holy Thorn which John Parry of Dolfach grafted for me last spring in the vicarage lower garden blossomed in an intense frost'. Mrs. Leather remarked in 1912 that the Bredwardine tree was dead, but listed others surviving at Colwall, Dorstone, King's Thorn, Rowlstone, Stoke Edith, Tyberton and Wormsley. One could add to these further specimens at Acton Beauchamp (Redmarley Farm), Eaton Bishop, Llangarron (Old Gore) and Orcop (Little Hill); and in Worcestershire Alfrick (Cherry Green), Hampton (near the remains of the cross), Newland (in the hedge of the garden at the Swan Inn), Ripple (The Grove) and Tardebigge.

Nearly all of these are now gone. The tree at Acton Beauchamp was cut down because of the nuisance occasioned by the large numbers of people who went to see it. The farmer soon afterwards broke an arm and a leg, and his house burnt down. At Orcop the thorn grew beside a ruined forge close to the Maltsters Inn (now The Stars) at Little Hill. In the late 1940's it attracted cars and coaches full of people on Twelfth Night, but interest

248

gradually waned, and the number of visitors fell to a handful. In January 1980 the tree blew down in a gale.

A story goes that it was once the custom to send the monarch a cutting each year from the Glastonbury thorn. One year Charles I was staying near Much Birch when his cutting arrived. He ordered it to be planted close by, and the place came to be called King's Thorn. Others were propagated from it, and there is one descendant by a narrow lane at Little Birch.

The *Worcester Journal* graphically described in 1959 how the tree at Ripple flowered at midnight:

Slowly, slowly, the buds unfold and in half an hour the holy tree is white and glistening as a hawthorn tree in main moonlight. ... Until one o'clock the tree remains in bloom, then softly the petals drop like white snowflakes and the tree is black and gaunt and common once more.

Another of the profusion of Twelfth Night customs was that of wassailing cider apple trees. Cider was poured over their roots, guns were fired three times through the branches, and songs sung:

> Here's to thee old apple tree,
> Whence thou mayest bud,
> Whence thou mayest blow {blossom},
> Whence thou mayest bear apples enow.

After many years in abeyance the ceremony was revived in 1987 at Much Marcle. The initiative came from Weston's Cider, whose managing director, Mr. Michael Roff, commented twelve months later: 'Maybe it is just a coincidence but the crop of cider fruit this year has proved to be one of the best in living memory'.

Subsequently the event grew steadily. In 1991 some 300 people, fifty of them with torches, marched from the old cider mill up the slope to the orchard. In addition to wassailing the Leominster Morris Men danced, and also performed a mumming play. Thirteen fires were lit and one, the Judas fire, was extinguished. A great deal of mulled cider was drunk at Weston's willing expense, and the occasion now seems firmly fixed in the calendar once more. Indeed, the report in the *Hereford Times* in January 1991 of 'an ancient custom dating back to Anglo-Saxon times' was already starting to imply a venerable tradition.

Such revivals seem to have the habit of catching on elsewhere. Four years after Much Marcle, Breinton—just up the Wye from Hereford— started its own apple tree wassail, on Twelfth Day rather than Twelfth

Night. (In fact, Much Marcle adopts the nearest Saturday to Twelfth Night). After taking a leading part in the wassailing the Breinton Morris Men go on a singing and dancing tour of the local public houses. Morris dancers were also involved in the now-defunct ritual of Plough Monday.

February

Eighty years ago Mrs. Leather described the custom of sending valentines as 'dying, not yet extinct'. She would have been surprised at the profusion of greetings now sent, and scandalised at such things as strippagrams. Country people used to believe that even the birds chose their mates on St. Valentine's Day (14 February).

Depending on the date of Easter, Lent begins on a Wednesday between 3 February and 9 March. The previous day is Shrove Tuesday, which used to be the occasion for horseplay, mischief-making and cruel sports such as (at Bromsgrove and Worcester) throwing sticks at tethered cockerels. More sedate was the custom at Cradley of the children's assembling at noon and joining hands to encircle the church. A Jack-a-Lent is mentioned in Worcester's chamberlain's accounts for 1653 as part of the Shrovetide procession. The figure, of straw and cast-off clothes, was dragged through the streets and then either burned or shot to pieces. It was thought to stand for Judas, but may originally have represented the old year.

The pancake bell once gave the signal to begin frying pancakes. Upton-on-Severn had a bell at 11 a.m. for 'pans on' and another at noon for 'pans off'. A Worcestershire rhyme ran:

> Hark I hear the pancake bell,
> And fritters make a gallant smell.

The custom of making pancakes on Shrove Tuesday now seems to be waning—but one makes such comments at one's peril. Mrs. Leather observed that Mothering Sunday was 'by no means forgotten, but declining'. Now it is flourishing as never before. In earlier times this was the occasion in Mid-Lent when grown children, particularly girls, were expected to visit their mothers. Taking a simnel cake as a present, and being given a celebratory meal in return, preferably of veal.

March

Easter Day is a moveable feast depending on the moon and falling between 22 March and 25 April. Good Friday was thought to be a particularly auspicious day for planting, especially for the seeds of stocks; if these were set as the sun went down their flowers would be double. Bread or hot-cross buns baked on Good Friday might be saved and hung up for good luck. After being kept until the following Easter they could be grated into a liquid which was then drunk to ease stomach-ache. Hot-cross buns were once baked only on a Good Friday but now they are on sale in some bakers' shops and supermarkets for several weeks.

Bakers themselves kept some buns, reminding people that as Christ was on his way to be crucified a washerwoman threw some dirty water over him whereas a woman carrying newly baked bread wiped him dry and gave him a loaf. Christ then said 'From henceforth blessed be the baker and cursed be the washer'. It follows that washing clothes should be

Heaving—as it was in the eighteenth century

251

Heaving—as is

avoided on Good Friday, a belief which lingered until the 1940's at Broadwas, Offenham and no doubt elsewhere. It was even considered unlucky to leave suds in a tub or boiler over Good Friday.

The rolling of decorated hard-boiled eggs by children at Churchill Gardens in Hereford was instituted on Good Friday in 1975 and has continued each year ever since. This is an example of a custom consciously transplanted from elsewhere but taking root locally.

A favoured Easter diversion was heaving, pronounced 'aving or 'oving, depending on one's area. Originally this had a religious significance to do with Christ's rising from the dead, but it became a secular celebration. In Herefordshire women were hoved on Easter Monday by other women. A party would go round farms and houses, the youngest girl carrying a bunch of flowers. They went in and sang 'Jesus Christ is risen again', then each woman in the household was in turn put in a chair and lifted. Her feet were sprinkled with drops of water from the girl's flowers, which were dipped in a basin beforehand. On Easter Tuesday the men conducted a similar exercise.

Perhaps at a later stage the practice of one sex's lifting the other came in. This was certainly the case in Worcestershire where in some places—Alvechurch and Hartlebury, for example—women were lifted on the Monday; others—Kidderminster and Worcester—on the Tuesday. At Hartlebury farmers' wives believed that if their maidservants were heaved they would break no crockery during the ensuing year.

Heaving continued at Worcester until the 1850's, its last outposts being the slum areas of Birdport and Dolday (which were later cleared of houses and are now respectively a car park and bus station). At Kidderminster the women, gaily dressed for the occasion, would bedeck a chair with ribbons and stretch a rope across the street. Any man then passing—and one wonders how many men did pass by accident—was seized, put in the chair, raised aloft, and turned three times. After being returned to earth he was kissed by all the women and released on making a contribution towards the 'thirsty amazons'' evening of drinking and dancing. Next day it was the men's turn to take the active role. In 1834 the custom was adapted to political campaigning: the popular M.P., Richard Godson, was heaved by women at forty-seven public houses and given—it was calculated—2,160 kisses.

Heaving lasted longer than anywhere else in the factories and pubs of Kidderminster, but even there it was only a memory by the turn of the nineteenth century. In Herefordshire 'it degenerated into wickedness, and is now discontinued', according to a comment of 1887. Detailed documentation is unfortunately not provided.

A century later heaving was revived, and featured at the Ledbury Folk Fair in 1989. This was the week before Easter. Women and men took turns to lift each other on the same day. Kissing was restored to the ceremony, and the spectators contributed to a collection for charity. In the next two years the decorated chairs had increased to three, including one from Worcester, so it seems that the custom in adapted form may again return to the calendar. Only time will tell.

April

All Fools' Day (1 April) continues to have an appeal, though it is far from being a major festival. On St. Richard's Day (3 April) well dressing used to take place at Droitwich (see chapter 3). Tenbury Fair is held on 22 April, and Orleton Fair on the following day (St. George's Day), which are the traditional dates in those localities when the cuckoo is expected to be first heard. At Monnington on May Eve (30 April) people renewed the birch and rowan twigs nailed outside barns and houses to keep witches at bay. Rogationtide—Rogation Sunday, the fifth after Easter, can fall in April or May—was the classic time for beating parish bounds (see chapter 3).

May

May Day was once one of the highlights of the year. After the Restoration some of its customs gravitated to 29 May but others remained. In Worcestershire it was known as Robin Hood's Day. There is a story—also ascribed to Leicestershire—that Bishop Latimer was riding down from London when he decided to make a stop at a Worcestershire village and preach there. He found the church locked. After half an hour a key was produced, with the comment 'Sir, this is a busy day for us. We cannot hear you now; it is Robin Hood's day. The parish are gone about to gather for Robin Hood. I pray you hinder them not'. The reference is no doubt to the Robin Hood pageants or plays of which a relic lingered at Hartlebury in the May Day gathering of the Foresters' Club whose members assembled at the Mitre Oak public house before processing through the village led by people dressed as Robin Hood, Maid Marian and Friar Tuck.

1 May was a holiday for those farm labourers attending a hiring fair (see chapter 8) in search of a new master. In Herefordshire the expression 'maffering' meant 'gone to May Fair' and, by extension, having a good time. Hereford May Fair is still held though now purely for pleasure rather than the sale of goods which was the case in much earlier times. The earliest extant charter—and fairs were permitted only by charter from the king or some great noble—dates from the early twelfth century, though this may have confirmed an even earlier grant, for the event was also known as St. Ehelbert's Fair. The rights were vested in the bishop, which gave the alternative name of Bishop's Fair. Tolls could be levied on goods. Those offending during the nine days of the fair could be brought to summary trial before a Court of Piepowder, whose name derives from the French, *pieds poudrés* (duty feet), which was an apt designation for the fair-goers. Successive bishops of Hereford (or rather their bailiffs) ran the fair for many centuries, starting every year on 19 May, until the rights

Maypole at Upper Chilstone, Madley (Alfred Watkins)

passed to Hereford Corporation in 1838. Even then the bishop received an annual payment of twelve and a half measures of the best wheat in compensation. In 1951 a full civic proclamation of the fair took place, in commemoration of the Festival of Britain which was held that year.

At Hereford May Day was also the occasion for madrigal singing from the top of the cathedral tower. The custom lapsed for almost a century before being revived in 1988. Still in Hereford, sweeps and milkmaids celebrated on 1 May. Writing in 1879, 'Nonagenarian', recalled:

We used to go every May-day to Broomy-hill, and dance round the May-pole, and play at stool-ball, and have cake and cider; and the milk-women used to dance with the milk-pails on their heads. They used to dress the pails with all sorts of beautiful silver things, which they borrowed, and they used to shine in the sun, and as the women danced so these spoons and cream jugs, and all these things, used to make music along with the fiddle.

On the same day on Sweeps' Green at Broomy Hill the chimney sweeps 'took their brooms and made merry'. At Evesham:

the streets were crowded, and a number of sweeps issued from the Bewdley (the part of the town where they principally resided), dressed in fantastic attire, made of gaily coloured ribbons, paper, etc., hats of various shapes; also carrying various instruments of their craft, accompanied with a gaily-decorated vehicle, in which was seated the Queen of the May and the Little Boy Sweep.

The only place in the whole country where such a festival is now held is Rochester in Kent, where it was revived just a few years ago.

The classic May ritual involving 'joy and gratitude to providence on the return of spring' was described by John Duncumb in 1804:

On the first day of May, the juvenile part of both sexes rise early in the morning, and, walking to some neighbouring wood, supply themselves with green branches of trees. Returning home, the boughs are placed against the doors and houses, and are kept there during the remainder of the day.

In addition, maypoles—often birch trees—were brought back. One was photographed at Upper Chilstone (Madley) in 1924. Some Worcestershire villages—Bayton, Hartlebury and Offenham, for example—had permanent maypoles.

The May ceremonies were often criticised on the grounds that they provided too many opportunities for immorality and drinking. Later there was a trend towards making them into children's events. The village of Hallow a few miles up the Severn from Worcester revived its May Day customs in the early 1950's, claiming to celebrate in 'the good old-fashioned way'. A photograph of 1951 shows the plaiting of ribbons by the dancers, but this practice was introduced from the continent by John Ruskin as late as 1888.

After the battle of Worcester in 1651 the future Charles II eluded pursuing parliamentary soldiers by hiding in an oak tree at Boscobel House in Shropshire; birds—one version says an owl—perching in the tree remained undisturbed, and flew off only at the approach of the troopers who concluded that no one could be hiding there. When Charles was formally restored to the throne on 29 May (in 1660) this date, combined with commemorative oak leaves and sprays, came to be regarded in many places as the real May Day.

Until well within living memory children sported sprigs of oak on Oak Apple Day (the same 29 May), in default of which their fellows would sting their bare arms or legs with nettles. One village keeps up the custom still: Dilwyn. As late as the 1930's every beehive at Three Hills in Worcestershire was decorated with its own spray of oak. At Bromyard 'you'd see Maypoles all the way down Sheep Street, decorated with oak boughs and flowers, and people dancing round them, all wearing oak leaves'. Every house in Bosbury had its spray of oak over the door, and at Kingsland a great bough was hoisted to the top of the church tower. The same was done at Alvechurch and Clent.

At the Restoration there were extraordinary rejoicings in Worcester. However, Charles II never returned to the 'Faithful City', which in the eighteenth century became strongly Whig and Hanoverian. In the 1790's the Tory faction revived the practice of decking the Guildhall with oak boughs and holding processions on 29 May. The latter lasted until the 1860's, and the day was taken as a good opportunity by the people of Dolday. 'Gangs of "largesse" gatherers perambulated the adjoining streets, some of the males wearing exaggerated crinolines—if it be possible to exaggerate a fashionable garment of that description'. Even the decoration of the Guildhall lapsed but was revived in 1938, and continues to this day.

Another Oak Apple Day revival takes place at Upton-on-Severn, where on the nearest Saturday to 29 May the town crier starts proceedings at 10.15 a.m. In addition to a fair, archery, skittles, a pig roast and a barn dance, there is processional dancing from Old Street, through High Street,

At the Upton Festival, 1990

Dunns Lane and Waterside. People wear seventeenth century dress. Morris dancers and street entertainers perform. Charitable agencies raise funds at a multitude of stalls. The whole event is organised by the Upton-on-Severn Tourist Association.

Children's dancing is also included in the Upton programme. The scene would have been familiar to an observer of 1893 who wrote:

On May-pole day, the 29th of May, the children, assisted by their parents, decorate a pole with may-blossom and with flowers. ... The May-pole is carried from house to house by two or three strong lads and, at intervals, is set up and held in an upright position ... while the children join hands and dance round it, singing:

> All around the May-pole we will trot,
> See what a May-pole we have got;
> Garlands above and garlands below,
> See what a pretty May-pole we can show.

A very similar celebration is still held at Elmley Castle where on Spring Bank Holiday Monday—this recent Bank Holiday, the last Monday in May, is very close to Oak Apple Day—the Women's Institute also holds a wayside market, asserting an ancient right.

At the Spring Bank Holiday in 1991 the Bishop Heys Ladies Morris side revived the tradition of maypole dancing at Bredwardine, Dorstone and Hay-on-Wye. As well as morris, they performed three different maypole dances.

Finally, the Heart of Oak Friendly Society at the village of Fownhope has (or used to have) its club gathering on the nearest Sunday to Oak Apple Day. Sticks bearing wooden oak apples and fresh flowers are paraded to the church for a service, preceded by the club's banner and oak bough with red, white and blue ribbons.

June

Whitsunday, seven weeks after Easter, falls between 14 May and 10 June. Trinity Sunday is the first after Whitsun.

Until 1850 'Ditching the Mayor of Bewdley Street' took place at Evesham during Whit Week. The man chosen as a kind of mock mayor was taken down the street on a cart. If he could hang on when the crowd tried to dislodge him he was taken back for more drinks until such time as he could cling to the cart no longer and was tipped into a ditch at the bottom of the street.

June was a great month for wakes and fairs. Grafton on the slopes of Bredon Hill had a gathering for games and competitions on Whit Monday. John Drinkwater frequently stayed at the village, which inspired two of his poems, 'At Grafton' and 'Dreaming John at Grafton'. Broadway Wake followed on Whit Tuesday and Wednesday, and still exists as a fair on the village green. An example from Herefordshire is King's Caple, which held its Club Feast, including dancing and nine-pin bowling, on Whit Tuesday.

On Trinity Sunday came Claines Week, despite attempts to suppress it because of 'scenes of fighting, drunkenness and debauchery'. Cropthorne, also in Trinity Week, offered a wealth of traditional sports. In the back-sword or single-stick contests the first to draw blood was the winner, so fighters drank a mixture of vinegar and gunpowder which they believed would inhibit bleeding. People ducked into water to take oranges in their mouths and into flour to retrieve treacle-covered coins. Two boys with hands tied behind their backs simultaneously tried to eat a bun hanging from a string. Races included wheelbarrow (blindfold), sack, old men's, old women's, boys' and girls'. To win a leg of mutton one had to shin up a greasy pole and collect a bunch of flowers from the top. There were wrestling, shin-kicking, quoits, skittles, and nine-pins. Hornpipes and jigs were danced to the music of fiddle, flute and tambourine. The wake was organised for over forty years by C.F. Stratton, landlord of the New Inn.

Brampton Bryan or Bron Fair was on 22 June. Until 1970 a horse fair was held under a charter of Henry III dating from 1252. The delicacy of the day was Bron Fair Cakes, similar to Shrewsbury Cakes.

On Midsummer Eve (23 June) the people of Church Street in Kidderminster still enjoy their Feast of Peace and Good Neighbourhood which is claimed to date from time immemorial. Funds have been periodically topped up by legacies such as the £150 left for investment in 1776 by a local bachelor, John Brecknell. The items provided are a farthing loaf and a twopenny plum cake for every child and unmarried person born in Church Street; a piece of cake for all residents; and pipes, tobacco and ale for all the men living there.

Midsummer Day was the occasion for Bromsgrove's horse and pleasure fair, perhaps because 24 June is also the Feast of St. John. The horse fair lapsed in the early twentieth century but the pleasure fair continues. So does the Court Leet which meets on the Saturday after 24 June, though its high bailiff, ale-taster and the like now have only ceremonial functions.

Pershore Fair is held on 26 June (the Feast of St. Edburga) and the two days following. By ancient custom anyone hanging out a bush (or bough, or even a cabbage) had the right to sell beer during the fair, until the magistrates intervened in 1865 and declared the practice illegal.

Some of the functions of the old fairs and wakes are now filled by agricultural shows such as the enormous Three Counties Show held on a premanent site near Malvern in mid-June.

July

On the second Sunday of July it was the custom at Chaddesley Corbett to put any stranger 'through the whoop'. The procedure followed is unclear since those in the village who remember it are reticent about giving details. Presumably it was a way of demanding largesse.

Wakes and fairs continued in July. At Huntington (near Kington) from 1403 till 1956 a fair associated with St. Thomas à Becket was held during the month. Richard de Brito, one of Thomas's murderers, built the church and dedicated it to him in an attempt at expiation. St. Thomas's relics were translated on 7 July, and the fair held on the 18th. the difference in dates perhaps being due to the change in the calendar again. Originally all forms of livestock were sold; latterly, only horses, including the mountain ponies known as 'munts'. The animal reaching the highest price of the day was ceremonially ridden through the public house in the village.

Richard de Brito as a further penance paid for the north chapel to be built in the old church at Dorstone. His workmen are said to have been housed in the village at the Pandy Inn, which claims to be the oldest licensed premises in Herefordshire.

Other fairs of the month include Ross (19-21 July, St. Margaret's Day, its eve and morrow), Hartlebury (the first Sunday after 25 July; now gone) and Clent (28 July, St. Kenelm's Day; see chapter 3). The modern Bromyard Gala is also held in July.

August

On Lammas Day (1 August) common land which had been fenced off while hay grew was thrown open again for pasture. The meadows by the River Lugg at Lugwardine—in 1991 the subject of an enquiry over a plan for a by-pass for Hereford—preserve many features of the mediaeval system. Land is still in strips, with boundaries marked by 'mere stones', many of which bear their owners' initials, and some are dated. The management of the meadows is overseen by the commoners' association which carries on the function of the old manorial court.

Guarding the Lammas Bread, the first made from the grain of the new harvest. From a misericord at Ripple

September

The Bromyard Folk Festival, founded in 1967 on the initiative of Dave Jones, is held during the third week. From an initial budget of £125 it grew to a multi-thousand pound event, and one of the premier festivals for traditional folk music. Jones continued to organise it for 24 years until his untimely death in 1991. Each year, a gathering of some 2,000 people from all over the country is entertained by singers, musicians and morris dancers. The festival-goers are far from passive, and many—perhaps most—join in the singing, dancing and story-telling, not to speak of the drinking.

Until the middle of the nineteenth century the Lawless Hour was kept up at Kidderminster on the first Monday after Michaelmas Day (29 September). The understanding was that the high bailiff left office at noon but his successor did not take over till 1 p.m. With no one formally in charge of the town, officers could make no arrests for damage to property nor, within limits, for personal injury. The ringing of the town bell at noon unleashed, to the ritual cry of 'kellums, kellums', volleys of old shoes, cabbage stalks and other missiles in a bout of good-natured strife.

At times the battle became unduly violent but when magistrates attempted in 1822 to curtail the festivities a serious riot ensued. The town authorities continued to support the custom, and provided large quantities of apples which were thrown to the crowd.

October

This was one of the classic months for mops (see chapter 8).

Hallowe'en (30 October) was feared rather than celebrated in the past, but parties are a fairly common occurrence now. However, they seldom include the attempts at divining a future husband which used to be made on the day by young women (see chapter 4). Some children have taken to going round in fancy dress, knocking on doors and demanding a 'trick or treat'. The practice has been condemned as an import from America but it originally travelled there from this country.

November

Guy Fawkes Night (5 November) is still a lively, popular festival, though some of the rhymes and chants associated with it have fallen out of use. In Herefordshire boys marched round shouting:

> Remember, remember the fifth of November,
> Gunpowder, treason and plot.
> Remember, remember the fifth of November
> Shall never be forgot.

The Worcestershire equivalent was chanted by gangs of men and boys as they went round houses asking for fuel for their fire. They thumped on the ground with sticks for emphasis, particularly on the words plot, forgot and faggit. The last couplet is as clear a threat as today's trick or treat:

> O don't you remember the fifth of November
> Is gunpowder, trayson and plot?
> I don't see the rayson why gunpowder trayson
> Should ever be forgot.
> A stick and a stake for Queen Victoria's sake,
> I pray, master, give us a faggit;
> If you don't give us one we'll take two,
> The better for us and the wuss for you.

Until the twentieth century an even more elaborate song was sung:

> Guy Fawkes and his companions did contrive
> To blow the Houses of Parliament up alive,
> With three-score barrels of powder below
> To prove old England's wicked overthrow;
> But by God's mercy all of them got catched
> With their dark lanterns and their lighted match.
> Ladies and gentlemen sitting by the fire,
> Please put hands in pocket and give us our desire;
> While you can drink one glass we can drink two,
> The better for we and the worse for you.
> Rumour, rumour, pump-a-derry,
> Prick his heart and burn his body,
> And send his soul to Purgatory.

On St. Martin's Day (11 November) until at least the 1980's a squad of infantry paraded colours through the ruins of St. Stephen's Without at Worcester. The original troop was recruited by Colonel Montagu of Pershore for Wellington's march on Badajoz in 1812. Opposite the church seven felons were gibbeted in 1704, and some who go near on February evenings experience a feeling of dread.

St. Clement's Day (23 November) is followed two days later by St. Catherine's Day. The former was one of the ancient quarter days. The Dean and Chapter of Worcester Cathedral used to close their audit on the latter, marking the occasion by a distribution of spiced wine in the 'Cattern Bowl' to residents in the college precincts.

Worcestershire children went round singing on both days, a custom apparently not observed in Herefordshire. As early as 1827 a correspondent wrote to William Hone about a celebration common in his native Worcestershire:

On the afternoon of St. Clement's day, a number of boys collected together in a body, and went from house to house; and at the door of each house, one, or sometimes more, would recite, or chaunt, the following lines -

> Catherine and Clement, be here, be here;
> Some of your apples, and some of your beer;
> Some for Peter, and some for Paul,
> And some for him that made us all.
> Clement was a good old man,
> For his sake give us some;
> Not of the worst, but some of the best,
> And God will send your soul to rest.

Sometimes grown men would go in like manner, and, to such, the people of the house would give ale or cider; but to the boys they gave apples, or, if they had none to spare, a few halfpence. Having collected a good store of apples, which they seldom failed to do, the boys repaired to some of their houses, where they roasted and ate the apples; and frequently the old would join the young, and large vessels of ale or cider would be brought in, and some of the roasted apples thrown hot into it, and the evening would then be spent with much mirth and innocent amusement; such as, I sorrow to think, have departed never to return.

Yet the custom did continue at Alvechurch, for example, until 1900. Just a few years earlier this account came from Hartlebury:

'Catten and Clementing', by the youths of this parish and the adjoining parish of Chaddesley, is still indulged in on the night of 23rd. November, by the lads going round to the principal houses and repeating the following verses, but the last verse is used in connection with the same at Hartlebury only: and the boys occasionally take with them a 'Hoberdy' lantern, that is a light placed within a hollow turnip, having eyes, nose and mouth cut therein, which gives them a weird appearance.

> Catherine and Clement come year by year,
> Some of your apples and some of your beer,
> Some for Peter, some for Paul,
> Some for the merry boys under your wall.

Peter was a good old man,
For his sake give us some;
None of the worst, but some of the best,
And pray God send your souls to rest.
Butler, butler, fill the bowl,
Dash it up against the wall;
Up the ladder, and down the can,
Give us a red apple and we'll be gone.
   A plum, a plum, a cherry, a cherry,
   A cup of perry will soon make us all merry.
We go a Cattin, a Cattin we go,
From Hitton to Titton, as soon you shall see;
From Hitton to Pitton, Hartlebury all three,
Round by old Kiddy, and good Hillintree;
Then down to old Arley, Astley and Shrawley go nimbly,
And finish up at Holt, Hallow and Grimley.

Some places—Harvington, Leigh, Offenham—preferred St. Catherine's Day itself for their collecting.

December

St. Thomas's Day (21 December) was another of the occasions during the winter when people were by tradition allowed to collect. The activity was called thomasing, gooding or mumping. In Herefordshire a sack of wheat was set at every farmhouse door and any woman who called to ask was given a quartern measure of it. In the Stourbridge area of Worcestershire old women and widows asked for a 'gaud'—possibly meaning a celebratory gift—or 'good'. They curtsied and said 'Please to remember St. Thomas'. It was considered unlucky to refuse. Other collectors sang:

Bud well, bear well,
God send spare well.
A bushel of apples to give
On St. Thomas's morning.

At Evesham the words were:

A wissal, a wassal about the town:
Got any apples, throw them down.
Jug's white, ale's brown;
This is the best house in the town.

265

Holly and ivy and mistletoe bough,
Give me an apple and let me go.
Up the ladder and down the wall,
Up the stocking and down the shoe.
Got no apples, money'll do;
Got no money, God bless you.

According to local author Fred Archer a boy who may have been the last of the thomasers sang before dawn at Ashton-under-Hill in 1963:

Here I come a-thomasin',
A-thomasin', a-thomasin'.
Here I come a-thomasin'
So early in the morning.

The first words of the Evesham song are a corruption of 'wassail', a word of ancient pedigree meaning 'be well' or 'good health'. The wassail bowl typically contained lambs' wool—a mixture of hot ale, spices, sugar and roasted apples, to which eggs and thick cream were sometimes added. In some family gatherings during the festive season each person in turn took an apple from the bowl and ate it, then drank the health of the company.

Wassailers also toured houses and farms with their bowl, which might hold up to two gallons. In Herefordshire they flourished in the neighbourhood of Bromyard. Led by their captain they sang various songs and carols, but always:

Wassail, wassail, round the town,
Your bread is white, your ale is brown.

At each house their bowl would be replenished with punch made from hot cider, gin, nutmeg and sugar. The wassailers were also given toast and money. A Worcestershire variant of their song begins:

Wassail, wassail, all over the town,
Our toast it is white and our ale it is brown.
Our bowl is made of the white maple tree,
With the wassailing bowl we'll drink to thee.

On Christmas Eve bees were thought to sing in the hive. At Tenbury the cows knelt in the byre at midnight (as oxen did elsewhere on Twelfth

Night), and twelve fires were lit to bring twelve months of fruitfulness. The old mistletoe bough which had hung in the kitchen for a year was taken down and replaced with a new. In Herefordshire, though, new mistletoe was not brought in until New Year's Day (and was taken down with the rest of the decorations at Candlemas). Ivy and holly were brought in on Christmas Eve, holly especially being unlucky at any other time. The Yule log would also be drawn to the fireplace. People were careful to retain some fragments of it for a year; among other things they warded off lightning.

At Bewdley on Christmas morning it was the custom to allow servants and apprentices to lie in bed while the mistress of the house got up to begin the work. The bellman (mentioned in a local rhyme quoted in chapter 1) went round the town to make known his request for a tip by singing:

> Arise, mistress, arise,
> And make your tarts and pies,
> And let you maids lie still;
> For if they should rise
> And spoil your pies
> You'd take it very ill.
> Whilst you are sleeping in your bed,
> I the cold wintry nights must tread.
> Past twelve o'clock. Ehe!

Then he called 'Good morning, masters and mistresses all. I wish you all a merry Christmas'.

On Christmas Day the morris dancers or mummers (see chapter 11) might come round, or carol singers (chapter 9). At the village of Blakemere a holy thorn bloomed at midnight (as others did on Twelfth Night). Boxing Day was once the time for shooting pigeons in Worcestershire. A different kind of slaughter was the killing of the wren, a most unlucky bird to kill on any other day. John Masefield remembered from his youth that 'some young savages still killed the wren on St. Stephen's Day' (26 December). A happier tradition at Lower Ballingham was a broom dance at the inn on the same morning, to the accompaniment of a fiddle normally kept behind the bar.

On New Year's Eve a farmer at Queenhill, near Upton-on-Severn, until the 1950's put out all his loose money on the grass in front of the house to bring him luck in the ensuing year. In both counties farm workers went into public houses to 'bury Old Tom'. There seems to be no full description of the proceedings in existence, but they involved a mock funeral followed by dancing, cider-drinking and singing. There were all kinds of songs, but this one was never missed out:

> We wish you a merry Christmas, a happy New Year,
> A pocket full of money and a cellar full of beer,
> And a good fat pig to serve you all the year.

Bibliography

Unless otherwise stated the place of publication of books listed is London.

Allies, Jabez *On the Ancient British, Roman, and Saxon Antiquities and Folk-lore of Worcestershire* (London and Worcester, 1852)

Amphlett, Dorothy *Worcestershire Folklore* in F.B. Andrews, *Memorials of Old Worcestershire* (1911)

Amphlett, John *A History of Clent* (1907)

Anderson, Joseph *The Witch on the Wall. Medieval Erotic Sculpture in the British Isles* (Copenhagen and London, 1977)

Anderson, William *Green Man* (1990)

Anderton, Thomas *Letters from a Country House* {Hagley Hall} (1891)

Anon. *Manuscript Song Book* (Hereford Record Office, AD 41/1)

　　　Old Meg of Herefordshire for a Mayd Marian (London, 1609; Malvern, 1982)

　　　Worcestershire Folklore, in *The Three Pears Worcester Arts Magazine*, no.4 (1929), 6-9

Archer, Fred *The Secrets of Bredon Hill* (1971)

　　　When Adam was a Boy (1979)

Aubrey, John *Brief Lives*, ed. Oliver Lawson Dick (Harmondsworth, 1962)

Bannister, A.T. *The Place-names of Herefordshire. Their origin and Development* (Hereford, 1916)

Bannister A.T. *Sutton Walls and the Legend of St. Ethelbert*, in the *Woolhope Transactions* (1917), 221-6

Barnard, E.A.B. (ed.) *Notes and Queries concerning Evesham and the Four Shires* (2 vols, 1911)

Bede, Cuthbert {Edward Bradley} *Modern Mumming*, in *Notes and Queries*, 2nd ser., 40 (1861), 271-2

Bentley, Samuel *History and Description of the Parish of Bosbury* (1891)

Berkeley, Mrs. *Some Local Superstitions*, in *Reports and Papers of the Associated Architectural Societies*, 36, pt 1 (1921), 103-116

Berkeley, M. amd Jenkins, C.E. (eds) *A Worcestershire Book* (Worcester, 1932)

Brassington, W. Salt *Historic Worcestershire* (Birmingham, Leicester, Leamington and London, n.d. ? 1894)

Briggs, K.M. *The Fairies in Tradition and Literature* (1967)

Bright, Allan H. *Colwall and the Neighbourhood*, in *Woolhope Trans.* (1921-3), 178-184

Broadwood, Lucy, and Fuller Maitland, J.A. (eds) *English County Songs* (1893)

Brunvand, Jan Harold *The Choking Doberman and Other 'New' Urban Legends* (Harmondsworth, 1987)

Burton, John E. *A History of Bewdley* (1883)

Bushaway, Bob *By Rite. Custom Ceremony and Community in England, 1700-1880* (1982)

Capes, Canon *The Bishop's Fair* (Hereford, n.d.)

Cave, E.L. *The Burning of the Bush*, in *Woolhope Trans.* (1898), 5-8

Cawte, E.C., Helm, Alex, and Peacock, N. *English Ritual Drama* (1967)

Chamberlain, Mrs. *A Glossary of West Worcestershire Words* (1882)

Clay, W.K. (ed.) *Four Folk Songs from Hartlebury, Worcestershire* (Kidderminster, n.d. ? 1909)

Coleman, D.J. *A Historical Study of the Village of Orcop in Herefordshire* (Typewritten thesis in Hereford City Library, 1967)

Corbett, Edward C. *Some Notes on the Folklore of Worcestershire*, in *Worcestershire Naturalist Club Transactions*, 5, pt 2 (1912), 348-62

Some Worcestershire Fairy Tales, in *Worcestershire Archaeological Society Transactions*, 2 (1943-5), 22-29

Crawford, Phyllis *In England Still* (Bristol, 1938)

Dayus, Kathleen *Her People* (1982)

Defoe, Daniel *A Tour through the Whole Island of Great Britain* (Harmondsworth, 1971; orig. 1724-6)

Devlin, J. Dacres *Helps to Hereford History, ... The Mordiford Dragon; and other subjects* (1848)

Duncumb, John *Collections towards the History and Antiquities of the County of Hereford* (2 vols, Hereford, 1804)

Dunn, George *George Dunn. The Minstrel of Quarry Bank*, ed. Roy Palmer (Dudley, 1984)

Edminson, Vera L. *Ancient Misericords in the Priory Church, Great Malvern* (Worcester, n.d.)

Fletcher, A.W. *Eckington. The Story of a Worcestershire Parish* (1933)

Fletcher, H.L.V. *Herefordshire* (1948)

The Wye Valley (1968)

Folklore, Myths and Legends of Great Britain (1973)

Fosbroke, Thomas Dudley *Ariconensia; or Archaeological Sketches of Ross, and Archenfield* (Ross, 1821)

The Wye Tour (Ross, 3rd ed., 1826)

Gaunt, Peter *The Cromwellian Gazetteer* (Gloucester, 1987)

Gibbings, Robert *Coming Down the Wye* (1942)

Goodyear, G.H. *Stourbridge Old and New* (1908)

Grigson, Geoffrey *The Englishman's Flora* (St. Albans, 1958)

Grindrod, Charles F. *The Shadow of the Raggedstone* (1888)

Gwilliam, H.W. *Old Worcester. People and Places* (2 vols, Worcester, 1977)

Worcestershire's Hidden Past (Bromsgrove, 1991)

Hackwood, F.W. *Oldbury and Round and About in the Worcestershire Corner of the Black Country* (Wolverhampton and Birmingham, 1915)

Haggard, Andrew *Dialect and Local Usages of Herefordshire* (1972)

Havergal, F.T. *Herefordshire Words and Phrases* (Walsall, 1887)
    Records Historical and Antiquarian of the Parish of Upton Bishop (Walsall and Hereford, 1883)

Hazlitt, W.C. *Dictionary of Faiths and Folkore* (1905)

Heins, Nigel *Sad Story* in *Hereford Times*, 14 Aug. 1986
    The Robed Ghost of Hereford in *Hereford Times*, 26 Dec. 1991
    Silver John in *Hereford Times*, 20 Feb. 1992

Herefordshire Federation of Women's Institutes *The Herefordshire Village Book* (Newbury and Hereford, 1989)

Hickin, Norman E. *The Natural History of an English Forest. The Wild Life of Wyre* (Shrewsbury, 1978)

Hole, Christina *British Folk Customs* (1976)
    Witchcraft in England (1977)

Holloway, John (ed.) *The Oxford Book of Local Verses* (Oxford, 1987)

Hone, William (ed.) *The Every-day Book and Table Book* (3 vols, 1826-38)

Hopkinson, Jean (ed.) *A Pocketful of Hops* (Bromyard, 1988)

Hurle, Pamela *Hanley Castle. Heart of Malvern Chase* (London; Chichester, 1978)
    Upton. Portrait of a Severnside Town (Chichester, 2nd ed., 1988)

Huskinson, A. *Kellums or the Lawless Hour* in *Worcestershire Countryside*, 1, no.8 (1948), 201

Johnson, Andrew, and Punter, Stephen *Aspects of Herefordshire* (Logaston, 1987)
    Aspects of Worcestershire (Logaston, 1989)
    Walks and More (Logaston, 1990)

Johnson, Richard *The Ancient Customs of Hereford* (London and Hereford, 1868)

Jones, Dave *The Roots of Welsh Border Morris* (Putley, 1988)

Jones, John, Morgan, June, and Morgan, Ernest (eds.) *Dorstone 1890-1990* (Dorstone, 1990)

Jones, Lavender *Customs and Folklore of Worcestershire* (1970)
    A Nest of Singing Birds. The Life and Work of Ella Mary Leather of Weobley (n.p., 1978)

Jones, P. Thornesby *Welsh Border Country* (1938)

Jordan, George *Bewdley* (Manuscript in Worcester City Library, 1864)

Joyce, F. Wayland *Tenbury. Some Record of its History* (Oxford, 1931)

Judge, Roy *The Jack-in-the-Green. A May Day Custom* (Cambridge, 1979)

Keates, Jonathan *The Companion Guide to the Shakespeare Country* (1979)

Kilvert, Francis *Kilvert's Diary*, ed. William Plomer (3 vols, 1940)

Klausner, D. *Records of Early English Drama: Herefordshire, Worcestershire* (Toronto, 1990)

Ledbury, E.J. *Worcestershire Superstitions* in *Folkore*, 6 (1895), 305

La Trobe, John Antes *The Music of the Church* (1831)

Lawson, Emily M. *The Nation in the Parish, or, Records of Upton-on-Severn* (1884; orig. 1869)

Leather, E.M. *The Folk-lore of Herefordshire* (Hereford, 1912; East Ardlsey, 1970; Hereford, 1991)

Scraps of English Folklore in *Folklore*, 37 (1926), 296-9

Leeds, Winifred *Herefordshire Speech* (Leominster, 1985)

Lees, Edwin *Pictures of Nature in the Silurian Region around the Malvern Hills and Vale of Severn* (1856)

Leicester, Hubert A. *Forgotten Worcester* (Worcester, 1930)

Worcester Remembered (Worcester, 1935)

Little, B. *Oak-apple Maying* in *Warwickshire and Worcestershire Magazine*, 11, no. 2 (1954-6), 46-7

Llewellin, F.G. *The History of Saint Clodock: British King and Martyr* (Manchester, 1919)

Lloyd, J.W. *The Burning of the Bush* in *Woolhope Trans.* (1901), 104-5

Lones, T.E. *Scraps of English Folklore (Worcestershire)* in *Folklore*, 25 (1914), 370; 36 (1925), 85-93

Masefield, John *Grace before Ploughing. Fragments of Autobiography* (1966)

So Long to Learn. Chapters of an Autobiography (1952)

Wonderings (1943)

Massingham, J.H. *The Southern Marches* (1952)

Mawer, A., Stenton, F.M., and Houghton, F.T.S. *The Place-names of Worcestershire* (Cambridge, 1927)

Mee, Arthur *Herefordshire* (1948, 3rd ed.)

Morgan, F.C. *Hereford Cathedral Church Misericords* (Hereford, 1975)

Herefordshire Printers and Booksellers, in *Woolhope Trans.* (1939-41), 106-27

Printing in Herefordshire, Part II, in *Woolhope Trans.* (1974), 230-38

Herefordshire Printers and Booksellers, in *Woolhope Trans.* (1971), 274-5

Morgan, W.E.T. *A Few Folk- and other Stories*, in *Woolhope Trans.* (1924), 96-103

Mountney, Michael *The Saints of Herefordshire* (Hereford, 1976)

Munthe, Malcolm *Hellens. A Herefordshire Manor* (1957)

Murray-Aynsley, M. *Scraps of English Folklore, XVI: Herefordshire*, in *Folklore*, 39 (1928), 381-2

Noake, John *Guide to Worcestershire* (1868)

Notes and Queries for Worcestershire (1856)

Rambler in Worcestershire (1851)

Worcester in Olden Times (1849)

Worcestershire Nuggets (1889)

Worcestershire Relics (1877)

Noake, M.V. *May Day at Hallow* in *Worcestershire Countryside*, 1 (1951), 197-8

'Nonagenarian' Letters in *Hereford Times*, 15 Apr. and 20 May 1879

Northall, G.F. *English Folk-rhymes* (1892)

Oldham, Jean *The Legend of Silver John* Kington History Society Papers, 1 (1977-8)

Opie, Iona, and Tatem, Moira *A Dictionary of Superstitions* (Oxford, 1989)

Palfrey, H.E. *Foleys of Stourbridge* in *Trans. Worcs. Arch. Soc.*, New Ser., 21 (1945), 1-15

Palmer, Roy *Britain's Living Folklore* (Newton Abbot, 1991)

    The Folklore of Warwickshire (1976)

    (ed.) *Folk Songs Collected by Ralph Vaughan Williams* (1983)

    (ed.) *Songs of the Midlands* (East Ardsley, 1972)

Palmer, R.E. (Roy) *The Funny Rigs of Good and Tender-hearted Masters in the Happy Town of Kidderminster. Anno 1828*, in *Trans. Worcs. Arch. Soc.*, 3rd Ser., 3 (1970-2), 105-113

Palmer, Roy (ed.) *Poverty Knock* (1974)

Palmer, Roy, and Pye, Roger *Treasure Trove, or "The Enchanted Piss-Pot"*, in *English Dance and Song* (Spring 1992)

Parry, Richard *The Further Recordings of Richard Parry, the Kington Historian*, ed. John Southwood (Kington, 1984)

    The History of Kington (Kington, 1845)

Pevsner, Nikolaus *The Buildings of England. Herefordshire* (Harmondsworth, 1963)

    The Buildings of England. Worcestershire (Harmondsworth, 1968)

Poole, William *Old Mops Mended, Not Thrown Away* (Hereford, n.d.)

Quinion, Michael B. *A Drink for Its Time. Farm Cider Making in the Western Counties* (Hereford, 1979)

Radford, E. and M.A. *Encyclopaedia of Superstitions* (n.d. ? 1947)

Raven, M. and J. (eds) *A Good Christmas Box* (Wolverhampton, 1967; orig. Dudley, 1847)

Reade, Hubert *Ghosts of Much Dewchurch* in *Woolhope Trans.* (1927-9), 156-65

Roberts, S.F. Gavin *A History and Description of Ledbury Parish Church* (Ledbury, 6th ed., 1990)

Rouse, W.H.D. *Tokens of Death*, in *Folklore*, 4 (1893), 258

Salisbury, John *A Glossary of Words and Phrases used in South-east Worcestershire* (1893)

Seaton, Douglas *A History of Archenfield* (Hereford, 1903)

Sharp, Cecil *Cecil Sharp's Collection of English Folk Songs*, ed. Maud Karpeles (2 vols, 1974)

Sharpe, Frederick *The Church Bells of Herefordshire* (Brackley, 1976)

Sherard, Robert H. *The White Slaves of England. II, The Nailmakers of Bromsgrove; III, The Chainmakers of Cradley Heath*, in *Pearson's Magazine* (1896), 167-173; 408-414

Sherwood, Martha M. *Life, Chiefly Autobiographical*, ed. S. Kelly (1854)

Shoesmith, Ron *Alfred Watkins. A Herefordshire Man* (Logaston, 1990)

Simpson, Jacqueline *The Folklore of the Welsh Border* (1976)

Smith, Brian *A History of Malvern* (Leicester, 1964)

Smith, L.D. *Carpet Weavers and Carpet Masters. The Hand Loom Carpet Weavers of Kidderminster, 1780-1850* (Middle Habberley, 1986)

Sprackling, Graham *Field Names in the Parish of Ewyas Harold, Herefordshire* (n.p., n.d.)

Stanton, Geo. K. *Rambles and Researches among Worcester Churches* (London and Bromsgrove, 2 vols, 1884-6)

Stanton, L.M., and Partridge, J.B. *Worcestershire Folklore*, in *Folklore* (1915), 94-7

Taylor, Antoinette *An English Christmas Play* {from Broadway}, in *Journal of American Folklore*, 22, no. 86 (1909), 389-94

Thomas, Keith *Religion and the Decline of Magic* (Harmondsworth, 1973)

Thompson, E.P. *Customs in Common* (1991)

Tiddy, R.J.E. *The Mummers' Play* (Oxford, 1923)

Tongue, Ruth (ed.) *Forgotten Folk-tales of the English Counties* (1970)

Tonkin, J.W. *Herefordshire* (1977)

Tree, W.W.A. *Some old Worcestershire Customs*, in *Worcs. Nat. Club Trans.*, 5, pt 2 (1912), 203-223

Vaughan Williams, Ralph (arr.) *Eight Traditional English Carols* (1919)
Five Variants of Dives and Lazarus (1940)
Twelve Traditional Carols from Herefordshire (1920)

Vaughan Williams, Ursula *RVW. A Biography of Ralph Vaughan Williams* (Oxford, 1988)

Waite, Vincent *Malvern Country* (1968)

Watkins, Alfred *The Old Straight Track* (1987; orig, 1925)

Walters, H.B. *The Church Bells of Worcestershire*, in *Worcs. Arch. Soc. Trans.*, Old ser., 25 (1899-1900), 549-91; new ser., 2 (1923-5), 1-58; 5 (1927-9), 111-47; 6 (1927-9), 1-61; 7 (1930-1), 1-40; 8 (1930-1), 1-38

Westwood, Jennifer *Albion. A Guide to Legendary Britain* (1985)

Whitlock, Ralph *Here Be Dragons* (1983)

Williams, Alan *The Hauntings of Hoarwithy*, in *Herefordshire County Life*, no. 7 (Dec. 1978), 40-1

Williams, Alfred Rowberry *Legends of the Severn Valley* (n.d.)

Williams, Phyllis *Bromyard. Minster, Manor and Town* (privately printed, 1987)

Willis-Bund, J.W. *The Legendary History of Worcestershire*, in *Reports and Papers of the Associated Architectural Societies*, 31, pt 2 (1912), 585-612

Worcestershire Federation of Women's Institutes, *The Worcestershire Village Book* (Newbury and Worcester, 1988)

Wright, Geoffrey N. *Discovering Epitaphs* (Aylesbury, 1972)

INDEX

278

279

281

283